Phil
Wills

PAN-AFRICANISM

PAN-AFRICANISM

The Idea and Movement, 1776-1991

SECOND EDITION

P. OLISANWUCHE ESEDEBE

HOWARD UNIVERSITY PRESS

Washington, D.C.

1994

Howard University Press, Washington, D.C. 20017

Manufactured in the United States of America

This book is printed on acid-free paper.

10   9   8   7   6   5   4   3   2   1

Library of Congress Cataloging-in-Publication Data

Esedebe, P. Olisanwuche.
    Pan-Africanism : the idea and movement, 1776–1991 /
    P. Olisanwuche Esedebe. — 2nd ed.
        p.   cm.
    Includes bibliographical references and index.
    ISBN 0–88258–186–4 : $15.95
    1. Pan-Africanism—History.   2. Nationalism—
Africa—History.
    3. Blacks—Race identity—History.   4. Organization of
African Unity.   I. Title.
DT30.E77   1994
320.5'49'096—dc20
                                              94-8375
                                                 CIP

Contents

Preface

In spite of the fast-growing literature on Pan-Africanism, not much that is really new has emerged in the preceding decade. Most of the published works seem to repeat or confirm, albeit in greater detail, what has been said before. Quite often attention is focused on personalities and organizations whose commitment to Pan-Africanism is doubtful. Closely connected with this misplaced emphasis is the tendency to rely heavily on the records of the European colonial regimes and to list the publications of Pan-African leaders and pressure groups instead of integrating the substance of such material in the text itself. Is it still necessary to point out that all the colonial powers were hostile to the movement and did their utmost to discredit and even suppress it? Unless we pay more attention to the documents, utterances, and exertions of the Pan-Africanists themselves, ask new questions, or provide more satisfactory answers to old ones, we cannot make meaningful contributions. A new question that may be asked—in fact it is just beginning to be asked—is about the attitude of African descendants in Asia and the Middle East to the phenomenon. Latin American aspects have hardly been investigated. Until such significant gaps are filled, any dogmatic generalizations must be suspect.

Another reason why interpretations of the phenomenon cannot be conclusive at present is the handicap imposed by the nature of contemporary history. No historian writes with complete detachment. But there is a kind of detachment possible for historians of the past, which contemporary historians can hardly attain. As the narrative approaches the present day, the contemporary historian's temptation to take sides—however unconscious—becomes increasingly uncontrollable. Few, if any, contemporary writers can discuss the Nigerian civil war, for example, without being unduly influenced by national, party, or personal self-interest.

A further difficulty facing contemporary historians is that they are denied the advantage of hindsight. Only developments they expect to have a long-term impact will appear to be significant, and this on the basis of mere assumptions of the future course of events.

The interpretations offered in this book are therefore tentative. The study itself grew out of my doctoral thesis, "A History of the Pan-African Movement in Britain, 1900–1948," presented to the University of London in 1968. In 1972 I was fortunate to win a Senior Fulbright Fellowship, which enabled me to do further research in the United States, having already used sources in England. As a result of my postdoctoral research in American and African archives, I have broadened the scope of the dissertation to include major developments outside of Britain from 1750 to 1900, and between 1948 and 1963.

Those who helped me in one way or another during my research are so many that it is impossible to name all of them. I would like to thank, in particular, the staff of the following institutions: King's College Library, Library of the London School of Economics and Political Sciences, Institute of Commonwealth Studies, Senate House Library—all of London University; British Museum; Public Record Office (London); Ethiopian Embassy, London (Information Section); Rhodes House Library (Oxford); National Library of Scotland; New York City Public Library; Columbia University (New York); Howard University Library (Washington, D.C.); Library of Congress (Washington, D.C.); Fourah Bay College (University of Sierra Leone) Library; Ghana National Archives (Accra and Cape Coast); George Padmore Research Library (Accra), and Institute of African Studies (Legon, Ghana).

I am indebted to the late Mr. George Bennett of the Institute of Commonwealth Studies, Oxford, for suggesting the theme of my doctoral dissertation as well as Dr. Christine Moody and the late Mr. Reginald Bridgeman, both of whom allowed me the use of documents in their possession. To Mrs. Violet Creech-Jones, Lord Brockway, Dr. Malcolm Joseph-Mitchell, Professor Kenneth Little, Dr. Hugh W. Springer, and Dr. Richard Pankhurst, I am grateful for the readiness with which they answered my queries. My gratitude also goes to Professor J. E. Flint, who supervised the greater part of my thesis at King's College, London, before going to Dalhousie University (Canada), Professor Gerald S. Graham, Professor George Shepperson, and Mr. Douglas H. Jones for their kindness and guidance during the absence of my supervisor.

My research was made possible by grants from three major sources: the Commonwealth Scholarship Commission in the United Kingdom, who sponsored my doctoral research in England; the Nigerian Federal Government, who sponsored my field work in West Africa; and the United States Government, who awarded me a Fulbright Fellowship enabling me to consult some important documents in America.

I greatly appreciate the comments and criticism of those friends who read my thesis or the draft of this book in whole or in part: Mazi Ray Ofoegbu, Dr. Sunday O. Anozie, Dr. N. M. B. Bhebe, and Mr. John Conteh-Morgan.

Finally, I owe a special debt to Mr. Harry Caulker for typing the manuscript and to my wife for her unflinching support and assistance in checking the typescript.

Abbreviations

AAPC	All-African Peoples' Conference
ACS	American Colonization Society
ADB	African Development Bank
ADF	African Development Fund
AEC	African Economic Community
AEDBA	Arab Economic Development Bank for Africa
ANC	African Natioanl Congress
APU	African Progress Union
CAO	Committee of African Organizations
CEAO	Communauté Economique de l'Afrique de l'Ouest
CM	Council of Ministers (Organization of African Unity)
CO	Colonial Office, London
CPSSDCA	Conference on Peace, Security, Stability, Development, and Cooperation in Africa
EAC	East African Community
EACSO	East African Common Services Organization
ECA	Economic Commission for Africa
ECOMOG	ECOWAS Monitoring Group
ECOWAS	Economic Community of West African States
FNLA	Frente Nacional de Libertação de Angola
FO	Foreign Office, London
FRELIMO	Frente de Libertação de Moçambique
GCARPS	Gold Coast Aborigines' Rights Protection Society (Gold Coast ARPS)
IAFA	International African Friends of Abyssinia
IASB	International African Service Bureau
IGO	Inter-Governmental Organizations
KFAED	Kuwait Fund for Arab Economic Development
LCP	League of Coloured Peoples
LDRN	Ligue de la Défense de la Race Nègre

MNC	Mouvement National Congolais
MPLA	Movimento Popular de Libertação de Angola
NAACP	National Association for the Advancement of Colored People
NCBWA	National Congress of British West Africa
NCNC	National Council of Nigeria and the Cameroons
OAU	Organization of African Unity
PAC	Pan-Africanist Congress
PAF	Pan-African Federation
PAFMECA	Pan-African Freedom Movement for East and Central Africa
PAFMECSA	Pan-African Freedom Movement for East, Central, and Southern Africa
PAIGC	Partido Africano de Independencia de Guinea e Cabo Verde
POLISARIO	People's Front for the Liberation of Saquiet el-Homra and Rio de Oro
RDA	Rassemblement Démocratique Africain
SADCC	Southern African Development Coordinating Conference
SWAPO	South West African Peoples' Organization
WANS	West African National Secretariat
WASU	West African Students' Union
UAPAD	United Aid for Peoples for African Descent
UAS	Union of African States
UDEAC	Union Douanière et Economique de l'Afrique Centrale
UNIA	Universal Negro Improvement Association
UNITA	Uniao Nacional Para a Independencia Total de Angola
UPC	Union of the Peoples of the Cameroons
ZANU	Zimbabwe African Peoples' Union
ZIPRA	Zimbabwe Peoples' Revolutionary Army

Terms

African	All persons of African descent including indigenous Africans.
Exile	All people of African origin living permanently or temporarily outside Africa.

PAN-AFRICANISM

1

Origins of Pan-African Ideas

DESPITE THE FLOOD of books and articles on Pan-Africanism in recent years, the study of the phenomenon is still in its infancy. Writers tend to bury its aspirations and dynamics in a welter of fascinating but largely irrelevant details. Not surprisingly, there is still no agreement on what it is all about. Explanations that some African scholars and politicians give often differ from those suggested by African descendants abroad. Sometimes the continental Africans themselves advance conflicting interpretations.

In the 1930s the veteran African American scholar and agitator W. E. B. Du Bois stated that the Pan-African movement aimed at an intellectual understanding and cooperation among all groups of African descent in order to bring about "the industrial and spiritual emancipation of the Negro people."[1] At the third annual conference of the American Society of African Culture held in 1960 at the University of Pennsylvania, several speakers expressed conflicting opinions.[2] Rayford Logan, a black American historian, saw the phenomenon in terms of self-government by African countries south of the Sahara. Disagreeing, the Nigerian journalist and politician Anthony Enahoro insisted that it included the economic, social, and cultural development of the continent, the avoidance of conflict among African states, the promotion of African unity and influence in world affairs. The Senegalese publicist Alioune Diop felt that it was more or less synonymous with the concept of "African personality" or "negritude." In the opinion of the well-known British journalist Colin Legum, Pan-Africanism "is essentially a movement of ideas and emotions; at times it achieves a synthesis: at times it remains at the level of antithesis."[3]

For the more recent writers Pan-Africanism seems to mean anything. This was probably why Adekunle Ajala[4] failed to define it in his 440-odd-page book. Accepting George Shepperson's dichotomy, Robert G. Weisbord[5] uses Pan-Africanism with a capital P when referring to "this twentieth-century movement" and pan-Africanism with a small p to describe "a general movement of international kinship and numerous short-lived movements with a predominant cultural element." Kenneth King[6] extends the term to include the appeal for Africans of educational institutions run by black Americans in the United States as well as the exertions of white missionaries, philanthropists, and even politicians like ex-President Theodore Roosevelt of America, who believed that the education of Africans and that of African Americans constituted a single interdependent problem. Whereas J. Ayodele Langley[7] thinks that Pan-Africanism is a protest, a refusal, a demand, and a utopia born of centuries of contact with Europe, the German historian Imanuel Geiss[8] believes that it is an irrational concept, a matter of vague emotions. The historian's cynical assertion appears to be borne out by the several definitions suggested by V. Bakpetu Thompson in his book.[9] Thompson sees Pan-Africanism as a struggle in which Africans and others of African blood have been engaged since their contact with modern Europe. Elsewhere in the same study he declares that Pan-Africanism and the concept of African personality are interchangeable, that Pan-Africanism is a campaign to rehabilitate the valuable aspects of African culture, and that the phenomenon means the political unification of the continent.

None of these explanations seems adequate. Some of them are actually misleading. A more accurate definition is by no means easy to formulate. It cannot be given in a neat and short sentence. Before offering a working definition, it will be helpful to list the major component ideas, namely, Africa as the homeland of Africans and persons of African origin, solidarity among people of African descent, belief in a distinct African personality, rehabilitation of Africa's past, pride in African culture, Africa for Africans in church and state, the hope for a united and glorious future Africa. All these elements or combinations of them form the principal aims of twentieth-century Pan-African associations; they pervade the resolutions of Pan-African meetings held outside and inside the continent since 1900; they permeate the utterances and publications of men like W. E. B. Du Bois, Marcus Garvey, George Padmore, Kwame Nkrumah, Julius Nyerere, and Stokely Carmichael. With some simplification we can say that Pan-Africanism is a political and cultural phenomenon that regards Africa, Africans, and African descendants abroad as a unit. It seeks to regenerate and unify Africa and promote a feeling of oneness among the people of the African world. It glorifies the African past and inculcates pride in African values. Any adequate definition of the phenomenon must include its political and cultural aspects. How can a phenomenon that has been institutionalized in the Organization of African Unity (OAU) still remain a utopia? And what is irrational about seeking the solidarity of the African world and inculcating pride in Africa's past and culture?

The present debate on the nature of Pan-Africanism stems largely from three unfortunate tendencies. There is the tendency to overplay one aspect of the phenomenon at the expense of another. A second source of confusion is the rather heavy reliance on the records of the European colonial administrations, all of which were hostile to the movement and did their utmost to suppress or even destroy it. Linked with this tendency is the practice of enumerating the publications of Pan-African leaders and organizations instead of integrating the material in the text itself. Thus, in his book Geiss speculates on the originator of the term *Pan-African* and the identity of Benito Sylvain. Yet the answers are contained in the Schomburg Collection listed in the author's bibliography. The careful reader will also notice that the text of Geiss's study does not show any substantial use of the works of, for example, Edward W. Blyden. Geiss's preference for the compilations of European liberals and their societies may have misled him into thinking that Pan-Africanism is an irrational concept; all the same, his work serves the useful purpose of revealing sources in German, Portuguese, and even English unknown to many previous writers.

Like Geiss, Langley is open to the charge of excessive reliance on non-Pan-African documents, in this case, the despatches and minutes of British colonial officers in West Africa and London. If he had so much as glanced through Akweke Nwafor Orizu's *Without Bitterness*,[10] Mazi Mbonu Ojike's *My Africa*,[11] and S. D. Cudjoe's

Aids to African Autonomy,[12] and paid attention to the exertions of
R. N. Duchein, founder and president of the Pan-African Unification Organization, he would probably not have made the sweeping
statement that the West African nationalist elite "reinterpreted Pan-
Africanism to suit their economic and political interest, particularly
when ideology and interest clashed."

This brings us to a third cause of the disagreement on what Pan-
Africanism is all about: the failure to distinguish between what is
Pan-African and what is not. In their eagerness to demonstrate that
Pan-Africanism is not synonymous with the activities of Du Bois,
Padmore, and others, many recent commentators have gone to the
extreme of raking up obscure figures of doubtful Pan-African stature. It is a mistake to suppose that every anticolonial activity is a
manifestation of Pan-Africanism. Thus, Ato Kifle Wodajo, an Ethiopian writer, thinks that "in Africa itself the seeds of Pan-Africanism were implanted the moment the first alien coloniser set foot on
her soil."[13]

A similar opinion was expressed by the African American John
H. Clarke, at the Second World Black and African Festival of Arts
and Culture held in Lagos from 15 January to 12 February 1977. In
his words:

> For a period of more than a hundred years, African warrior nationalists,
> mostly kings . . . out-manouvered and out-generaled some of the best
> military minds of Europe. They planted the seeds of African indepen-
> dence for another generation to harvest. Their Pan-Africanism was
> more military than intellectual, but it was Pan-Africanism.[14]

In this view every African agitator would be a Pan-Africanist; the
1896 House Tax uprising in Sierra Leone led by Bai Bureh, as well
as the Aba Women's Riot of 1928, would qualify as Pan-African
episodes. But the evidence suggests that Bureh and the Aba women
were solely concerned with the narrow interests of their localities,
not with the wider Pan-African world.

It is the view of the present writer that only persons committed
to the ideals of Pan-Africanism and activities clearly linked with the
Pan-African movement deserve notice. A good example of this kind
of link is Nkrumah's famous statement that the independence of
Ghana would be meaningless unless it was linked with the total
liberation of the continent.

Just as writers quarrel over what Pan-Africanism stands for, so too they clash on its periodization. Geiss feels that Pan-Africanism, in its strictest sense, started in 1958 when Nkrumah summoned two Pan-African meetings in Accra, the first to be held on African soil. On the other hand, Langley has warned us against "the tyranny of dates and labels" and maintains that "Pan-Africanism is not a movement that should be boxed and frozen into epochs and categories." Disregarding his own prescriptions, he goes on to suggest in the same study that "the small gathering at Kumasi in 1953 can be seen as a new phase in the evolution of an idea and as the real beginning of the Pan-African movement in Africa."[15] Langley's inability to defend his own declarations emphasizes the necessity for periodization, however tentative.

If we accept the need to periodize, what features of the phenomenon shall we consider to be of decisive importance? Should we ignore Pan-African sentiments or notions and concentrate on such concrete aspects as Pan-African conferences and pressure groups? By rebuking those who "in the absence of concrete evidence, assemble any number of incidents and ideas and call it Pan-Africanism,"[16] Langley appears to be advocating the elimination of Pan-African sentiments. If so, is it still necessary to state that every concrete thing, concrete evidence included, begins as an idea? Not only do Pan-African sentiments and notions constitute an integral part of Pan-Africanism, they also help us to date its inception. The question of date is important because the essential features of any phenomenon will be judged differently if they are differently delimited. Our opinions on the nature of Pan-Africanism will vary according to whether we assume that it came into existence in the eighteenth, nineteenth, or twentieth century.

When Pan-Africanism began, however, and who launched it will never be known. Hence it is futile to try, as some writers have attempted, to ascribe the phenomenon to any one person or trace its origin to a particular year. Of course, the term *Pan-African* and its derivative *Pan-Africanism* were not coined at the time the phenomenon they describe emerged. This is hardly surprising, for labels are sometimes invented after a movement has had time to establish itself. Just as a baby does not need baptism to exist, so, too, a creed does not require a label to be a fact of life. Though the words *Pan-African* and *Pan-Africanism* became popular after the 1900

London congress, their substance had been thought out long before. In discussing the origin of Pan-Africanism, what one should look for is the period when the sentiments or concepts underlying it first attracted attention.

Pan-African thinking originally began in the so-called New World, becoming articulate during the century starting from the declaration of American independence (1776). It represented a reaction against the oppression of blacks and the racial doctrines that marked the era of abolitionism. It also found expression in the independent church movement in the New World and Africa as well as in resistance to European colonial ambitions in Africa.

Although the principles of the American Revolution implied civil rights for all, black Americans continued to suffer disabilities because of their race and complexion.[17] Alexis de Tocqueville's description of the predicament of blacks in the United States will probably never be bettered. An extensive tour of America enabled the French lawyer to observe firsthand the plight of African descendants there. What he saw drove him to remark that the black American made a thousand fruitless attempts to ingratiate himself with men who despised him. He adopted his oppressors' values, echoed their opinions, and hoped by imitating them to form a part of their society. Having been indoctrinated from infancy into believing that black men were naturally inferior to whites, he accepted the myth and became ashamed of his personality. He saw evidence of inferiority in each of his features and if it were in his power he would gladly rid himself of everything that distinguished him from a white man.

Despairing of ever attaining equal status with other racial groups, the African American began to think seriously of returning to the fatherland. In 1787 a committee of the African Lodge, whose Grand Master was Prince Hall, sent a petition to the Legislative Assembly of Massachusetts. Despite the egalitarian principles enshrined in the national constitution hammered out in Philadelphia that year, men of African blood continued to suffer discrimination, which they feared would remain the case so long as they and their children lived in America. Since they were poor and therefore in no position to return to Africa without help, the petitioners urged the legislature to assist them and other blacks who wished to emigrate.

The petition was ignored, and Prince Hall was obliged to fight for civil liberties on American soil itself.

With the adoption of the Philadelphia Constitution, which among other things regarded a black slave as being equal to three-fifths of a person, African Americans reopened the issue of emigration. In 1789 the Union Society of Africans in Newport lamented the fact that Americans of African descent were treated as strangers and outcasts. The society also drew attention to the "heathenish darkness and barbarity" engulfing the ancestral continent.

As a young man, Paul Cuffe, a half-Indian, half-black-African Boston merchant and devout Quaker, had campaigned for the rights of black Americans in his native state of Massachusetts. When this met with little or no success, he switched his efforts to Sierra Leone in particular and Africa in general. His aims were to promote selective emigration to Sierra Leone and to save Africa from the scourge of the slave trade by helping Africans to develop a viable economy based on local products. Once Christianity and commerce had taken root in Sierra Leone, it would become the task of blacks there to spread these blessings to other parts of the continent.

In 1808 Cuffe obtained the support of the African Institution, a British humanitarian organization dominated by former directors of the Sierra Leone Company and still influential in running the affairs of the colony. Three years later, Cuffe visited Sierra Leone, where he made careful plans for emigration. He also seized the opportunity to establish the Friendly Society of Sierra Leone "to open a channel of intercourse" between Negro America and Sierra Leone; as an example of his good faith, he bought a house in Freetown.[18] When he returned to America, he urged African descendants in Baltimore, Boston, New York, Philadelphia, and Westport, Connecticut, to support colonization in Africa. In 1815 he made another trip to Sierra Leone, taking about forty blacks in family groups, largely at his own expense. In the letters they wrote back to America, these repatriates advised other exiles to follow their example.

On his return, Cuffe gave the benefit of his experience to the founders of the American Colonization Society (ACS). Founded in December 1816 by white American liberals and designed to finance the deportation of free blacks, the ACS received funds from private individuals, church groups, state legislatures, and a donation of

$100,000 from the United States Congress.[19] Cuffe was chosen to lead emigrants to be sent by the society, but he died before the first expedition left for West Africa.

Among the second batch of emigrants was Reverend Lott Cary (1780–1828), an ex-slave in Richmond, Virginia, who ransomed himself and two children for $850.[20] To found a "colony which might prove a blessed asylum to his degraded brethren in America, and enlighten and regenerate Africa" became Lott Cary's burning ambition. Between 1817 and 1857, the first forty years of its existence, the ACS sponsored the resettlement in Liberia alone of about thirteen thousand African Americans, "the pioneers of African Redemption."

As citizens in a prosperous country with enormous mineral and agricultural resources, many black Americans lived in the hope that tomorrow would be a better day. Sustained by this optimism, many free black Americans hesitated or even refused to support schemes seeking to remove them from the country. They proclaimed the United States as their home and land, which their fathers had built and defended against invaders.

One of the expressions of opposition to the ACS came from the Annual Convention of the Free Colored People, first held in Philadelphia in 1830 and afterward in that and other cities annually until the Civil War (1861–65). The anticolonization case found a classic expression in an oration delivered in July 1830 by Peter Williams, pastor of St. Phillips Episcopal Church, New York.[21] His argument may be summarized as follows.

No people in the world possessed so high a respect for liberty and equality as the citizens of the United States. Yet no people held so many slaves or made such fine distinctions between man and man. Thus, the freedom Americans had fought for was illusory. The rights of men now depended on the color of their skins. Though officially delivered from the letters of slavery, black Americans "are oppressed by an unreasonable, unrighteous, and cruel prejudice, which aims at nothing less than the forcing away of all the free colored people of the United States to the distant shores of Africa." Admittedly some supporters of the American Colonization Society were genuinely interested in the regeneration of Africa through evangelization and the suppression of slavery and the slave trade. All the same many leaders of the society, "those who are most active and most influential in its cause," had openly declared the removal of the free colored population of the country as the actual objective.

Surely Africa could be uplifted without sending all the free people of color in the United States there. Was it not both illogical and hypocritical to state that Africa would benefit from the return of its children in exile and with the same breath denounce the same exiles as the most "vile and degraded people in the world"? How could vile and degraded men build a virtuous and progressive Africa?

Equally ridiculous and inconsistent was the suggestion of colonizationists about "improving the character and condition of the people of color in this country by sending them to Africa." The "barbarous" environment of Africa was deemed more suitable for improvement than American society

> where schools and colleges abound, where the gospel is preached at every corner, and where all the arts and sciences are verging fast to perfection . . . We are NATIVES of this country, we ask only to be treated as well as FOREIGNERS. Not a few of our fathers suffered and bled to purchase its independence; we ask only to be treated as well as those who fought against it. We have toiled to cultivate it, and to raise it to its present prosperous condition; we ask only to share equal privileges with those who come from distant lands, to enjoy the fruits of our labour. Let these moderate requests be granted and we need not go to Africa nor anywhere else to be improved and happy. We cannot but doubt the purity of the motives of those persons who deny us these requests, and would send us to Africa to gain what they might give us at home.[22]

In maintaining that many a white American liberal was not really concerned about the relative backwardness of the African continent, Peter Williams was quite right. But he missed the point when he demanded the "improvement" of blacks in the United States rather than in the jungles and disease-ridden villages of Africa. The point was that most white Americans, the males in particular, saw in the growing free black American population a threat to their sexual security. For them the black man was at bottom a rapist, forever lusting after white women. This libel is adequately documented in the study *Slavery, Race and the American Revolution* by Duncan J. McLeod.[23]

The migration of free blacks to the middle and northern states after the Revolution was largely prompted by legislation in the

South that made emigration a condition of emancipation. Virginia passed such a law in 1806, thereby precipitating much of the fear in other populations. Within a year of Virginia's action, Delaware, Kentucky, and Maryland all introduced measures denying permanent residence to free blacks from other states.

At the same time congressional debates on the abolition of the slave trade in 1806–07 were marked by vehement opposition to the increasing free black population. And in 1809, during a debate on the enforcement of the act, Representative Taylor of South Carolina contended that it was not the intention of the law of 1807 "to increase our population in free blacks. It was not to set free the people of this description that the law had to be passed, but to prevent them from being brought here at all."[24] Is it not significant that the act abolishing the slave trade failed to provide for the liberation of those illegally imported? In the words of Duncan J. McLeod, "The formation of the American Colonization Society was a direct response to the urge to limit free black numbers."[25]

However, hopes of better conditions for blacks held out by the outbreak of the American Civil War together with Abraham Lincoln's Emancipation Proclamation (1863) seemed to prove the opponents of emigration right. As a result, the enthusiasm to return to Africa flagged. But by the end of Reconstruction (1877) these hopes were totally shattered. The yearning for the fatherland once more rose to the surface. This desperate craving, abundantly documented in the *African Repository*,[26] found expression in the Liberia exodus organizations that emerged in South Carolina and the utterances of Bishop Henry M. Turner.

The back-to-Africa idea also appealed to African descendants in the West Indies. Slave escapes and disturbances used to lead to uproars in which free blacks were obliged to show documentary evidence in support of their status, for every person of that complexion was described a slave, as the Antiguan legislature ruled in 1783, until legal proofs to the contrary were produced.

In his autobiography published toward the end of the eighteenth century, Olaudah Equiano, otherwise known as Gustavus Vasa the African, complains bitterly about the perpetual fear of reenslavement and the impunity with which supposedly emancipated blacks were universally insulted and robbed, "for such is the equity of the West Indian laws, that no free negro's evidence will be admitted in their courts of justice."[27] At about the age of ten Equiano had been taken from his native Igboland in Nigeria by slave traders to the southern states of America. He was then sold to a planter in the West Indies. He worked there and aboard ships operating between the Caribbean and England before he saved enough money to buy his freedom in 1776. As a free black he found the West Indies so disgusting and unsafe that he concluded that unless he left the region he would not be actually free. He eventually made his way to England, where he married Susan Cullen of Ely (near Cambridge) on 7 April 1792. Before his marriage Equiano had helped in organizing the repatriation of some liberated African slaves to Sierra Leone. But an indiscreet letter attacking some of the white organizers of the expedition robbed him of the chance of returning to Africa.

When the British Emancipation Act became effective in 1838, the desire to quit the scene of humiliation and the zeal to regenerate the African race through missionary work seized many an African descendant. The following year, one Thomas Keith set out from Jamaica with only a letter of recommendation from his pastor to be a missionary to his brethren.[28] Four years later several families, some going as evangelists and teachers, others as settlers, sailed from the same territory with one Alfred Saker and landed in the Cameroons.[29] By 1858 they had become so numerous as to constitute a distinct colony, Victoria.

In Barbados, a West Indian Church Association was launched under whose auspices persons of African origin returned to the parent continent. Among them was John Duport, a young man from Saint Kitts, who in 1855 went to West Africa to do missionary work in the Rio Pongas area of what is now Guinea Republic. With the help of local chiefs and traders, Duport was able to start a school at Falangia. "A stream of others followed; some stayed, others were forced by ill-health to return, and others died."[30]

Liberia also attracted the attention of Afro-West Indians. Among them may be mentioned the Jamaican journalist John B. Russwurm. At first, in common with the well-known black American, Frederick Douglass, he opposed emigration to Africa in general and the American Colonization Society in particular. But, unlike Douglass, he changed his mind, subscribing to the view that Africans in exile could help themselves and their race best by giving strong support to Liberia. Not surprisingly he went to Liberia and founded a newspaper, the *Liberia Herald*, in 1830.

In Latin America, the urge to emigrate to the fatherland was not as compelling as in the United States and the Antilles. Here the situation differed. The treatment of slaves might have been more brutal in the Portuguese and Spanish colonies than in the Dutch, English, and French Caribbean islands and possibly the North American settlements. Nevertheless, in Latin America slaves had a greater chance of securing their liberty.[31] There was no doubt about their fitness for freedom. Thus, in colonial Brazil, notorious for its barbarous treatment of slaves, blacks performed nearly all the menial tasks, but with manumission they filled openings in private and public employment. Racial relations were free of prejudice to such an extent that a French diplomat remarked in a despatch of 1835 that Brazil was a mulatto monarchy with nothing pure except the royal blood.[32]

If miscegenation made for integration, it was by no means the decisive factor. The crucial factor is to be found in the relatively open nature of Latin American society. Here the emancipated Negro was really a free person, being by law the equal of all other free citizens. It is important to note that when slavery was ended in Brazil (1888), the crowd in the gallery showered flowers on the members of the legislature, and throughout the night the masses danced in the streets of the capital city, Rio de Janeiro.[33]

All the same, it would be a mistake to suppose that the African exiles in Latin America completely escaped the back-to-Africa fever. Throughout the nineteenth century, pockets of Afro-Brazilians now and again crossed the Atlantic to settle in Whydah (Dahomey) and Lagos (Nigeria). Equally significant was a remark made in 1891 by an English clergyman, the Reverend Francis P. Flemynge

> that over a million Negroes were eager to go back to Africa: He was so moved by compassion that he decided to form an " 'African Repatriation Relief Society' for the purpose of collecting funds to give free and assisted passages to these poor creatures from Brazils [sic] and Havana to Africa."[34]

A detailed and documented study of the activities of African descendants scattered all over Asia still needs to be done. But judging from the scanty evidence now at our disposal, it seems that though Afro-Asians still cherish memories of the fatherland, they have remained unaffected by the Pan-African movement. This apparent indifference has been attributed partly to the comparatively humane treatment meted to them, partly to their conversion to Islam and assimilation into the local culture, and partly to ignorance of Pan-African developments.[35]

A second factor behind the emergence of Pan-African consciousness was the racial doctrine associated with the long debate over the Atlantic slave trade. With the colonization of the American hemisphere, the Aristotelian hypothesis that some humans are by nature slaves and others free was used to justify the enslavement of the aboriginal Amerindians and later Africans. Thus, in the sixteenth century, the Spanish propagandist Juan Gines de Sepulveda claimed that the Amerindians' inability to resist the Spanish adventurers proved not only their natural inferiority but also their need of a strong and wise government to be provided, presumably by the Spaniards. The myth of natural servitude obtained a new lease on life from the closing decades of the eighteenth century through the entire nineteenth.

Two main currents of racial theory may be distinguished: the evolutionary and the teleological. An example of the evolutionary argument was Thomas Arnold's view of history advanced in 1841. In his inaugural lecture as Regius Professor of History at Oxford, Arnold saw history as a kind of relay race among a small team of gifted peoples, each of whom produced their best, passing on their achievements to greater successors. Thus, what the ancient Greeks handed to the Romans the Romans in turn passed on to the Northern Europeans. To him, modern history appeared to be not only a step in advance of ancient history but the last step. Since no gifted race remained to receive the seed of modern European civilization, the uncreative mass of mankind must either assimilate the elements of European culture "so completely that their individual character is absorbed, and they take their whole being from without; or, being incapable of taking in higher elements they dwindle away when brought into the presence of a more powerful life and become at last extinct altogether."[36] It struck the professor's reviewer that three centuries of close contact with the powerful Europeans had failed to exterminate the Africans in exile; on the contrary, "they have actually advanced under circumstances the most hostile to advancement."[37] If the test of history was the capacity to survive, continued the reviewer, the Africans at home had shown themselves quite capable of survival in the tropics, where Europeans could not live. Was it not possible then that Europeans might one day pass on the products of their work to a superior race of Negroes?[38]

According to the teleological school, the Creator deliberately made men unequal. To whites he gave intelligence to enable them to direct wisely the activities of the others. To nonwhites (these usually meant blacks) he gave strong backs fortified with a weak mind and an obedient temper so that they might labor effectively under the supervision of white masters. This interpretation proved extremely popular in the United States, where it served as a principal defense of Negro slavery. Although physical anthropologists and other pseudoscientific racists were soon to vie with one another in the minute measurement of skulls and facial angles, they never abandoned the old use of skin color as a guide to the degree of superiority or nearness to the apes. Because Europeans erected the hierarchy of races, they naturally placed whites on the top. The darker races were ranked below in order of darkness.

The middle of the nineteenth century witnessed a revival of the teleological argument. This event was marked by the appearance of virulently racist publications, notably by the Englishman Thomas Carlyle, the Edinburgh anatomist Robert Knox, the French sociologist Arthur de Gobineau, and the American naval officer Commander A. H. Foote. While Knox held that "the true black or negro race" reached the zenith of its ability centuries before and had become stagnant,[39] Foote denied them any achievement worth mentioning. If everything Africans and their descendants had accomplished from time immemorial, he wrote contemptuously, were to be destroyed or forgotten, the world would lose no great truth, no profitable art, no exemplary form of life.[40] Civilization and culture, Gobineau maintained, were the exclusive creation of the superior races, arguing that superiority and inferiority were not due to environment but were innate.[41]

In his infamous *Occasional Discourses on the Nigger Question* written in 1849, Carlyle asserted: "That, you may depend on it, my obscure Black friends, is and was always the Law of the World, for you and for all men: To be servants, the more foolish of us to the more wise; and only sorrow, futility, and disappointment will betide both, till both in some approximate degree get to conform to the same."[42]

Insinuations about the alleged permanent inferiority of the black man and assertions that he had contributed little or nothing for the comfort of humanity posed a challenge that educated elements of the African diaspora picked up. Olaudah Equiano reminded the conceited and polished European that his ancestors were once, like the Africans, uncivilized and barbarous. Pride in his African origins moved Equiano to praise his people, the Igbo, for their resourcefulness, integrity, and intelligence. He went so far as to claim that deformity was almost unknown among them. Equiano blamed the European adventurers for much of the intercommunal conflict among Africans, and by drawing attention to conditions in eighteenth-century Europe, he drove home the point that violence is not peculiar to black men.

Some African Americans, such as the astronomer Benjamin Banneker, pointed to their contemporary achievements to show that the popular notions about the African were false. The West African scientist James Africanus Beale Horton provided evidence from his own medical and educational career to refute the allegation of Negro inferiority, showing by the experience of his own people, the Sierra Leone Creoles, that there could be a swift change from apparent barbarity to a civilized condition in a single generation.

Equiano, Banneker, and Horton wanted to demonstrate that African backwardness was neither inherent nor permanent but due to adverse circumstances and lack of opportunity. Delving into the African past itself, David Walker, another African-American, not only affirmed the potential equality of the races but cited the glories of ancient Egypt as examples of the African's contributions to civilization.

Following the example of his fellow American, David Walker, the Reverend James Theodore Holly produced in 1857 a forty-six page booklet with the title *A Vindication of the Capacity of the Negro Race for Self-Government and Civilized Progress, As Demonstrated by Historical Events of the Haytian Revolution and the Subsequent Acts of That People Since Their National Independence.*[43] Though marred by emotional language, which can be excused by the nature of his subject, the pamphlet is analytical, coherent, and persuasive, based firmly on history not myth. Its object is threefold. One, as the title implies, is to refute "the vile aspersions and foul calumnies that have been heaped upon my race for the last four centuries, by our unprincipled oppressors; whose base interest, at the expense of our blood and our bones, have made them reiterate, from generation to generation, during the long march of ages, everything that would prop up the impious dogma of our [supposed] natural and inherent inferiority."[44] A second purpose was to convert those philanthropists who secretly doubted the equality of the races and often betrayed themselves when pressed to accept the logical consequences of their avowed beliefs. The third aim must be quoted in extenso if we are not to miss its Pan-African dimension:

> to inflame the latent embers of self-respect that the cruelty and injustice of our oppressors, have nearly extinguished in our bosoms, during the midnight chill of centuries, that we have clanked the galling chains of slavery. To this end, I wish to remind my oppressed brethren, that dark and dismal as this horrid night has been and sorrowful as the general reflections are, in regard to our race; yet, notwithstanding these discouraging considerations, there are still some proud historic recollections, linked indissolubly with the most important events of the past and present century, which break the general monotony, and remove some of the gloom that hang over the dark historic period of African slavery, and the accursed traffic in which it was cradled.[45]

At the end of his exposition Holly proudly announced, with much justification then, that the African exiles in Haiti "have already made a name, and a fame for us, that is imperishable as the world's history."[46] The more blacks searched their past, the greater their admiration of African culture tended to grow.

Several works written by European abolitionists helped to promote the cause of the Negro history movement. One, which immediately became a standard source of pro-Negro arguments, was penned by the Englishman Wilson Armistead and published in 1848 in Manchester under the title *A Tribute for the Negro: Being a Vindication of the Moral, Intellectual and Religious Capabilities of the Coloured Portion of Mankind; With Particular Reference to the African Race*. Another was contributed by H. G. Adams. Published in London in 1852, it was entitled *God's Image in Ebony: Being a Series of Biographical Sketches, Anecdotes, etc. Demonstrative of the Mental Powers and Intellec-*

tual Capacities of the Negro Race. The use of biographical sketches to answer racists remained fashionable for a long time as can be seen from *Memoirs of West African Celebrities* and *African Leaders, Past and Present*, both of which appeared at the beginning of the present century and were written by the Gold Coast clergyman S. R. B. Attoh Ahuma and the neglected Nigerian pamphleteer, Adeoye Deniga, respectively.[47]

Racial antagonism was also aroused in the process of the evangelization of Africa, where it strained relations between the local clerics and their European counterparts. It culminated in a movement that sought to Africanize Christianity and tended toward the formation of independent African churches on the model of the African Methodist Episcopal churches in America. *Ethiopianism* is the term usually employed to describe this phenomenon, which emerged in Africa in the last third of the nineteenth century. There is no agreement about whether the term should apply to the South and central African separatist churches[48] or only to a type of the South African variety[49] or be used in a Pan-African sense.[50] If secession was not everywhere a feature of Ethiopianism, at least two other factors were. One was the determination to save cherished indigenous values from the destructive influences of the foreign missions. The other was the principle of "Africa for the Africans" in opposition to European interference. For these reasons it seems justifiable to use the term in the wider Pan-African sense.

Influenced by the racists of the day, many a nineteenth-century European missionary behaved as if conversion and general acceptance of the African way of life were mutually exclusive. Hence most of the correspondence they sent home bristled with accounts of what they described as the wickedness and abominable customs of pagan society. Though some of their letters were published in reputable journals mainly to stimulate missionary subscription, they became an unwitting source of racism.

Separation began to manifest itself in West and South Africa from the 1870s. As early as 1872 a minor secession from the Hermon Congregation of the Paris Mission occurred in Basutoland. Twelve years later Nehemiah Tile broke away from the Wesleyan Mission to form the Tembu Church with Ngangelizwe, the Chief of the Tembu, as its visible head. "The cause of this important secession was not only opposition to European control, but also a positive desire to adapt the message of the Church to the heritage of the Tembu tribe. As the Queen of England was the head of the English church, so the Paramount Chief of the Tembu should be the *summus episcopus* of the new religious organization."[51]

One of the oldest Nigerian independent churches, the United Native African Church, was established on a resolution "that a pure Native African Church be founded for the evangelization and amelioration of the race, to be governed by Africans."[52] The UNA Church was not the product of a schism from a particular denomination. It was set up by men of several denominations as a purely African missionary effort.

Another secession occurred in German Cameroon where the Native Baptist Church broke away from the Basle Mission in 1888–89.[53] This religious phenomenon appeared late in East and central Africa becoming active during the period 1900–30 when the European colonialists had already begun to entrench their positions. In both regions the movement tended not only to center on prophets but also to be the focus of political agitation. Thus, under the leadership of John Chilembwe in Nyasaland it culminated in an uprising there;[54] in the Belgian Congo (Zaire) its leader Simon Kinbangu was imprisoned while the Ugandan Malaki Musajjakawa (whose disciples were called *Bamalaki* or Malakites) was deported. The Portuguese consistently restricted the entry of Protestant missions into their territories on the ground that they were the advance-guard of African nationalism.[55]

Thus the humiliating and discriminatory experiences of the African diaspora, the racism that accompanied the campaign for the suppression of the Atlantic slave trade, the independent African church movement as well as European imperialism, all represent the main sources of and conditions giving rise to Pan-African consciousness and ideas. If the ideas seemed vague at first, they received a more articulate expression at the hands of the West Africans J. A. B. Horton, the Reverend James Johnson, and Edward W. Blyden, an Afro-West Indian who later adopted Liberian nationality. Lesser pioneer Pan-African theorists include the African American Anglican divine Alexander Crummell, the Haitian diplomat and publicist Benito Sylvain, and the Nigerian clergyman Orishatukeh Faduma and Mojola Agbebi.

Born in June 1835 in Gloucester village (Sierra Leone) to an Igbo recaptive, James Africanus Beale Horton was educated partly in Sierra Leone and partly in England where he adopted the name Africanus to show his African identity. After studying medicine at King's College, London, and the University of Edinburgh he was commissioned in the British Army where he served for twenty years in West Africa. But his interests were not confined to military and medical matters. Indeed, his knowledge of the classics, history, and anthropology was remarkable for a man of any race. His best-known work is *West African Countries and Peoples, British and Native. With the Requirements Necessary for Establishing That Self-Government Recommended by the Committee of the House of Commons, 1865; And a Vindication of the African Race* published in London in 1868. Several ideas that are Pan-African in scope can be found in this book. One is the notion of a great African past. Africa in ages past, he proudly recalls

> was the nursery of science and literature; from thence they were taught in Greece and Rome so that it was said that the ancient Greeks represented their favourite goddess of Wisdom—Minerva—as an African princess. Pilgrimages were made to Africa in search of knowledge by such eminent men as Solon, Plato, Pythagoras; and several came to listen to the African Euclid, who was at the head of the most celebrated mathematical school in the world and who flourished 300 years before the birth of Christ. The conqueror of the great African Hannibal made his associate and confidant the African poet Terence.[56]

Africa, Horton goes on, produced many of the famous theologians of the early Christian church, notably Origen, Tertullian, Augustine, Clemens Alexandrinus, and Cyril. Horton's reasoned reassessment of the ancient history of Africa exposed the profound ignorance of Foote in particular and racists in general. Thus, Horton helped in no small measure to restore the self-confidence of blacks, which was necessary for the further progress of the cause of Pan-Africanism. Wherever Africans found themselves, he emphasized, they tended to flourish even in the face of unspeakable odds. From this he inferred that they were "a permanent and enduring people" contrary to the vaporings of Arnold. The refutation of Foote and Arnold, though Horton fails to name them, rendered the highway of Pan-Africanism much clearer, firmer, and safer.

The rejection of the theses of Foote and Arnold also enabled Horton to hope for a grand African future, another key Pan-African concept. A careful analysis of world history revealed to Horton the long-established fact that change was an ordinance of nature. No condition was permanent. There existed a natural law of evolution and dissolution. Under this law "nations rise and fall; the once flourishing and civilized degenerates into a semibarbarous state; and those who have lived in utter barbarism, after a lapse of time become the standing nation."[57]

Despite the speculations of Robert Knox, Africans "must live in the hope, that in process of time, their turn will come, when they will [again] occupy a prominent position in the world's history, and when they will command a voice in the council of nations."[58] There was no reason why the same race that had churches and repositories of learning and science, that governed ancient Egypt and was the terror of no less a city than ancient Rome should not once more stand on its legs.[59] It was in recognition of the permanent and enduring character of the African race, he thought, that the Committee of the House of Commons had come to embrace "that great principle of establishing independent African nationalities as independent as the present Liberian Government."[60] The African nationalities Horton had in mind were West African ethnic groups and communities such as the Fanti and Ga of the Gold Coast, the Igbo and Yoruba of present-day Nigeria, as well as the Sierra Leone Creoles. African states as we now know them had not yet emerged. All the same, he would still have welcomed them, for he looked beyond autonomous ethnic communities, however viable, to a united West Africa.

Horton's idea of a university was also West African in scope. Such an institution he hoped would serve not only to cure Africans of the poison of innate inferiority but also to exploit the unused human and economic resources of the region. He was farsighted and broadminded enough not to exclude foreign agencies completely from his program for African regeneration, arguing that "it is impossible for a nation to civilize itself; civilization must come from abroad. As was the case with the civilized continents of Europe and America, so it must be with Africa; which cannot be an exception to the rule."[61]

Another significant Pan-African theorist was James Johnson, a schoolmate of Africanus Horton at Fourah Bay College, Freetown. Like Horton, he was a Sierra Leonean of Nigerian extraction. Unlike

Horton, he couched his ideas in religious language. Also a contemporary of Edward W. Blyden, Johnson was a highly respected cleric of the CMS. Though his radicalism often embarrassed that church, his obsession with the parochial interests of Sierra Leone and Nigeria makes him a lesser African leader than E. A. Ayandele, his biographer, claims.[62] To say this is not to deny the Pan-African dimension of some of the clergyman's statements.

Johnson subscribed to the belief in a glorious African past, which he traced back to the time when the Christian church held sway in North Africa and when such indigenous divines as Tertullian, Augustine, and Cyprian lent color and dignity to the crown of Christendom. His religious training led him to attribute the decline of this golden age to the failure of North Africans to spread Christianity throughout the continent. In spite of this setback he looked forward to a grand future. "Africa is to rise once more," he declared in 1867 and "she will take her place with the most Christian, civilized and intelligent nations of the Earth."[63] The Native Pastorate created by the CMS in Sierra Leone in 1861 was for him an agency "for the development of a future African Existence" and the nucleus of a continental African church uniting the various Christian sects. In his view such a church would pave the way to a monolithic African society and foster the growth of African solidarity.

Johnson justified the campaign for an independent church on the ground that Africans were a distinct people with peculiar traits. It was no surprise that they should condemn the habit of uprooting the African convert from his cultural milieu and treating him as a tabula rasa on which foreign material must be written. No consideration, he bitterly complained, was given to the African way of life. Convinced that the Creator did not wish to confound the races, he demanded the "African must be raised upon his own idiosyncrasies."[64] Johnson is here arguing a case for the preservation of the African personality. But he does not use the phrase itself, for it had not yet been coined by Edward W. Blyden, who is probably the greatest exponent of Pan-African concepts.

It must not be supposed that Blyden was the originator of Pan-African ideas. Nor can we say with certainty that he was the most original. But to suggest as J. D. Hargreaves has done that "his numerous essays and orations do not really cohere into an intellectual whole"[65] is to betray one's superficial acquaintance with their

contents. Of course, it is possible to point to one or two inconsisten-
cies, but they do not affect the essence of his Pan-African aspirations.

The real point about Blyden's Pan-African ideas is not their logical consistency or inconsistency but their questionable originality.
So striking is the similarity between his arguments and those of
Africanus Horton and Alexander Crummell that one is tempted to
ask, Who copied whom? If it is hard to determine how much Blyden
owes to his two distinguished contemporaries, there is no doubt
that his writings are the most elegant, articulate, and forceful,
reaching a wider audience. According to the Englishman Bosworth
Smith, hitherto no voice had come "audible at all events to the outer
world, from Africa itself."[66] It was in the pages of Blyden's tracts,
he goes on, that the great dumb, dark continent had begun to speak
at last.[67] A contemporary African newspaper, the *Lagos Weekly Record*, described Blyden as an oracle on both sides of the Atlantic, "the
highest intellectual representative and the greatest defender of the
African race."[68] The well-known Gold Coast lawyer and nationalist
J. E. Casely-Hayford, who as a schoolboy in Sierra Leone knew
Blyden, was making the same point when he said that the claim of
Blyden to the esteem of all thinking Africans rested not so much on
the special work he did for any particular section of the African
world as on the general service he rendered to the race as a whole.
For more than a quarter of a century Blyden sought to reveal every-
where the African to himself and, most important of all, to lead him
back to self-respect and confidence.[69]

Edward Wilmot Blyden was born of "pure Negro descent from
the Eboe [Igbo] tribe"[70] in August 1832 on the Danish West Indian
island of St. Thomas. His parents were Romeo and Judith Blyden,
believed to have been born about 1794 and 1795, respectively, on St.
Eustatius, another Danish Caribbean island. It was the father of
Romeo and grandfather of Edward W. Blyden who came to the West
Indies from Igboland. Because of the poor circumstances of his
parents, Blyden was at first meant for the tailoring profession. But,
consumed with love for the ancestral continent and a desire to
contribute toward its advancement, he sailed to the United States
in search of education that would equip him to work in Africa.
Because he was black, American institutions of higher learning refused to admit him. Turning his mind to the budding Republic of

Liberia, he emigrated there in January 1851 with the aid of the New York Colonization Society to become a journalist, a Presbyterian minister of religion, diplomat, scholar, and above all, a Pan-African propagandist.

Blyden served as editor of the *Liberia Herald* for one year before he attained the age of twenty and later of *The Negro* launched in Freetown in 1872. A correspondent to the *Lagos Weekly Record*, he was at the time of his death in Sierra Leone (1912) a resident editor of *The African World*, an English periodical. On various occasions he held the office of commissioner to the descendants of Africa in the United States and the West Indies, minister of the interior, secretary of state, and ambassador to London and Paris. As a scholar, Blyden excelled in the classics and mathematics. He taught himself Hebrew, for he was anxious to read the earliest versions of the Bible, especially passages containing references to the African people.

In 1861 he became professor of Greek and Latin at Liberia College, Monrovia, and president of the college twenty years later. He first attracted public attention in England through a letter he wrote to William E. Gladstone, British chancellor of the Exchequer, in appreciation of his Budget of 1860. Gladstone used to carry this letter in his pocket in order to show it to his friends. It was eventually read in the House of Lords by Lord Brougham with the following comment: "The writer of this letter was engaged in the honourable office of teaching, and his quotations from Latin and Greek showed that he had, as he represented, devoted himself to the study of the ancient as well as the modern languages. . . . A better composed or better reasoned letter was never written."[71]

In recognition of his erudition, social and academic honors flowed to him from all corners of the globe. He was made fellow of the American Philological Association (1880), corresponding and honorary member of the Society of Sciences and Letters of Bengal (1882), vice president of the American Colonization Society (1884), vice president of the Africa Society of England as well as an honorary member of the highly exclusive Athenaeum Club of London. He was decorated with the Coronation Medal of King Edward VII and Queen Alexandra of Great Britain as well as by the governments of France and Turkey.[72]

More than in scholarship Blyden's fame lies in the sophisticated but articulate manner he presented Pan-African concepts. Himself a victim of color prejudice, Blyden naturally challenged the racial doctrines about the Negro. Many of his tracts, notably "Hope for Africa,"[73] "The Negro in Ancient History,"[74] and "Africa's Service to the World,"[75] as well as his address "Study and Race,"[76] are brilliant repudiations of nineteenth-century racism. He observed that all peoples who had risen from obscurity had had the same opposition of contempt to contend against. And "when our adversaries . . . pour their indignities, and fasten their disgraceful epithets upon us, let us take comfort in the thought," he urged, "that we are now beginning to enjoy the means which their ancestors were obliged to possess before they could rise from their obscure, ignoble and ignorant condition."[77]

No one in the days of Caesar or Tacitus could have predicted that the savage wildness of the German would give place to the learning and culture the people subsequently exhibited. When Cicero dismissed the Britons as unfit to serve as slaves, who would have dared to suggest, without appearing to insult the intelligence of decent men, that that people would be among the leading powers of the earth? If it was true that there was innate ability in certain races to rise in the scale of civilization, why did the Britons, when Greece and Rome flourished in all their grandeur, remain insignificant and unknown? There abounded tribes in whose veins coursed "the renowned Caucasian blood, sunk to-day in a degradation as deep, and in an ignorance as profound as any tribe in Africa."[78] If civilization was inborn in the Caucasian, every land inhabited by him ought to be in a high state of civilization. Why then were the peasantry of all the European countries so far down in the scale of civilization? Why did Greece, Italy, Portugal, Spain, and Turkey, which once flourished, sadly degenerate? "Why did not their Caucasian nature, if it did not urge them onward to higher attainments, keep them in the same leading position among the nations?"[79]

Demosthenes and Cicero, Caesar and Alexander, saw no serener sky and felt no more genial breeze than their degenerate posterity. The stars remained as beautiful and bright as when Homer and Virgil felt their inspiration. What then caused the difference? To a large extent, Blyden explained, men were the creatures of the circumstances in which they lived. Very often what they achieved depended more on the surrounding influences than on their personal qualities. The African formed no exception to this universal rule. Between him and the other men, there was not that difference which racists labored to establish. The African was in the rear of the European "not because of any essential difference existing in [his] nature, but only on account of differing circumstances."[80] The wonder, Blyden contended, was that despite the numerous obstacles being continually thrown in the path of his advancement, the African was not more backward.[81]

Appealing to the Bible and classical writers including Homer, Herodotus, Pindar, and Aeschylus, Blyden endeavored to show that ancient Africans were held in higher esteem than their contemporaries. Homer, who like Herodotus traveled in Egypt, made frequent mention of them. So fascinated was he by the fantastic achievements of these people that Homer raised their authors above mortals, making them associates of the gods.[82] Jupiter, and sometimes the entire Olympian family, was often made to betake himself to Ethiopia (i.e., Africa) to converse with and partake of the hospitality of the "blameless Ethiopians."[83]

To Africa the kings and philosophers of antiquity also resorted, either to gaze upon its wonders or to gather inspiration from its arts and sciences or to consult the Oracle of Jupiter, Ammon. From time immemorial the Ethiopians had been generous helpers. Out of its abundance, ancient Egypt furnished grains to the starving population of Europe. In modern times the "discovery" of the New World without Africa would have been useless, for neither the aboriginal Amerindian nor the European adventurers possessed the physical labor power to exploit the dazzling wealth before them. No history of modern civilization would be complete without a reference to the "black stream of humanity, which has poured into America from the heart of the Soudan."[84]

Nor could it be denied that the material development of England was aided beyond measure by the same black stream. "By means of Negro labor sugar and tobacco were produced; by means of sugar and tobacco British commerce was increased; by means of increased commerce the arts of culture and refinement were developed. The rapid growth and unparalleled prosperity of Lancashire are partly owing to the cotton supply of the Southern States, which could not have arisen to such importance without the labour of the Africans."[85] Contrary to the fulminations of the racists, then, Africans possessed not only an enviable past, though slightly marred by aberrations of barbarism; they had also made immense contributions to the general progress and happiness of humankind. Blyden expressed the hope that European writers would drop their discredited speculations and ridiculous assertions, at least now that the Atlantic slave trade had been suppressed and the necessity to deny the humanity as well as the attainments of Africans no longer existed.[86] Misled by the false theories of racists, "superficial teachers in Africa" were trying to Europeanize the African, that he might by losing, if possible, his identity "escape the doom which according to their amiable theology hangs over him—a curse which so far as he is concerned never had any existence—a miserable fiction, a wild phantasy [*sic*] of exploded commentators."[87] When "God lets men suffer and gives them to pain and death, it is not the abandoned, it is not the worst or the guiltiest, but the best and the purest, whom He often chooses for His work, for they will do it best."[88]

Blyden's admiration of the African past partly led him to take enormous pride in African culture. The phrase "African personality" was first used not by Kwame Nkrumah but by Blyden in a lecture, "Study and Race," read before the Young Men's Literary Association of Sierra Leone.[89] Among other things he regretted that there were Africans, especially those trained abroad, who were so unpatriotic as to advise

> "Let us do away with the sentiment of Race. Let us do away with our African personality and be lost, if possible, in another Race." This is as wise or as philosophical as to say, let us do away with gravitation, with heat and cold and sunshine and rain. Of course the Race in which these persons would be absorbed is the dominant race, before which, in cringing self-surrender and ignoble self-suppression they lie in prostrate admiration.[90]

Such admonition was unworthy of any true patriot whose plain duty, according to Blyden, is to defend and cultivate the peculiarity of his race.[91] Africans had been assigned a place in the universe; there was no room for them as something else. Of course, he was aware that some Africans and their descendants assumed the disgusting posture of "cringing self-surrender" through fear of offending European friends who might otherwise ostracize them. Nonetheless, he considered it more honorable to be ridiculed for being oneself than applauded for aping foreigners.[92] The African at home, he explained,

> needs to be surrounded by influence from abroad, not that he may change his nature, but that he may improve his capacity. Hereditary qualities are fundamental, not to be created or replaced by human agencies, but to be assisted and improved. Nature determines the kind of *tree*, environments determine the *quality* and *quantity* of the fruit. We want the Negro's eye and ear to be trained by culture that he may see more clearly what he does not see, and hear more distinctly what he does not hear. We want him to be surrounded by influence from abroad to promote the development of his latent powers, bring the potentiality of his being into practical or actual operation. He has capacities and aptitudes which the world needs, but which it will never enjoy until he is fairly and normally trained. In the music of the universe each shall give a different sound but necessary to the grand symphony.[93]

Little wonder he told an annual conference of the American Colonization Society that the young nation of Liberia would not be a copy of the United States; it would discover a method for its own development and it would be different from that of the Anglo-Saxons.[94]

To prevent the European agencies from destroying the African cultural heritage, Blyden pressed for the establishment of a West African university as well as a West African church to be controlled by Africans. He corresponded with J. Pope Hennessy, administrator in chief of the British West African Settlements, on the issue of a higher institution of learning.[95] Blyden proposed a curriculum based on the study of Greco-Roman classical civilization, mathematics, and African subjects, including African languages. Hennessy recommended the scheme to Lord Kimberley, secretary of state for the colonies. This led to the conversion of Fourah Bay College, originally founded as a theological institution in the 1820s, to a university college affiliated with Durham University, England. In the preface to the second edition of his major work, *Christianity, Islam and the Negro Race*, published after the correspondence with Hennessy, Blyden states that the book was meant for Negro youths eager to know the history, character, and destiny of their race. His *African Life and Customs*, which appeared four years before he died, further stimulated interest in African traditions.

Like James Johnson, Blyden supported the idea of Africanizing Christianity. Following a dispute between the CMS and Samuel Ajayi Crowther, the first African Anglican bishop, he called for the formation of an independent church. Such a church, he insisted, must be African, not a copy of the Anglican Church, adding that the "great incubus upon our development has been our unreasoning imitation."[96] In the same breath he warned against the danger of moving to the opposite extreme of shunning anything foreign merely because it is foreign. There were many good things in other peoples' customs; these, Africans should isolate and cherish.

Blyden's demand was among the reasons why the United Native African Church was set up in Lagos in 1891. Defending "native Christianity" at the Congress on Africa held in Atlanta, Georgia, four years later, Orishatuke Faduma maintained that there was no absolute connection between spiritual salvation and European usages.

Hence he discarded his foreign name, William James Davies, just as Mojola Agbebi (formerly D. B. Vincent) and the Gold Coaster S. R. B. Attoh Ahuma (formerly S. R. B. Solomon) had done. This was why Faduma demanded at the congress "a Christian life and thought expressed in Africa, not after the manner of a Frenchman, an American, or an Englishman but assimilated to Africa."[97] It was also for this reason that Blyden sometimes preferred Islam to Christianity. Islam, he often remarked, "possessed inherent elements of strength suited to the African in his environment, his racial character and traditions."[98]

Finally, Blyden also shared the hope of a grand African future. He conceded that suffering had been a conspicuous feature of the recent history of the African world. "But the future," he predicted confidently, "will have a different story to tell. The Cross precedes the Crown."[99] To quicken the regeneration of the continent Blyden advocated the establishment of what he called "an African Nationality." In common with most of his contemporaries he entertained no doubt that the African diaspora would ever become first-class citizens in the New World. Whites had for a long time had the upper hand. The educational institutions, banks, ships, and the media of propaganda belonged to them. The laws were framed and enforced by them. They also controlled the security forces. Given such an impregnable position it was impossible, so it seemed to Blyden, to dislodge them.

For him the only realistic solution was to be found in the creation of an African nationality. Africa's wealth was being appropriated by outsiders while its own sons, its legitimate owners, languished in poverty abroad. If the expertise these sons were wasting in trifling occupations were thrown into the ancestral continent, the result would be a strong and respectable African power. For three hundred years, he recalled, their skill and industry had been mainly responsible for the development of the Western Hemisphere while in Africa itself there was still no country powerful enough to check the continual threat from European nations to the sovereignty of Haiti and Liberia. As long as Africans remained disunited, he warned, they must expect to suffer from the whims and caprices of other peoples. He urged:

> We need some African power, some great centre of the race where our physical, pecuniary and intellectual strength may be collected. We need some spot whence such an influence may go forth in behalf of the race as shall be felt by the nations. We are now so scattered and divided that we can do nothing. The imposition begun last year (1861) by a foreign power upon Haiti, and which is still persisted in, fills every black man who has heard of it with indignation, but we are not strong enough to speak out effectually for that land. When the same power attempted an outrage upon the Liberians, there was no African power strong enough to interpose. So long as we remain thus divided, we may expect impositions. So long as we live simply by the sufferance of the nations, we must expect to be subject to their caprices. . . . We must build up negro states; we must establish and maintain the various institutions; we must make and administer laws, erect and preserve churches, and support the worship of God; we must have governments; we must have legislation of our own; we must build ships and navigate them; we must ply the trades, instruct the schools, control the press, and thus aid in shaping the opinions and guiding the destinies of mankind.[100]

Implicit in Blyden's African nationality is complete autonomy in political, economic, and religious affairs. His proposals anticipated much that first Marcus Garvey and later Kwame Nkrumah would advocate in the twentieth century. Perhaps it is not farfetched to see in the proposals the thin edge of the concept of Black Power as well as the idea of an Organization for African Unity backed by a high command.

It was partly in response to Blyden's call that many an exile returned to the fatherland in general and Liberia in particular during the nineteenth century. This motive is abundantly illustrated by an appeal issued in 1893 by the African American colonists of Maryland County in connection with a boundary dispute between Liberia and France. "We are not foreigners," they boasted,

> we are Africans and this is Africa. Such being the case we have certain natural rights—God-given rights—to this territory which no foreigner can have. We should have room enough, not only for our present population, but also to afford a home for our brethren in exile who may wish to return to their fatherland and help to build up this Negro nationality.[101]

The idea of a Negro nationality or an African nationality received further extension and elaboration at the hands of Timothy Thomas Fortune (1856–1928), an African American publicist. Though at first he opposed the back-to-Africa campaign, at the end of his life he became editor of Garveyite publications. Like the Reverend James Johnson he believed that European intervention in Africa would ultimately lead to solidarity and unification of the continent.

While James Johnson saw the Native Pastorate set up by the CMS in Sierra Leone as the embryo of a continental African church, the nucleus of a future African existence, Fortune foretold that the proliferation of African nationalities arising from the European partition would culminate in some sort of a united states of Africa. Speaking at the Atlanta Congress of Africa of 1895 he insisted that Africans

> will be forced into this federation in self defence, as the American colonists were. History repeats itself. The nationalization of the African confederation which is a foregone conclusion from the facts in the case, will be the first step toward bringing the whole continent under one system of government. . . . It is written in the Holy Book that Ethiopia shall stretch forth her hand to God. Is it in the power of men to make of no effect the divine prophecy? Perish the thought. There shall yet be evolved out of the conflicting race elements on the continent of Africa a civilization whose glory and whose splendour and whose strength shall eclipse all others that now are, or that have gone before.[102]

Finally, we must cast a glance at the Haitian propagandist, scholar, and diplomat, Benito Sylvain (1868–1915). He is important not because of any novel ideas he propounded—his ideas were essentially those of his contemporaries—but because he is an interesting personality who deserves to be better known. In his book *Du Sort des indigènes dans les colonies d'exploitation* (Paris 1901), his titles are given as *officier de la marine haitienne, stagiaire de la marine française, aide de camp de sa majesté l'empereur d'Ethiopie, docteur en droit de la faculté de Paris, délégué général de l'association pan-africaine*. Other publications by him include *L'Etoile africaine: Bulletin de l'oeuvre du relèvement social des noirs*, the first number of which appeared in 1906, and *L'Oeuvre de la régénération africaine*.

Born on 21 March 1868 at Port-de-Paix (northwest Haiti), Sylvain took courses in naval studies at Collège Stanislas and later at L'Ecole Saint Charles, Saint Brienne, in France. Because of an 1887 edict forbidding foreigners to enter the French naval academy, he abandoned science in favor of philosophy, for which he gained a degree after a short period of intensive study. He attained similar distinction in journalism, repudiating attacks against the African race penned by the Frenchman Gaston Jollivet in *Le Matin* in 1888. The next year Sylvain served as secretary to the Haitian delegation in London. On his return to France in 1890 he challenged Charles Canivet, who had written a series of anti-African articles in *Le Soleil*.

Sylvain's replies were highly commended as a brilliant vindication of his maligned brethren and as an adequate refutation of those whom Sylvain himself nicknamed *aristocrates de la peau*. As a delegate to the Brussels Anti-Slavery Convention of Paris in 1891, he read a paper, "L'Evolution de la race noire," besprinkled with sentiment of Pan-African dimension. As the African American agitator James Theodore Holly had argued thirty-four years earlier, Sylvain maintained that the Haitian Revolution conclusively demonstrated the equality of the black and white races when the odds were even. Sylvain conceded the relative backwardness of Africa vis-à-vis Europe, but he maintained that this situation would not continue forever. From Africa shall radiate for the benefit of all humanity that sublime precept: Love your neighbor as yourself. Anticipating Blyden's lecture "Study and Race," Sylvain assured his audience that when Africa's hour of glory arrived, Africans would not abuse the opportunity to revenge themselves by suppressing less privileged peoples. Instead, Africans would endeavor to belie the monstrous aphorism: *homo homini lupus*. Referring to the historic Scramble for Africa, he regretted that whenever Europeans thought about Africa, it was to carve out portions of that continent for themselves with the result that international conferences had come to have no other purpose than to demarcate boundaries of territories the great powers had awarded themselves.

Benito Sylvain stands out as one of the last noteworthy exponents of Pan-African ideas. From 1893 onward, politically conscious men of African blood began to summon Pan-African conferences and to organize themselves in pressure groups, thus transforming Pan-African ideas into a movement.

1. *The Crisis*, November 1933, 247.

2. The proceedings of the conference have been published under the title *Pan-Africanism Reconsidered*, edited by the American Society of African Culture (Berkeley and Los Angeles: University of California Press, 1962).

3. Colin Legum, *Pan-Africanism: A Short Political Guide* (New York: Frederick A. Praeger, 1962), 14.

4. Adekunle Ajala, *Pan-Africanism: Evolution, Progress and Prospects* (London: Andre Deutsche, 1973).

5. Robert G. Weisbord, *Ebony Kinship: Africa, Africans and the Afro-American* (London: Greenwood Press, 1973).

6. Kenneth King, *Pan-Africanism and Education* (London: Oxford University Press, 1971).

7. J. Ayodele Langley, *Pan-Africanism and Nationalism in West Africa, 1900–1945* (London: Oxford University Press, 1973).

8. Imanuel Geiss, *The Pan-Africanism Movement* (London: Methuen, 1974).

9. V. Bakpetu Thompson, *Africa and Unity: The Evolution of Pan-Africanism* (London: Longman, 1969).

10. A. A. Nwafor Orizu, *Without Bitterness: Western Nations in Post-War Africa* (New York: Creative Age Press, 1944).

11. Mbonu Ojike, *My Africa* (New York: John Day, 1946).

12. S. D. Cudjoe, *Aids to African Autonomy* (London: College Press, 1949).

13. Ato K. Wodajo, "Pan-Africanism: The Evolution of an Idea," *Ethiopia Observer* 8 (1964): 166.

14. John H. Clarke, "The Development of Pan-Africanist Ideas in the Americas and in Africa Before 1900." Paper presented at the Second World Black and African Festival of Arts and Culture, Lagos, Nigeria, 15 January–12 February 1977. Text no. col. 5/03/USA. 12, 6–7.

15. Langley, *Pan-Africanism and Nationalism in West Africa*, 368.

16. Ibid., 8.

17. For details of some of the disabilities see P. O. Esedebe, "Pan-Africanism: Origins and Meaning," *Tarikh* 6 (1979): 13–17.

18. Hollis R. Lynch, "Pan-Negro Nationalism in the New World Before 1862," in *The Making of Black Americans*, vol. 1, ed. August Meier and Elliott Rudwick (New York: Atheneum, 1969), 46.

19. Leslie H. Fishel, Jr., and Benjamin Quarles, *The Negro American. A Documentary History* (Glenview, Ill.: Scott, Foresman, 1967), 145.

20. *African Repository*, March 1829, 11.

21. For a text of the discourse see Carter G. Woodson, *Negro Orators and Their Orations* (Washington, D.C.: Associated Publishers, 1925). See also Fishel and Quarles, *The Negro American*, 145–47.

22. Fishel and Quarles, *The Negro American*, 163–64.

23. Duncan J. McLeod, *Slavery, Race and the American Revolution* (Cambridge: Cambridge University Press, 1974).

24. Woodson, *Negro Orators and Their Orations*, 163–64.

25. McLeod, *Slavery, Race and the American Revolution*, 164.

26. See, for example, *African Repository*, October 1877, 114–16.

27. *Equiano's Travels*, abridged ed. (London and Ibadan: Heinemann, 1967), 84.

28. C. P. Groves, *The Planting of Christianity in Africa*, vol. 2 (London, 1954), 28; E. B. Underhill, *Alfred Saker* (London, 1884), 169–71.

29. Groves, *The Planting of Christianity*, 30.

30. Abioseh Nicol, "West Indians in West Africa," *Sierra Leone Studies*, n.s. 15 (June 1960): 18.

31. In Cuba alone in 1827, there were some twenty thousand more free persons of color than in the whole of the British West Indies. W. L. Mathieson, *British Slavery and Its Abolition* (London, 1926), 40. See also Frank Tannenbaum, *Slave and Citizen* (New York, 1947) and C. R. Boxer, *Race Relations in the Portuguese Colonial Empire* (London: Oxford University Press, 1963).

32. José Honorio Rodrigues, *Brazil and Africa*, trans. Richard A. Mazzara and Sam Hileman (Berkeley and Los Angeles: University of California Press, 1965), 80, 101, n. 118.

33. Frank Tannenbaum, *Ten Keys to Latin America* (New York: Vintage Books, 1962), 49.

34. Quoted in Edward W. Blyden, "The Return of the Exiles," *African Repository*, January 1892, 17.

35. Joseph E. Harris, *The African Presence in Asia: Consequences of the East African Slave Trade* (Evanston, Ill.: Northwestern University Press, 1971). See also a review of Harris's book by Vasant D. Rao in *Journal of Modern African Studies* 13 (1975): 356–58.

36. Thomas Arnold, *Introductory Lectures on Modern History* (Oxford: Clarendon Press, 1842), 37.

37. W. R. Greg, "Dr. Arnold," *Westminster Review* 39 (January 1843): 6.

38. Ibid., 6–33, passim.

39. Robert Knox, *The Races of Men* (London, 1850), chap. 6.

40. A. H. Foote, *Africa and the American Flag* (New York, 1854), 207.

41. Arthur de Gobineau, *Essai sur l'inégalité des races humaines*, 4 vols. (Paris, 1853, 1855).

42. Quoted in Philip D. Curtin, *The Image of Africa: British Ideas and Action, 1780–1850* (London: Macmillan, 1965), 380–81.

43. James Theodore Holly, *A Vindication of the Capacity of the Negro Race for Self-Government and Civilized Progress, as Demonstrated by Historical Events of the Haytian Revolution and the Subsequent Acts of That People Since Their National Independence* (New Haven, Conn., 1857).

44. Ibid., 5.

45. Ibid., 6.

46. Ibid., 44.

47. See Hollis R. Lynch, "West African Biography: A Historiographical Study," paper given at the African Historical Association meeting in New York, December 1971.

48. George Shepperson, " 'Pan-Africanism' and 'pan-Africanism': Some Historical Notes," 4–5, seminar paper given at the Institute of Commonwealth Studies, London University, April 1961; J. B. Webster, *The African Churches Among the Yoruba 1888–1922* (London: Oxford University Press, 1964), xiv–xv.

49. Bengt Sundkler, *Bantu Prophets in South Africa* (London: Oxford University Press, 1964), 53.

50. Jomo Kenyatta, *Facing Mount Kenya* (London: Mercury Books, 1962), 269.

51. Sundkler, *Bantu Prophets*, 38.

52. Quoted in Webster, *African Churches Among the Yoruba*, 68.

53. H. Rudin, *Germans in the Cameroon* (London, 1938), 340, 356.

54. For details see George Shepperson and Thomas Price, *Independent African: John Chilembwe and the Origins, Setting and Significance of the Nyasaland Native Rising of 1915* (Edinburgh: Edinburgh University Press, 1958).

55. Thomas Hodgkin, *Nationalism in Colonial Africa* (London: Frederick Muller, 1956), 98.

56. J. A. B. Horton, *West African Countries and Peoples . . . A Vindication*

of the African Race (1868; reprint, Edinburgh: Edinburgh University Press, 1969), 59.

57. Ibid., 60.

58. Ibid., 61.

59. Ibid., 60.

60. Ibid., 69.

61. Ibid., 175.

62. E. A. Ayandele, *Holy Johnson: Pioneer of African Nationalism, 1836– 1917* (London: Frank Cass, 1970). See P. O. Esedebe, "Holy Johnson," *Journal of African History* 13 (1972): 165–68.

63. Ayandele, *Holy Johnson*, 45.

64. Ibid.

65. John D. Hargreaves, "Blyden of Liberia," *History Today* 19 (August 1969): 568.

66. Bosworth Smith, *The Nineteenth Century*, December 1887, 793–94.

67. Ibid.

68. *Lagos Weekly Record*, 27 November 1890.

69. J. E. Casely-Hayford, *Ethiopia Unbound: Studies in Race Emancipation* (London, 1911), chap. 16, passim.

70. *Sierra Leone Weekly News*, 10 February 1912, 6; Edith Holden, *Blyden of Liberia: An Account of the Life and Labours of Edward Wilmot Blyden, LL.D. as Recorded in Letters and in Print* (New York, 1966), 19. Several important works still contain erroneous information about the nationality of Blyden's parents. George Padmore, *Pan-Africanism or Communism? The Coming Struggle for Africa* (London: Dennis Dobson, 1956), 54, claims they were from the Gold Coast, probably because of the author's friendship with Kwame Nkrumah; Legum, *Pan-Africanism: A Short Political Guide*, 20, suggests Togoland; Claude Wauthier, *The Literature and Thought of Modern Africa* (London: Pall Mall Press, 1966), 307, prefers Sierra Leone.

71. Quoted in Edward W. Blyden, *The African Society and Miss Mary H. Kingsley* (articles reprinted from the *Sierra Leone Weekly News*, March, April, May, and June 1901), introduction by Alice Stopford Green (London, 1901).

72. L. C. Gwam, "Dr. Edward Wilmot Blyden, M.A., D.D., LL.D. (1832–1912)," Ibadan, no. 15.

73. *African Repository*, September 1861, 258–71.

74. *African Repository*, June 1869, 161–72; July 1869, 193–201.

75. *African Repository*, October 1881, 109–25.

76. *Sierra Leone Weekly News*, 27 May 1893, 2–4.

77. *African Repository*, November 1862, 348.

78. *African Repository*, September 1861, 261.

79. Ibid., 263.

80. Ibid., 264.

81. Ibid.

82. *African Repository*, June 1869, 165.

83. *Iliad*, i, 423; xxiii, 206.

84. *African Repository*, October 1881, 114.

85. Ibid., 114–15.

86. Edward W. Blyden, *From West Africa to Palestine* (Freetown, 1873), 106.

87. *Sierra Leone Weekly News*, 9 April 1892, 3.

88. Edward W. Blyden, *The Origin and Purpose of African Colonization* (Washington D.C., 1883), 18.

89. Printed in *Sierra Leone Weekly News*, 27 May 1893, 2–4.

90. Ibid., passim.

91. Ibid.

92. J. Walter Cason, "E. W. Blyden's Contribution to the African Personality," *Cuttington Review* 3 (June 1962).

93. *African Repository*, January 1879, 3–4.

94. Blyden, *Origin and Purpose of African Colonization*, 18.

95. Edward W. Blyden, *The West African University* (Freetown, 1872).

96. For details see Webster, *African Churches Among the Yoruba*, and J. F. Ade Ajayi, *Christian Missions in Nigeria* (London: Longman, 1965); Edward W. Blyden, *The Return of the Exiles and the West African Church* (London 1891), 25–32.

97. J. W. E. Bowen, ed., *Africa and the American Negro: Addresses and Proceedings of the Congress on Africa* (Atlanta, 1896), 25–136, passim.

98. *West Africa*, November 1900, 225.

99. *Sierra Leone Weekly News*, 27 May 1893, 3.

100. Edward W. Blyden, *Liberia's Offering* (New York, 1892), 74–76.

101. Quoted in John D. Hargreaves, "Liberia: The Price of Independence," *Odu* (A Journal of West African Studies), n.s., no. 6 (October 1971): 14.

102. "The Nationalization of Africa," in Bowen, *Africa and the American Negro*, 199–204.

2

From Idea to Movement

THE CHICAGO CONGRESS ON AFRICA of 1893 may be taken as the beginning of Pan-Africanism as a movement. W. E. B. Du Bois's assertion that the Pan-African meeting summoned in London in 1900 put the word "Pan-African" in the dictionaries for the first time is largely responsible for the orthodox view that that gathering was the first Pan-African convocation ever. Actually, the Chicago Congress on Africa of which our authorities appear to be unaware has a better claim. Opened on 14 August 1893, it lasted for a whole week. Among the participants were Africans and persons of African descent in the New World, notably Alexander Crummell; Yakub Pasha, presumably an Egyptian; Bishop Henry Turner, an ardent advocate of the back-to-Africa movement and founder of the African Methodist Episcopal churches in Sierra Leone and Liberia; Bishop Alexander Walters of the African Methodist Episcopal Zion Church, who seven years later would chair the London congress; and the African American Frederick Perry Noble, secretary to the conference.[1] The American Colonization Society was represented by its secretary, J. Ormond Wilson, a retired educator. Other whites present included European scientists, explorers, and missionaries, most of whom had come to Chicago primarily for the World Columbian Exhibition held there that summer.

Edward W. Blyden and Booker T. Washington promised papers; that of the Reverend James Johnson was read by proxy. In all, one hundred papers were given, half of them by members of "the African race."[2] Some of the topics debated were "The African in America," "Liberia as a Factor in the Progress of the Negro Race," contributed by J. Ormond Wilson, and "What Do American Negroes Owe to Their Kin Beyond the Sea."[3] Turner seized the opportunity to urge African exiles to return to the fatherland. A few months before the congress he had warned that French encroachments on Liberia's frontier and the general "increase of whites all along since I last visited Africa" might culminate in the capture of the only spot (besides Haiti and Abyssinia) "upon the face of the globe [where] the black man can ever hope to be in power and demonstrate the ability of self-government."[4]

Commenting on the congress, the *Advance*, a Chicago newspaper, stated: "This great congress was unquestionably one of the most notable convocations of recent years in any country. We have had pan-Presbyterian, pan-Methodist, pan-Anglican, pan-missionary and pan-Congregational councils. . . . But none signified more than this pan-African conference."[5]

Anti-European feeling was also voiced at another congress on Africa called this time in Atlanta, Georgia, in December 1895 under the auspices of the Steward Missionary Foundation for Africa of Gammon Theological Seminary. Among those in attendance was the African American John Henry Smyth (1844–1908), a former United States minister resident and consul general to Liberia, who was honored by President Richard W. Johnson of Liberia with the title "Knight Commander of the Liberian Order of African Redemption." In his address, "The African in Africa and the African in America," Smyth attributed the appalling conditions in Africa to the activities of the European adventurers. "European contact," he lamented, "has brought in its train not merely the sacrifice, amid unspeakable horrors, of the lives and liberties of twenty million Negroes for the American market alone, but political disintegration, social anarchy, moral and physical debasement."[6]

It is partly against the background of this growing anticolonial sentiment among the African diaspora that the African Association was launched in England on 24 September 1897, mainly through the efforts of Henry Sylvester Williams, an Afro-West Indian barrister from Trinidad.[7] As the center of wide imperial and missionary interests, Great Britain was a natural focus for a protest movement. The organization aimed

> to encourage a feeling of unity; to facilitate friendly intercourse among Africans in general; to promote and protect the interest of all subjects

claiming African descent, wholly or in part, in British Colonies and other places especially in Africa, by circulating accurate information on all subjects affecting their rights and privileges as subjects of the British Empire, and by direct appeals to the Imperial and local Governments.[8]

The founders of the African Association were convinced that the time had come when the voice of blacks should be heard independently in their own affairs and that this could be best achieved by a pressure group with headquarters in London, the metropolitan capital.[9] Three patrons served it. They were J. Otonba Payne, an ex-registrar of the supreme court of Lagos; Dr. Mojola Agbebi, pastor of the United African Church, Lagos; and a lawyer, D. Augustus Straker, probably from the West Indies. The officers were the Reverend H. Mason Joseph, a master of arts from Antigua (president); H. Sylvester Williams (honorary secretary); Moses Da Rocha of Lagos (assistant secretary); and John Otonba Augustus Payne, the patron (treasurer).[10] Meetings of the organization took place at 139 Palace Chambers, Westminster.[11]

In his autobiography, Bishop Alexander Walters gives the credit of conceiving the idea of summoning the London congress to Henry Sylvester Williams.[12] But in a letter of 8 June 1899 to Booker T. Washington, Williams himself states that he had been "authorised by the Officers and Committee of Our Association to bring to your notice the proposed conference which you will notice in the enclosed Circular."[13] Washington was also requested to "make this known as widely as is possible."[14]

A similar letter was sent to Benito Sylvain.[15] By June 1900 a Pan-African conference committee had been created with the following officers: the Reverend H. Mason Joseph (chairman), the Reverend Thos. L. Johnson (vice chairman), Henry Sylvester Williams (general secretary), R. E. Phipps, a barrister (secretary for West Indies), Henry Plange (secretary for West Africa), Peregrino (secretary for South Africa), and Hector Macpherson (treasurer).[16]

What must now be regarded as the second Pan-African congregation eventually took place from 23 to 25 July 1900 under the chairmanship of Alexander Walters in the Westminster Town Hall. The objectives of the meeting were:

> First, to bring into closer touch with each other the peoples of African descent throughout the world; second to inaugurate plans to bring about a more friendly relation between the Caucasian and African races;

third, to start a movement looking forward to the securing to all African races living in civilized countries their full rights and to promote their business interests.[17]

Altogether about thirty-two delegates from various sections of the African world attended—men, women, and university students whose occupations or courses of study would normally place them in the middle class. Among the African American contingent may be mentioned Anna J. Cooper of M Street High School, Washington, D.C.; Anna H. Jones, a master of arts from Missouri; and Du Bois. Haiti was represented by Bishop J. F. Holly. Notable Afro-West Indians included the Reverend H. Mason Joseph; R. E. Phipps; G. J. Christian of Dominica; and J. E. Quinlan, a land surveyor from Saint Lucia.

From Africa came about ten representatives, the most prominent being J. Otonba Payne; James Johnson; the Sierra Leonean councillor, G. W. Dove; A. Ribero, a Gold Coast barrister; F. R. S. Johnson, formerly Liberia's attorney-general; and Benito Sylvain.

The Afro-West Indian Literary Society of Edinburgh was represented by Mr. Meyer, a West Indian medical student at Edinburgh University, and R. Akinwande Savage, a medical doctor from Lagos. The latter subsequently became an editor of the influential newspaper the *Gold Coast Leader* and at the end of the Great War helped J. E. Casely-Hayford to form the National Congress of British West Africa (NCBWA). Also in attendance were several exiles resident in England. They included John Alcindor, a Trinidadian medical practitioner trained at the University of Edinburgh, the Reverend Henry Smith about whom not much is known, and Henry Sylvester Williams.

Benito Sylvain and F. R. S. Johnson were made vice chairmen of the conference.[18] Some of the sessions were attended by three English Afrophiles, namely Bishop Colenso of South African fame; R. J. Colenso, a relation of the bishop; and G. B. Clark, a liberal member of Parliament.[19] Conspicuously absent was the veteran Pan-African theorist Edward W. Blyden, but some of his ideas on the African past and arguments for race individuality were echoed in the course of the deliberations.

The address of welcome was delivered by Dr. Creighton, the lord bishop of London. He assured the delegates that they enjoyed the sympathy and support of men of goodwill throughout the realm, expressing the hope that similar congresses would take place in the future. Alexander Walters opened the meeting with a paper entitled "The Trials and Achievements of the Coloured Race in America."[20] He set out the disabilities suffered by Negroes there, tracing their long struggle for the attainment of social, economic, and political liberties enjoyed by their white counterparts. Every form of violence and defamation was being used by white men to prevent the advancement of the colored population. Concluding, Walters explained that the purpose of the conference was "to organise, to better their condition, and to lay their claims before the white races, from whom they desired respect and recognition."[21]

In the evening the chief item was a paper, "The Necessary Concord to Be Established Between the Native Races and European Colonists," read by Benito Sylvain.[22] The African race, he said, had successfully proved its manhood. A race which in the face of formidable obstacles blocking its path of advancement had produced such men as Toussaint L'Ouverture, Alexander Dumas, Pushkin, and Emperor Menelik II deserved the respect of the rest of humanity. Britain was blamed for conniving at the abuses created by the concession systems and therefore held responsible for the antiliberal reaction characteristic of colonial policy in the preceding fifteen years. Before many years would pass the rights of the indigenous inhabitants must be recognized by every imperial power. In the meantime, he urged the metropolitan governments to end the practice of treating their subjects as serfs and maintained that no human power could stop the Africans in their social and political development.[23]

The next day, the congress debated the topic "The Progress of Our People in the Light of Current History." Opening it, F. R. S. Johnson gave a glowing but exaggerated account of the achievements of African American colonists in Liberia. In a speech more sensational than Johnson's and which was undisguised counterracism, John E. Quinlan asserted that there was scientific evidence in support of superiority of blacks over whites, both in "skin and skull."[24]

Another topic discussed during the morning sessions was "Africa, the Sphinx of History in the Light of Unsolved Problems." The first speaker on this issue was an African American student, M. D. Tobias, who summed up civilization as a system under which blacks slaved for the whites.[25]

The debate was continued in the evening, when two further papers were read. One with the title "Some Startling Historical Facts of the History of the Negro" was contributed by the Reverend Henry Smith. He dismissed as racist the theory that the black man descended from apes and monkeys. The idea is in fact not racist being part of the evolutionary doctrine of the time that all Homo sapiens are so descended. Smith went on to claim with obvious exaggeration and oversimplification that the great and the marvelous in ancient Egyptian civilization owed its stimulus and impetus to the neighboring southern city-states now known as Sudan, Ethiopia, and Nubia. "Just as the River Nile," he proceeded, "had its source and rise in Ethiopia and its ebb and flow in Egypt, so all that was great and distinguished—architecturally, religiously, and in the sense of civilization—had its rise in the lower country."[26] Contrary to popular impression, the Negro race had a grand and noble past and he hoped that it would have a yet grander and nobler future.[27] Smith recalled that Homer in the *Iliad* sang of these Africans beyond Egypt as favorites of the gods. The other paper, "A Plea for Race Individuality," was given by Anna H. Jones. She contended that the Negro's nature was artistic and religious. This artistic and spiritual disposition, she pleaded, must not be allowed to be soiled by the ephemeral materialistic civilization of the Anglo-Saxon.[28]

Part of the session of the third and last day of the meeting was devoted to a scrutiny of the colonial policies. Both G. J. Christian and Henry Sylvester Williams condemned the native policies in South Africa and the Rhodesias and insisted on reforms.[29] The rest of the session considered and adopted a report from a committee providing for the formation of a permanent Pan-African Association apparently to replace the African Association. The objectives of the new organization were:

1. to secure civil and political rights for Africans and their descendants throughout the world;
2. to encourage friendly relations between the Caucasian and African races;
3. to encourage African peoples everywhere in educational, industrial, and commercial enterprise;

4. to approach Governments and influence legislation in the interests of the black races; and

5. to ameliorate the condition of the oppressed Negro in Africa,
America, the British Empire, and other parts of the world.[30]

A central body or secretariat located at 61-62 Chancery Lane,
London, was set up. Officers were elected for a term of two years
as follows: Bishop Alexander Walters (president), Henry Sylvester
Williams (general secretary), and R. J. Colenso (general treasurer).[31]
An executive committee of four men and two women was elected
to help the secretariat. Three of the members were Anna J. Cooper;
the musician Samuel Coleridge-Taylor; and J. R. Archer, a prominent West Indian resident in London.[32] Emperor Menelik II and the
presidents of Haiti and Liberia were made honorary members of the
Pan-African Association.[33] There were provisions for the establish-
ment of branches in different parts of Africa, the Caribbean, and
United States, which were to be self-governing.[34] Among the officers elected for the branches were Benito Sylvain (Abyssinia),
J. Otonba Payne and N. W. Holm (Lagos), Edwin Vin Loch (Natal),
J. W. Williams and A. Lewis (Sierra Leone), and W. E. B. Du Bois
(Unites States).[35] The vacancies for Canada, Trinidad, Gold Coast,
Cape Town, Orange River Colony, Transvaal, and Rhodesia could
not be filled during the congress.[36] The members of the branches
were required to pay a shilling a year to meet local expenses and
each member four shillings annually to the secretariat in England.[37]
A conference of the association would be called every two years;
accordingly, it was decided that the next meeting would take place
in 1902 in the United States and another in Haiti in 1904.[38]

The gathering then adopted a draft statement, "To The Nations
Of The World," submitted by Du Bois on behalf of a subcommittee,
and despatched to sovereigns in whose territories persons of African origin might be found.[39] The problem of the twentieth century
was prophetically recognized as the problem of the color line, the
problem as to how far differences of race, as manifested in skin
color and hair texture, were going to be used as criteria for denying
more than half the population of the globe the right to share, to
their utmost ability, the blessings of modern civilization. It was
conceded that the darker races of the time lagged behind their
European counterparts. "This has not, however, always been the
case in the past, and certainly the world's history, both ancient and

modern, has given many instances of no despicable ability and capacity among the blackest races of men."[40]

Reacting against the Yellow Peril fantasy of the day, the congress pointed out that the so-called colored peoples were bound to exercise tremendous influence on the world by virtue of their numerical superiority. If blacks and other "backward" peoples were given the opportunity for education and self-government, this influence would be channeled along lines beneficial to all humankind. "But if, by reason of carelessness, prejudice, greed and injustice, the black world is to be exploited and ravished and degraded, the results must be deplorable, if not fatal, not simply to them but to the high ideals of justice, freedom, and culture which a thousand years of Christian civilization have held before Europe."[41]

The congress then suggested ways and means of achieving these high ideals of civilization. Discrimination on grounds of race and color must cease. The aspirations and interests of Africans must not be subordinated to the greed for gold, "their liberties taken away, their family life debauched, their just aspirations repressed, and avenues of advancement and culture taken from them."[42] Missionary enterprise must no longer be used as a screen to hide "the ruthless economic exploitation and political downfall of less developed nations, whose chief fault has been reliance on the plighted faith of the Christian Church."[43] Great Britain was invited to complete the noble work of Wilberforce, Clarkson, Buxton, Sharp, Livingstone, and Bishop Colenso by granting as soon as practicable the right of responsible government to its colonies in Africa and the Caribbean. The conscience of the United States was challenged to "rise and rebuke all dishonesty and unrighteous oppression toward the American Negro, and grant to him the right of franchise, security of person and property, and generous recognition of the great work he has accomplished in a generation toward raising nine millions of human beings from slavery to manhood."[44] France and Germany were reminded that the true worth of imperial dependencies "lies in their prosperity and progress, and that justice, impartial alike to black and white, is the first element of prosperity." The Congo Free State should become "a great central Negro State of the world" (i.e., an African nationality) whose prosperity should be measured not in terms of cash and commerce, but in the happiness and genuine advancement of its inhabitants.

Finally, the congress made an appeal to the nations of the world on the one hand and to persons of African extraction on the other. The Great Powers were requested to respect the integrity and autonomous status of Abyssinia, Haiti, and Liberia. At the same time the inhabitants of these countries as well as the African diaspora were exhorted to "strive ceaselessly, and fight bravely that they may prove to the world their incontestable right to be counted among the great brotherhood of mankind."[45] A separate memorial protesting against the condition of Her Majesty's subjects in the British Empire including South Africa was sent to Queen Victoria. The British secretary for the colonies in a reply assured "the members of the Pan-African Conference that, in settling the lines on which the administration of the conquered territories is to be conducted, Her Majesty's Government will not overlook the interests and welfare of the native races."[46] He also stated that a copy of the memorial had been communicated to the high commissioner for South Africa.

As an attempt to institutionalize Pan-Africanism, the Pan-African Association had great symbolic value and therefore was of considerable historical significance. But the achievements of the organization itself were short-lived. Its immediate achievement seems to be the journal *The Pan-African*, launched in October 1901 with the motto Light and Liberty. Edited by Henry Sylvester Williams, it was a monthly intended to disseminate information concerning the interests of the peoples of the African world. Though the journal promised to feature the progress and culture of the African world in subsequent issues, it did not survive the first number.

Earlier in March the same year Williams had traveled to the West Indies to involve his own people in the work of the Pan-African Association. A meeting was held toward the end of that month in Saint George's School, Kingston, Jamaica, with the aim of starting a local branch there.[47] During his absence from England some of his colleagues alleged there were no funds and dissolved the Pan-African Association. As a result of this arbitrary action, Alexander Walters and Henry Sylvester Williams hurried to London and on 13 September announced the continuation of the organization. The following were appointed members of the executive committee in replacement of those considered to have resigned: Bishop Small from Pennsylvania, the Reverend Henry Smith, J. Otonba Payne, the South African Tengo Jabavu, Lieutenant Lazare of Trinidad, and the medical practitioner Dr. R. N. Love, who was born in Nassau (Bahamas) and educated in England and on the European continent but spent many years in Jamaica fighting for the uplift of the black masses.[48] Williams was reelected general secretary until the next congress met in 1902. But the proposed conference never took place, and when Williams returned to the Caribbean, the Pan-African Association lapsed into obscurity.

By including colonial reforms in their resolutions, the London congress implicitly accepted the new order of European domination as a fait accompli. With the collapse of the Pan-African Association, individuals assumed the task of keeping Pan-African ideals alive and airing colonial grievances. During the ensuing decade the need to preserve African traditions became an obsession. Seizing the opportunity offered by the death of Mary Kingsley, Edward W. Blyden further elaborated the concept of the African personality in a series of articles written for the *Sierra Leone Weekly News*. Intended as a tribute to her courageous defense of the African way of life, they were subsequently reprinted in London as a pamphlet under the title *The African Society and Miss Mary H. Kingsley*.[49] To her, the African was a different kind of being from white men; his intelligence might even be found to be superior to theirs. But it was a different kind of intelligence incapable of moving along European lines of thought. Because of this difference it was wrong to regard African society as a childish groping toward the European model. "On the contrary, African religion, African morality and society were natural and proper expressions of African personality, and to try to improve them would produce only bastardization, corruption, and degradation."[50] No race, as a race, could make progress except along its own line of development.[51] Customs usually sneered at in Europe as a welter of cruelty, cannibalism, and barbarism she examined with sympathy. She rebuked the missionaries severely for attempting to empty the African mind of its content and refill it with Christian dogma, which tended to create more problems than it solved. In her last letter written on her way to South Africa and addressed to a Liberian newspaper, *The New Africa*, she complained that she had had to stand alone for two years fighting for Africa's freedom and institutions while Africans equally well and better educated in English culture had been prattling about religious matters to a pack of people who did not care about Christianity at all.[52]

Africans were exhorted to defend their institutions, to refute the stay-at-home politicians who thought that Africans were all awful savages or silly children to be dealt with only on a reformatory penitentiary line, to combat the false theories of missionaries, officials, and stray travelers "who for their own aggrandisement exaggerate the difficulties and dangers with which they have to deal."[53]

All this Blyden recalled with great emotion. In an address delivered before the Africa Society in 1903, Blyden, in answer to Miss Kingsley's strictures on the educated African, maintained that if an African trained on European lines was unable or unwilling to teach the outside world something of the institutions and inner feelings of his people, "if he cannot make his friends feel the force of his racial character and sympathise with his racial aspiration, then it is evident that his education has been sadly defective, that his training by aliens has done but little for him—that his teachers have surely missed their aim and wasted their time."[54]

At this time, too, Mojola Agbebi gave a sermon that won the admiration of Blyden and other prominent persons of African descent in the New World. The occasion was the celebration of the first anniversary of the African Church. Under the guise of exposing the defects of the version of Christianity being offered to Africans, Agbebi drew attention to the discrepancy between the words and deeds of the imperialists. What did one think, he asked, of a "religion which points with one finger to the skies, bidding you, lay up for yourselves treasures in heaven, and while you are looking up grasps all your worldly goods with the other hand, seizes your ancestral lands, levels your forests, and places your patrimony under inexplicable legislation."[55]

With the same breath he defended the African way of life. Hymnals were unnecessary for the propagation of the Christian faith. A hymn that induced solemnity in Saint Paul's Cathedral, England, might merely excite disgust in a church among the Kru of Liberia. The fact that everyone calls barbarian what is not his own usage reinforced his conviction that English hymns were actually unsuited to African aspirations; hence he thought it undesirable that Africans should dance to foreign music in their social festivities, sing to foreign music in their churches, march to foreign music in their funerals, and use foreign models to cultivate their musical talents.[56] Prayer books, harmonium dedications, pew constructions, surpliced choir, the white man's style, the white man's name, the white man's dress, all he dismissed as superfluities. For him the proper vehicle of thought of any country was to be found in its vernacular dialect. Africans must therefore cultivate an effective use of their mother tongue(s). Was not the grace bestowed on the day of Pentecost considered marvelous because every man heard in his native language the wonderful works of God?

The publication of Mojola Agbebi's sermon in the *Sierra Leone Weekly News* for 14 March 1903 provoked widespread comment. "This is the first time," exclaimed Blyden, "I have known of a native African . . . imbued with European culture, uttering views so radically different from the course of his training, but intrinsically African and so valuable for the guidance of his people."[57] The African American journalist, John Edward Bruce (1856–1923), who as a filing clerk in the 1880s first met Blyden in the rooms of the American Colonization Society, Washington, D.C., was no less impressed. Considering the sermon worthy of wider notice than it was likely to receive in the West African press, he republished it in the United States. In a congratulatory letter to Agbebi he wrote:

> I thank you with all my heart, dear good sir, and wish it were possible for me to shake your hand and tell you how proud I am of one, who is unquestionably an honour to the African Church and the African race. . . . I am black all over, and am as proud of my beautiful black skin, and that of my forebears, as the *blackest* man in Africa.[58]

The cult of the African personality reached its zenith in Edward Blyden's series of articles on "African Life and Customs" in the *Sierra Leone Weekly News*, from which they were reprinted in London in 1908 in book form under the same title. The articles represent a passionate analysis of the social, economic, and political arrangements evolved by the un-Europeanized African and under which he had lived and thrived from generation to generation. Under the African socioeconomic system "all work for each, and each works for all."[59] This communistic or socialistic order was not the result of an accident. Born of centuries of experience and the outcome of philosophical and faultless logic, its idea among all the ethnic groups was enshrined in proverbs. "Among the Veys, for example, a proverb runs thus, 'What belongs to *me* is destroyable by water or fire; what belongs to *us* is destroyable neither by water nor fire.' Again: 'What is *mine* goes; what is *ours* abides.' "[60]

Consequently, the surplus wealth accumulated under the native system by cooperative labor was regularly and in the most orderly manner shared among all concerned.[61] Compulsory spinsterhood was unknown and its recent introduction "is destined, wherever it seems to exist in practice, to disappear as an unscientific interference of good meaning foreign philanthropists with the natural conditions of the country."[62] If we are to trust the evidence of contemporary English periodicals, there were a little over five million unmarried women in Great Britain and the number was increasing. In London alone, there were eighty thousand professional outcasts.[63]

Under the African social system, Blyden boasted, there were no "women of the under world," no "slaves of the abyss." Every woman was above ground, sheltered and protected. The "Bundo" and "Porroh" institutions were held up for the emulation of Europeans. A Bundo society or school gives instruction in the normal and abnormal complaints females, particularly wives and mothers, were liable to suffer. All known remedies or sedatives for such ailments were taught, thus enabling a young girl to take care of herself in emergencies whether in the bush or in the town. The Porroh order was a similar society for males. By practicing polygamy, which enabled a mother's womb to recuperate for three years after each birth and ensured the production of a virile and vigorous race, Africa solved the marriage question for itself thousands of years ago. It has needed no revision and no amendment because "it was founded upon the law of Nature and not upon the *dictum* of any ecclesiastical hierarchy."[64]

In reply to the charges of bloodthirstiness and human sacrifice frequently leveled against African society, Blyden declared that those acquainted with history would agree that in its most brilliant period, Rome, which gave law to the civilized world, practiced extremely brutal customs. At that time, after Virgil and Cicero and Horace had lived and the reign of universal peace had prevailed under Augustus, hundreds of highly civilized Romans gazed upon combats of men with men, between whom no enmity existed, or of men with beasts. "Roman spectators encouraged men to butcher each other, not under the influence of any cause so respectable as superstition, but from a morbid love of amusement at the sight of blood."[65]

Even after the impact of Christianity had penetrated southern Europe, highly cultivated Spanish Christians delighted in shedding blood, sometimes on behalf of Christianity itself (i.e., the Spanish Inquisition), not to mention bullfights in the list of entertainments at Seville or an auto-da-fé in the square of Toledo. Compared with such scenes, Blyden emphasized, the alleged bloodthirst of the Africans appeared insignificant, the occasional blood spilled at human sacrifices a mere drop in the ocean, the public execution of criminals a mere child's play.

With regard to the punishment of crimes, the policy in Africa was to exterminate them as well as their perpetrators. Under the European system, so Blyden contended, the worst criminals were locked up for a few months and then released to continue to poison the moral and social atmosphere. The intention seemed to be not to eliminate the burglar but to invent instruments to defeat his enterprise. "Every day, then, hundreds of foes to the interests and peace of the community are turned loose, only to return to a career of war upon society."[66] The "75,000 thieves known to the Police in London" were of course ex-convicts who had undergone discipline or retribution in the prisons.[67]

The African method produced a deterrent effect upon the populace, at the same time ridding the society of the pernicious influence of a permanent criminal class. The universal absence of theft in the hinterland of the continent had been abundantly testified to by European travelers themselves. Blyden considered it a sad commentary on social conditions in Europe that some two thousand or three thousand homeless poor existed in the city of London.[68] Such a state of affairs could never be found in any part of Africa. "The African believes that the earth is the Lord's and the fulness thereof, and the sheep and the goats and the cows are all communal property, and no sheep would be allowed to go about bleating with filth and disease without being cared for."[69]

It was in defense of his institutions that the African fought internal wars, resisting men of his own community bent on aggrandizing themselves at the expense of the larger whole. "His wars against Europeans have also been in defence of his native Institutions which he regards as sacred."[70] Africans did not wish to see their communistic and cooperative system disturbed by indiscriminate foreign invasion. "And here we would ask those who have done us the honour to follow us thus far in this discussion, whether in social, economic, or industrial life, Europe has anything better to offer to the African than the system he has constructed for himself."[71]

Embedded in Blyden's analysis are germs of the now familiar concept of African socialism. In appreciation of the articles also published in the *Sierra Leone Weekly News*,[72] J. E. Casely-Hayford seized the opportunity to castigate the Europeanized African. In his opinion such a man was useless in the task of directing African life and African idiosyncracies along the line of natural and healthy development. "The superfine African gentleman, who at the end of every second or third year, talks of a run to Europe, lest there should be a nervous break-down, may be serious or not, but is bound in time to be refined off the face of the African continent."[73] Like Blyden and Africanus Horton, Casely-Hayford saw a university rooted in African soil as "the means of revising erroneous current ideas regarding the African; of raising him in self-respect; and of making him an efficient co-worker in the uplifting of men to nobler effort." He considered professorships in African languages to be the safest road to self-preservation. Casely-Hayford subsequently expanded these ideas into a book, *Ethiopia Unbound, Studies in Race Emancipation*.

This growing racial awakening and the sporadic excursions into the African past were channeled into the Negro Society for Historical Research. Launched by John E. Bruce and Arthur A. Schomburg, a Puerto Rican of African origin, in the United States in 1911, the year Casely-Hayford's book appeared in London, the society seems to have been inspired by the American Negro Academy started by Alexander Crummell on 5 March 1897.[74] In fact, Bruce and Schomburg were associated with the American Negro Academy. At one time the former was an executive member, the latter a president of the academy. Among the New World members of the Negro Society for Historical Research may be mentioned the philosopher Alain Locke, the first black American Rhodes Scholar at Oxford, editor of the anthology *The New Negro*[75] and a leading spirit of the Harlem Renaissance;[76] W. E. B. Du Bois; Marie Du Chatellier of

Panama; the Reverend William Forde from Costa Rica; and J. S. Moore of Bahia (Brazil).[77]

If Henry Sylvester Williams had not died the same year, he would probably have supported the new organization. The African members included King Lewanika of Barotseland (now an integral part of Zambia), who was made honorary president, Edward W. Blyden, J. E. Casely-Hayford, Mojola Agbebi, Moses Da Rocha, the South African F. Z. S. Peregrino, presumably one of the organizers of the London congress, and Duse Mohamed Effendi (later Duse Mohamed Ali).

Educated at King's College, London University, where he read history, Duse Mohamed was the son of an Egyptian army officer and his Sudanese wife. Offended by a statement on Egypt by Theodore Roosevelt of the United States, Duse Mohamed wrote his only book, *In the Land of the Pharaohs: A Short History of Egypt from the Fall of Ismail to the Assassination of Boutros Pasha*, acclaimed by the English press as the first book on Egypt by an Egyptian.[78] "His new fame got him the job to organize the entertainment for the First Universal Races Congress, which apparently he did with great success."[79] The congress sat in London from 26 to 29 July 1911 to discuss the relations between the so-called white and colored peoples with a view to fostering friendlier feelings and a heartier cooperation.[80] Among the participants were John Tengo Jabavu, Du Bois, Mojola Agbebi, and Edward W. Blyden. In their papers the first two analyzed the Negro problem, while Agbebi passionately defended African customs and institutions.

It is true that the Universal Races Congress, as its title attests, was no Pan-African conclave. Nevertheless, it had some relevance, however marginal, to the Pan-African movement. Its aim harmonized with an aspiration of the London Pan-African congress to improve relations between black and Caucasian peoples. Agbebi, Blyden, Jabavu, and Du Bois probably attended the Races Congress mainly to fulfill this objective of the 1900 Pan-African meeting.

It was the Races Congress that inspired Duse Mohamed to launch a journal in collaboration with J. E. Casely-Hayford. Called *The African Times and Orient Review: Politics, Literature, Art and Commerce: A Monthly Journal Devoted to the Interests of the Coloured Races of the World*, it ran for six years beginning in July 1912 and enjoyed a wide circulation in the United States, the West Indies, Egypt, East and West Africa as well as Europe and a number of Asian countries including India and Japan. Its chief support, however, came from West Africa, and it is believed that Casely-Hayford made substantial financial contributions to keep it in existence. African exiles like John E. Bruce, Booker T. Washington, and William H. Ferris (author of *The African Abroad*) contributed articles. Biographies of prominent men of African origin such as Mensah Sarbah of the Gold Coast, the Egyptian nationalist Mustapha Kamil, J. E. Kwegyir Aggrey, and the African American scholar William Scarborough, as well as the musician Samuel Coleridge-Taylor, formed a feature of the magazine. Another feature was the day-to-day reports and speeches on Africa made in the British Parliament.

The year Duse Mohamed launched his magazine was also the year Edward W. Blyden died in Sierra Leone. With the death of Blyden the stage was cleared for the appearance of new leaders. The first leader of Blyden's stature to emerge was Marcus Garvey. It was he more than any other person who introduced the ideas of an African nationality and the African personality, hitherto restricted to a handful of intellectuals, to the uninformed masses in the villages and streets of the African world.

After a sound elementary school education supplemented by an education course in the coastal town of Saint Ann's Bay, Jamaica, where he was born on 17 August 1887, he joined Benjamin's Printery in Kingston. He was so proficient that at twenty he became master printer and foreman of one of the largest local firms. This in itself constituted a spectacular achievement, since printing was a first-class trade in Jamaica at that time and some of the foremen of the big plants were imported from England and Canada. To keep pace with the ever-rising cost of living, the printers' union went on strike in 1909. Though Garvey was promised an increase in pay, he led the strike. "He did the job efficiently, organized public meetings and for the first time demonstrated those oratorical talents which were to magnetize the Negro people and stir the world."[81] The agitators received money from sympathetic American printers, but the union treasurer absconded with it, thereby shattering the morale of the strikers. As a result Garvey went to work at the Government Printing Office.

Still dissatisfied with the plight of the blacks around him, he gave up his new job to embark on an extensive tour that took him to about a dozen countries in South and Central America. The places he visited before returning to his native Jamaica in 1911 included Costa Rica, Panama, Ecuador, Nicaragua, Spanish Honduras, Colombia, and Venezuela. In Costa Rica and Panama he started the newspapers *La Nacionale* (which soon wound up) and *La Prensa* respectively. The conditions under which people of African blood in Costa Rica and Ecuador toiled drove him to protest to the British Council in each place. The British representative in Costa Rica told him nonchalantly that as consul he was powerless to change conditions there. The consul's indifference shook Garvey's being, leading him to the conclusion that whites did not consider the lives of black people to be as valuable as theirs and had no intention of protecting blacks or removing their disabilities.[82] During his travels he also learned about indescribable conditions in the ancestral continent itself from Jamaican and Barbadian ex-servicemen. As members of the West India Regiment these soldiers had been used by the British to subdue Africans and take their territories.[83]

All this made an indelible impression on his mind. He became possessed of a determination to end the duplicity of whites once and for all. In 1912, traveling through Spain and France, he went to England. While in Britain he joined the staff of *The African Times and Orient Review* just launched by Duse Mohamed. In an article he wrote for the journal, Garvey predicted that West Indians would be the instrument of uniting the African race "who before the close of many centuries will found an Empire"; to those who might laugh at his statement he posed the question: "Would Caesar have believed that the country he was invading in 55 B.C. would be the seat of the greatest Empire of the world?"[84]

It cannot be doubted that conversations with Duse Mohamed, as well as specimens of ancient African art he saw in the British Museum and his voluminous reading on the fatherland, helped to stir the Africanism in Marcus Garvey. Nor can one completely discount the influence on Garvey of the African Movement of the West African Chief Alfred Sam of the Gold Coast and Orishatuke Faduma, which caused considerable excitement in West Africa and the United States between 1914 and 1916. Among other things the African Movement aimed to maintain the cultural integrity of the African world and its economic independence; it sought to develop Africa industrially, to encourage the emigration of the best African

American farmers and technicians to West Africa, to develop banking and mining there, to build and acquire ships for transportation and dredging, and to establish modern institutions of higher learning.

Whatever Garvey owes to the African Movement and his association with Duse Mohamed seems to be outweighed by the inspiration he derived from his catholic reading and travels and from men like R. N. Love. In her privileged account, *Garvey and Garveyism*,[85] Amy Jacques Garvey points to Love as the first man of African blood to make a deep impression on her husband. A native of the Bahamas and executive member of the defunct Pan-African Association, Love was based in Jamaica, where he edited a paper called *The Advocate*. "Courageous and outspoken, he spent all his time and means in this work, and in the practice of medicine, especially among the poor."[86]

It was during his 1912–13 sojourn in England that Marcus Garvey formulated his plan of liberating the Negro race on a permanent basis.[87] He was conscious, as Blyden had been, that the members of the African world were unorganized with no meaningful commercial and industrial enterprises, unlike the Jews. "And what people could hold their own in these competitive days against groups and communities that ha[ve] vast accumulated reserves and therefore immense sustaining power?"[88] His travels had revealed that whether in the Western Hemisphere or Europe or even Africa, the Negro was treated like an animal possessing no political and economic rights. Would not a Negro national state, an African nationality, located in the fatherland and controlled by men of African blood solve all the problems of the members of the race wherever they might be? Would it not protect and give impetus to Negro commerce and industry "unfettered by any other motives but those of the welfare of the Negro race?"[89] Would the black man, then, not rise to any height merited by his ability instead of by the grace of his oppressors and detractors? For Garvey a people without authority and power was a race without respect. Also like Blyden, Garvey realized that it was impossible to erect such a nationality or polity without the rehabilitation of African values. Garvey therefore wanted the Negro to cultivate self-respect, race pride, and love of his dark skin, woolly hair, broad nose, and thick lips.

After presenting his ideas to some English liberals who approved

of them,[90] he went back to Jamaica in July 1914. With the support of
a J. A. Thorne, the plan of redeeming the African people was laid
before the public. The following month Garvey launched the Universal Negro Improvement and Conservation Association and African Communities' League,[91] which subsequently attracted world
attention as the Universal Negro Improvement Association (UNIA).
In a leaflet bearing the former title, Marcus Garvey explained that
in "view of the universal disunity existing among the people of the
Negro or African race, and the apparent danger which must follow
the continuance of such a spirit, it has been deemed fit and oppor-
tune to found a Society with a universal programme, for the purpose of drawing the people of the race together, hence the organization above-named."[92] All persons of Negro or African parentage
were requested to support the organization for the propagation and
achievement of the following general objects:

> To establish a Universal Confraternity among the race.
> To promote the spirit of race pride and love.
> To reclaim the fallen of the race.
> To administer to and assist the needy.
> To assist in civilizing the backward tribes of Africa.
> To strengthen the imperialism of independent African States.
> To establish Commissionaries or Agencies in the principal countries
> of the world for the protection of all Negroes, irrespective of nationality.
> To promote a conscientious Christian worship among the native
> tribes of Africa.
> To establish Universities, Colleges and Secondary Schools for the
> further education and culture of the boys and girls of the race.
> To conduct a world-wide commercial and industrial intercourse.[93]

Though Garvey met with little enthusiasm in his native island
and received little support from his English friends who were now
preoccupied with the Great War, he did not feel discouraged. "He,
however, kept on agitating single-handed and with his limited
means, until the end of 1916 when he sailed for New York to try his
luck in Harlem."[94] Exploiting the contemporary excitement about
the doctrines of "democracy" and "self-determination," which war-
aims propaganda, especially Woodrow Wilson's famous Fourteen
Points, had precipitated, Garvey put forward his plans for freeing
Africa.

Garvey's ideas won immediate approval partly because of the

fearless personality of the revolutionary and partly because the circumstances were propitious. During the Great War British and American spokesmen claimed that it was being fought in order to make the world safe for democracy. But with the end of hostilities they appeared to be unaware of the oppressive conditions facing the demobilized soldiers of African blood and their countries. Marcus Garvey only needed to open his mouth for the disillusioned masses to embrace him.

Thus the Universal Negro Improvement Association (UNIA) of New York fame was born. In January 1918 its organ, the *Negro World*, a weekly, appeared, remaining in circulation until 1933 when the *Black Man* succeeded it. In its first years the *Negro World* was published in English, French, and Spanish. Timothy Thomas Fortune became chief editor; Hucheshwar G. Mudgal, author of an important booklet, *Marcus Garvey: Is He the True Redeemer of the Negro?*[95] served as editor; William H. Ferris started a poetry section; and the Jamaican writers Claude McKay and John E. Bruce; and Duse Mohamed Ali functioned as columnists. Another newspaper, the *Daily Negro Times*, was soon launched. A flag for the race—a horizontal tricolor of red, black, and green—was adopted. An African national anthem set to martial music was produced:

> Ethiopia, thou land of our fathers,
> Thou land where the gods loved to be,
> As storm cloud at night sudden gathers
> Our armies come rushing to thee.
> We must in the fight be victorious
> When swords are thrust outward to gleam.
> For us will the victory be glorious
> When led by the red, black and green.

> *Chorus*

> Advance, advance to victory,
> Let Africa be free;
> Advance to meet the foe
> With the might
> Of the red, the black and the green.

> Ethiopia, the tyrant's falling,
> Who smote thee upon thy knees,
> And the children are lustily calling

From over the distant seas.
Jehovah, the Great One has heard us,
Has noted our sighs and our tears,
With His Spirit of Love has stirred us
To be one through the coming years.

O, Jehovah, Thou God of the ages
Grant unto our sons that lead
The wisdom Thou gave to Thy sages
When Israel was sore in need.
Thy voice thro' the dim past has spoken,
Ethiopia shall stretch forth her hand
By thee shall all fetters be broken
And Heaven bless our dear Motherland.[96]

Marcus Garvey struck African Redemption medals and created orders of chivalry with such titles as duke of the Nile; earl of the Congo; viscount of the Niger; baron of the Zambezi; knights of the distinguished service order of Ethiopia, Ashanti, and Mozambique. Though born a Catholic, Garvey set up an African Orthodox Church with Archbishop Alexander McGuire, a West Indian theologian, at the head. On the request of West African farmers and producers he created a Black Star Steamship Company to carry African merchandise to the United States.[97] Some African businessmen had complained of victimization, alleging that white shipping agencies as well as produce dealers invariably offered them very low prices for their goods.[98]

Africa for the Africans. Ethiopia Awake. Back to Africa. A Black Star Line. These were the slogans Garvey employed to capture the heart of the Negroes. In the jungles of the Congo in central Africa villagers described him as an African who had been lost in America but was about to return in order to save his brethren. The story is well known how the king of Swaziland in southern Africa told a friend that he knew the names of only two black men in the Western Hemisphere: the boxer Jack Johnson, who defeated his white opponent, and Marcus Garvey. When the governor of British Honduras banned the *Negro World*, Garveyites staged the July 1919 uprising in Belize.[99] In the United States, Hubert Harrison, journalist and founder of the Liberty League of Negro Americans, declared in a tract *When Africa Awakes* (1920) that the majority of the races would not acquiesce indefinitely to white supremacy and domination.[100]

He advised whites that whenever they read about the activities of the mullah, J. E. Casely-Hayford, and the Egyptian nationalist Zaghlul Pasha, or heard about Indian nationalist uprisings, of Black Star Lines, and of West Indian "seditions," they should remember that those fruits sprang from the seeds of their own sowing.[101]

By 1919 Garvey had formed branches of the UNIA all over the world. These branches held themselves in readiness for what was commonly but wrongly believed would be the first international convention of the Negro peoples of the globe. Plans for the convention included the drafting of grievances and a declaration of rights, the election of international officers, and the discussion of special reports on political and economic aspects of the African problem.

The convention eventually took place throughout the month of August in 1920 in Madison Square Garden, the largest auditorium in New York City. Delegates came from different regions of Africa, Brazil, Colombia, Haiti, Panama, and the West Indies, as well as Canada, England, and France. About twenty-five thousand representatives were inside the auditorium and thousands who could not be seated overflowed into the adjoining streets. In a long special address punctuated with applause, Garvey presented his case for African redemption. After five hundred years of oppression, Negroes were determined to suffer no longer. Despite promises made to Africans and their descendants during the Great War, they were deprived of all the democracy for which they had shed their blood. Black American soldiers returning from the battlefields of Europe were beaten or lynched in their uniforms in many southern states.[102] Since the other races had countries of their own, it was time the four hundred million Negroes of the world claimed Africa for themselves. If Europe was for the Europeans, Africa should belong to Africans and their descendants. Concluding, he warned that the African exiles were poised to return to their fatherland. He gave notice to the tenants, the European imperialists and colonists, to quit or face forcible eviction.

Officers of the Supreme Executive Council were then elected. The position of potentate, titular head of all the black people of the world, was earmarked for an African residing in the continent. The mayor of Liberia, Gabriel Johnson, was chosen in view of the plans of the UNIA to send the first batch of repatriates there.[103] George O. Marke, a Sierra Leonean civil servant educated at Oxford, became deputy potentate.[104] The office of provisional president went to Garvey.

Similar conventions took place between 1920 and 1925. During the quinquennium two major deputations were despatched. One went to Liberia to secure land for the settlement of the diaspora. The other delegation was sent in September 1922 with a five-page petition to the League of Nations, Geneva.[105] Signed by the executive officers of the UNIA on behalf of the Third Annual Convention of the Negro Peoples of the World, the petition recalled that the service rendered by the black race during the war of 1914–18 enabled the Allies "to defeat Germany in German East Africa, in German South-West Africa, in Togoland, the Cameroons, and other parts of the continent, as well as to defeat the common foe in Europe." As a reward for this "splendid service," the UNIA prayed the League to surrender to them "for the purpose of racial development, the mandates now given to the Union of South Africa; namely, German East Africa, and German South-West Africa."[106] The petitioners were confident that if the territories were ceded as requested, the UNIA would be able to bring them within two decades to a level of development that would "prove to the world and to the League our ability to govern ourselves."[107]

Overcome by impatience, a West African Garveyite unilaterally issued a circular dated 6 December 1922 to the European metropolitan governments affirming that "the Expression 'Africa for the Africans' is not merely a statement of fact but one of truth"[108] and deploring white supremacy as detrimental to the interest, peace, and happiness of the subject races. In the interest of world peace there should be a turning point. On the assumption that this was happening he deemed

> it necessary to point out that the whole Continent of Africa should come under a Monarchical Government having one "Common flag," a Union African Flag flying throughout the length and breadth of the Continent and replacing every other flag. An African Empire creates a position of an African King and Emperor which position should be assumed, and be done by an African Prince.
>
> There being none feeling himself called to do so I John H. Davies of 51 formally [*sic*] 43 Liverpool Street Freetown, Sierra Leone do hereby declare and make it known throughout the world that I have now done so.[109]

Having appointed himself king and emperor of Africa, John H. Davies ordered all foreigners, with the exception of those lawfully married to men or women of African blood, to leave. Colonial administrations were also ordered to hand over to "African Natives and Afro-Americans [*sic*] equal to the various positions."[110]

This circular was passed on to Sir A. R. Slater, the governor of Sierra Leone, by the governor-general of French West Africa asking the former to look into the matter.[111] In a reply, Governor Slater dismissed John Davies as a deranged mind who was not responsible for his actions, adding that steps had been taken to prevent the repetition of that offense.[112]

The fate of John Davies's circular foreshadowed the failure of the diplomatic initiative launched by the UNIA and the imminent decline of the movement itself. Despite its fantastic following, Garveyism was bound to suffer a setback, mainly because of the unfavorable international political situation of the time. Threats to expel the imperialists from Africa by force naturally alarmed the Western powers, even though the "provisional president" of the continent was unlikely to muster enough warships, submarines, and tanks to make good his boast. The French and British colonial authorities began to suppress the *Negro World*. To possess any Garveyite publication became a serious offense punishable by imprisonment. Yielding to pressure from the United States and the metropolitan powers, Liberia, which the UNIA had planned to use as a nucleus for the proposed Negro national state, suddenly dissociated itself from the Garvey movement.

Marcus Garvey also paid dearly for underestimating the machinations of several African American intellectuals, most of whom envied his worldwide popularity and boldness. When these intellectuals, among them well-known Harlem journalists, began to demand an investigation of his ventures, Garvey completely ignored them. Instead he concentrated his energy on demonstrating the moral and material benefits that the black world could derive from running steamships of their own. Prominent African Americans of Harlem were also among the first to demand his arrest. Such men included George W. Harris, editor of the *Amsterdam News* (Harlem), William Pickens and Robert W. Bagnal, officials of the National Association for the Advancement of Colored People, as well as Robert S. Abbott, editor-publisher of the *Chicago Defender*.[113] After serving a short prison sentence for allegedly misusing the United States mail, he was deported to his native Jamaica, where he encountered even greater intrigues and harassment from the local black elite.

With the removal of the redeemer from the United States, Garveyism suffered a setback from which it is only just beginning to recover, thanks to the changed world political situation. In the words of Claude McKay, "Marcus Garvey had dreamed of a vast model colony in Liberia. But it was Harvey Firestone who realized the dream with his extensive [rubber] plantations."[114]

Nonetheless, it would be mistaken to suppose that Marcus Garvey achieved nothing. Apart from rehabilitating the color black, he shook the black masses of the diaspora into an awareness of their African origins. Without setting foot on African soil he created for the first time a real feeling of international solidarity among Africans and persons of African stock.

This feeling of solidarity had already begun to manifest itself as early as 1917, when West Indian and West African students in London formed the Union for Students of African Descent, primarily for literary and social activities.[115] An organization called the African Progress Union (APU), also based in London, appeared the next year with the aim of promoting the social and economic welfare of the Africans of the world.[116] Among the members of the APU were Duse Mohamed Ali and Counsellor J. R. Archer, an influential West Indian in the Battersea District of London.

It was also partly because of the impact of Garveyism, although he disapproved of its propaganda tactics, that W. E. B. Du Bois convened a series of Pan-African meetings between 1919 and 1927. Following the procedure adopted by Henry Sylvester Williams in connection with the 1900 Pan-African Conference, Du Bois addressed a memorandum on New Year's Day 1919 to prominent personalities of African blood, among them the Senegalese, Blaise Diagne, on the necessity for a Pan-African congress.[117] The proposed congress was expected to consider reports on the conditions of Negroes in various parts of the globe, to "obtain authoritative statements of policy toward the Negro race from the Great Powers," to make representations on behalf of the Negro people to the Paris Peace Conference, and to lay down principles for the development of the Negro race. The principles were political rights for all educated persons of African extraction and their children, economic development in the colonies primarily for the benefit of the indigenous inhabitants, political reforms based on local traditions "with the object of inaugurating gradually an Africa for the Africans," recognition of the sovereign status of Haiti, Abyssinia, and Liberia, and the development of the former German dependencies under the supervision of the League of Nations.[118] The proposed conference was also expected to set up a permanent secretariat with headquarters in Paris charged with the task of "collating" the history of the Negro race; encouraging the appreciation of Negro art and literature; following political, social, and economic developments in the African world; publishing articles, pamphlets, and proceedings of the congress under discussion; and organizing another Pan-African meeting in 1920.[119] Finally, the memorandum suggested that a preliminary conference be held at once to consider the proposals just outlined and others that might be advanced. "This plan was acceptable not only to the representatives of the various Negro peoples gathered in France, but it was also welcomed by the French [government]"[120] thanks to the influence of Diagne, who during the Great War was a cabinet minister in the French government headed by Georges Clemenceau.

Du Bois eventually called a Pan-African meeting in Paris. Held from 19 to 21 February 1919 in the Grand Hotel, Boulevard des Capucines, it was attended by fifty-seven delegates drawn from different sections of the African world.[121] Fifteen territories were represented, notably Abyssinia, Liberia, Haiti, the United States, San Domingo (Dominican Republic), French Caribbean, British Africa, French Africa, Egypt, and the Belgian Congo.[122] Also in attendance was J. R. Archer, a participant at the 1900 Pan-African Conference and president of the African Progress Union. The importance that the European colonial administrations attached to the Paris gathering was reflected by the high calibre of their representatives. France was represented by the chairman of its Foreign Affairs Committee; Belgium by a member of the Belgian Peace Delegation named Van Overgergh; Portugal by Friere d'Andrade, formerly minister of foreign affairs.[123] The United States government sent William E. Walling and Charles Edward Russell.[124]

As chairman and one recently elevated by the French government to the position of commissioner-general of native affairs and who had married into one of France's most distinguished families, Blaise Diagne not surprisingly opened the proceedings with praise for the French colonial system. C. D. B. King, president-elect of Liberia and Liberian delegate to the Paris Peace Conference, gave an inspiring account of his country's aspirations and accomplishments, expressing the hope that the people of African descent would feel proud of that republic. "Let us," he concluded, "be considered a home for the darker race in Africa."[125] The representatives of the American government as well as Gratien Candace, deputy from Guadeloupe in the French Chamber, unequivocally condemned discrimination on grounds of race. Two other deputies from the West Indies, Boisneuf (Gaudeloupe) and Lagrosillière (Martinique), expressed disappointment at the refusal of white Americans to treat as equals black men "who in common with themselves were giving their lives for democracy and injustice."[126] While the delegates of the Belgian and Portugese colonial authorities talked about imminent reforms, the chairman of the French Foreign Affairs Committee claimed that his country adopted the policy of equality and liberty for all men regardless of race even before the French Revolution, boasting that there were no less than six colored deputies in the French Parliament, among them the chairman of the congress who also served on his committee.[127]

In compliance with Du Bois's preconference memorandum, resolutions were passed providing for another Pan-African meeting and demanding reforms. The Great Powers were asked to issue an international code, similar to that being proposed for labor, for the protection of Africans.[128] A permanent bureau should be set up by the League of Nations to ensure the enforcement of the code. The inhabitants of Africa and the peoples of African descent must henceforth be governed according to certain principles. These included the abolition of forced labor; the right of Africans "to participate in the government as fast as their development permits, in conformity with the principle that the government exists for the natives, and not the natives for the government"; the right of every child to learn to read and write in his language; the regulation of capital investment and concessions to prevent exploitation of the African people; and the holding of land with its mineral resources in trust for the community who at all times should have effective ownership of as much land as they could profitably develop.[129] Viewed against the contemporary obsession with the doctrine of self-determination as expressed in Woodrow Wilson's Fourteen Points, these demands seem moderate.

More radical and therefore more in tune with the postwar agitation for freedom were the resolutions adopted at the 1921 London Pan-African Congress held at the Central Hall, Westminster, from 27 to 29 August with further sessions in Brussels and Paris the next month. In attendance were medical doctors like the Sierra Leonean, Ojo Olaribigde, practicing in England, and Vitallian, a former physician to Emperor Menelik II; seasoned trade unionists like Albert Marryshaw from Grenada who later became member of the Legislative Council there; diplomats like Helen Curtis, Liberian consul to Brussels, and Dantes Bellegarde of the Haitian delegation, Paris; students and dons like the Nigerian undergraduate Ibidunni Morondipe Obadende and José de Magalhaes of Angola, a professor at the Lisbon School of Tropical Medicine, a deputy for São Tomé in the Portuguese Parliament, and president of an African pressure group called the Liga Africana;[130] businessmen like the Nigerian Peter Thomas and Nicola de Santos-Pinto, a mulatto planter also from São Tomé and member of the Liga Africana. Morocco was represented by a Mr. Arnold, an English liberal familiar with the social and political conditions there; South Africa by Mr. and Mrs. J. L. Dubé; East Africa by Norman Maclean Leys, a British medical officer well known for his antisettler views and opposition to colonial rule;[131] and the Belgian Congo by Mfum Paul Panda, leader of the Union Congolaise and "spokesman for black Belgium."[132] Gratien Candace, described by Du Bois as "more French than the French,"[133] and Isaac Béton, a school teacher in Paris, represented Guadeloupe; Jean Razaief, Madagascar (now Malagasy). The British government sent two observers, Colonel Beckles Wilson, publicity agent of the Gold Coast, and Captain Fitzpatrick of the Nigerian Political Service. The delegates of the African Progress Union (APU), which made the arrangements for the London sessions, included John Alcindor and J. R. Archer, both of whom attended the 1900 conference, as well as the Liberian Robert Broadhurst, secretary of the APU, and J. A. Barbour-James (British Guyana) who had served in the Gold Coast as a surveyor.

Among the representatives of the NAACP may be mentioned Du Bois, Walter F. White, an African American journalist and grad-

uate of Atlanta University, and Jessie Redmon Fauset, trained at
Cornell University and the Sorbonne and literary editor of *The Crisis*,
organ of the NAACP. Unlike the American participants, those who
came from West Africa did so mostly as individuals and not as the
representatives of organizations. Others came from Swaziland, Jamaica, Martinique, French Congo, Trinidad, the Philippines, and
Liberia.[134] Altogether 110 delegates took part in the 1921 Pan-African
meeting, and in addition to these there were no less than one thousand visitors.[135] Compared with the Pan-African convention summoned in New York the previous year by Marcus Garvey, the attendance at the 1921 conference appears unimpressive.

John Alcindor, chairman of the APU, presided over the opening
session in London. In his address he thanked the American delegates "who had financed the conference, and travelled thousands
of miles to maintain an entente cordiale between the Africans and
African-descended people."[136] They would ventilate their grievances and devise ways and means of removing them. The enemies
of the African race were very often the Africans themselves, who
he thought lacked character, education, and cohesion. Observers
were beginning to see that "all was not well with Africa and the
Africans." It was the duty of the African to speed up this awakening
of public conscience and galvanize it into activity by means of a
wise propaganda.[137]

Then followed an account by Du Bois of the Pan-African movement since 1900 and the numerous obstacles that had to be sur-
mounted. It was of the utmost importance that Negro leaders of
thought should come together and inform themselves of the different aspects of the Negro problem. The conference had been called
to discuss segregation, the racial problem of America and South
Africa, the land question, especially in Africa, and the methods of
cooperation among the peoples of the African world. In view of the
reluctance of the Great Powers to allow a discussion of their domestic problem in the colonies, the French and the British authorities
had been assured that the gathering was neither "directed towards
revolution" nor financed by the Soviet Union as was then commonly
assumed that any movement of that nature must be.[138]

Of the many speeches on race relations, the most touching was
that contributed by Peter Thomas. Little children in the streets of
London embarrassed him with shouts of "There's the nigger."

Though he did not feel insulted, he wanted that expression expurgated from the English language. Harmony between the races in the British Empire demanded that children should be taught from their cradle days to respect fellow human beings regardless of their complexion. As a loyal British subject, he deprecated the metropolitan government's habit of misinterpreting any articulation of grievances by subjects as "a seething, underground current of disloyalty."[139]

Turning to segregation, he argued that "it meant separating one class of mankind from another." On the steamer an observant stranger would notice how West Africans were confined to one side. Probably unaware that European domination was largely imposed by superior force of arms, Peter Thomas lamented that if West Africans had not received Europeans with kindness, the invaders would not have had the power to introduce the vicious policy of segregation. "With their intense spiritual nature they were prepared to forget a wrong, and to forgive, but they could not go on forgiving."[140] Recalling that the riches of West Africa were used to develop Liverpool, he urged the authorities to increase educational and industrial facilities to improve the standard of living of the people.[141]

Presenting the case of East Africa, where he worked as a medical officer for sixteen years, Norman Maclean Leys described how the indigenous inhabitants of Rhodesia, Nyasaland, Uganda, and Kenya (the first two are in central Africa) were being dispossessed of their lands. In these places, practically no African had any legal right of ownership or security of tenure in communal or even individual land. In Kenya alone, the land already alienated to white settlers amounted to nearly five million acres. It was the policy of the imperial regime to induce those living on lands that had been alienated to leave their homes and work for the white settlers. That policy was carried out by the influence of the colonial government over local chiefs, who were in their pay, thus enabling the secretary of state for the colonies in London to deny that forced labor was being used in British dominions. Wages were fixed by the joint action of the white employers. The standard wage was six shillings a month or two pounds of rice or maize a day. If the congress wanted to defend the interests of the East Africans, Leys advised, now was the time to do so.

Two concrete proposals stood out clearly in the welter of ideas exchanged: one concerned cooperation among the peoples of African stock, the other dealt with their political future. With regard to the question of cooperation, Albert Marryshaw (Grenada) warned that what was needed was not dazzling oratory but actions. Men of African blood must be prepared to dip their hands into their pockets; they must make financial sacrifice to help one another.[142] A Nigerian lawyer, L. B. Augusto, urged that a start could be made by going to the aid of Liberia, which appealed to the United States for a loan of five million dollars in January 1918.[143] "Let us," he pressed, "lend the solid weight of the newly conscious black world towards its development."[144]

Combining the League of Nations idea with the political aspirations of the National Congress of British West Africa (NCBWA) and the back-to-Africa movement of Marcus Garvey, Ibidunni Morondipe Obadende (Nigeria) advocated the formation of a League of the Negroes of the World with headquarters in Liberia and branches in other parts of the globe where persons of African descent might be found. From this league was to emerge a union of all "the West African countries, extending from Senegal to Portuguese West Africa, including [the] Belgian Congo, or as far as possible under the name of the United States of West Africa on the basis of alliance with the European Powers who have helped in developing those Colonies and Protectorates."[145]

Thus Obadende's "African Programme" in the end turned out to be a charter for West Africa only. The program itself rested on the naive assumption that the imperialists would eagerly surrender their acquisitions. Despite its naiveté, the scheme was significant, for it showed what kind of future some of the delegates envisaged for Africa: a united Africa, free of alien influence. It is important to note that something of Obadende's program was reflected in the resolutions.

The resolutions may be divided into four main sections as follows: a general criticism of the colonial system and relations between the "colored" and "white" races; detailed criticisms of the major imperialist powers; a plea for the continued respect for the sovereignty of Abyssinia, Haiti, and Liberia; and lastly a challenge to the rest of the world. The first part of the manifesto regretted that relations between the various groups of humanity were determined principally by the degree in which one could subject the other to its service, "uprooting ruthlessly religion and customs, and destroying government, so that the favoured few may luxuriate in the toil of the tortured many."[146] What was needed was a fair distribution of world income between the exploiting and the exploited peoples.

A second part of the document contained criticisms of some aspects of the colonial activities of Belgium, Great Britain, Portugal, Spain, and France. France was commended for placing "her cultured black citizens on a plane of absolute legal and social equality with her white, and [for having] given them representatives in her highest legislature."[147] At the same time, France was urged to widen the political basis of its native government, to restore "to her indigenes the ownership of the soil," and rebuked for exposing African labor to the "aggression of established capital" and for "compelling black men without a voice in their government to fight for France."

A third section of the manifesto warned that the continued existence of the autonomous Negro states was "absolutely necessary to any sustained belief of the black folk in the sincerity and honesty of the white."[148] The continued occupation of Haiti by the United States was condemned.

Finally, the resolutions called upon the rest of the world to choose one of the following alternatives:

> either the complete assimilation of Africa with two or three of the great world states, with political, civil and social power and privileges absolutely equal for its black and white citizens, or the rise of a great black African State founded in Peace and Goodwill, based on popular education, natural art and industry and freedom of trade; autonomous and sovereign in its internal policy, but from its beginning a part of a great society of peoples in which it takes its place with others as co-rulers of the world.[149]

Commenting on the conference, a London journalist paid tribute to the humor that marked its proceedings.[150] This cordial atmosphere was absent in the Brussels sessions held from 31 August to 2 September 1921. The resolutions passed unanimously at the London meeting aroused opposition when Du Bois proposed their adoption.[151] As chairman, Blaise Diagne, whose cooperation in 1919 had made the Paris congress possible, now refused to submit

Du Bois's motion to the vote. The Senegalese politician was determined to see that nothing revolutionary was done by the gathering.
Ignoring the overwhelming majority support for Du Bois's motion,
he proclaimed adopting a declaration submitted by the Belgian liberal, Paul Otlet. The convocation did not break up in confusion
thanks to the restraint of Du Bois, who desisted from pressing the
matter. The Otlet manifesto was, at bottom, a diversionary document demanding among other things the establishment of scientific
institutes to investigate the development of the Negroes.[152]

At the Paris session the London resolutions were substantially
rephrased on the insistence of Blaise Diagne, who rejected blunt
references to the metropolitan powers. With the end of the deliberations in September, the congress sent a committee, among them
Du Bois and the Haitian diplomat, Dantes Bellegarde, to Geneva to
present a petition to the League of Nations.[153]

What was the reaction of the Europeans to the 1921 Pan-African
meeting? It was a mixed one. The fact that so many black luminaries
from remote corners of the globe were exchanging ideas on disabilities imposed by white arrogance and intolerance not surprisingly
aroused suspicion of a revolution and fear of black domination. As
Walter White relates, there were secret agents of the British Colonial
Office at the London sessions "and the same surveillance was encountered in Belgium and France."[154] The *Manchester Despatch* commented that the white people did not naturally look forward with
joyful emotions to the day when a prolific black race would rise to
power, "but the time may come when we shall have to submit
ourselves to the tender mercies of our dusky conquerors."[155] Reflecting the postwar disillusionment with European civilization, the *Public Opinion* of London declared that no white man could have attended the conference and retained his smug complacency; the days
of the superrace were numbered; the theory of the permanent and
necessary inferiority of the Negro seemed then to be untrue from a
practical, as it had always been from a Christian, standpoint.[156]

Several newspapers took a less gloomy view. *L'Humanité* of Paris
remarked that the black and mulatto intelligentsia proved by its very
existence that the black race was not inherently inferior. How could
Europeans consider inferior to white men these orators with their
clear thought and their ready words? asked the paper.[157] It was the
Pan-Africanists' sincerity of purpose that most impressed many a

European commentator. According to the *Daily Graphic* (London) the delegates

> were so intensely in earnest, both the men and women, so absolutely convinced of the justice of their cause, their right to a citizen's franchise, to representation in the world's councils, to everything in fact, that civilized humanity offers to the[ir] sons, regardless of race, colour and creed.[158]

Nearly all the newspaper correspondents paid a glowing tribute to the exertions and eloquence of Du Bois. For instance, the Belgian *Echo de la Bourse* was convinced that whether one liked him and his program or not, one must "bow to his brilliant intellect and his devotion to the black race."[159] The fact that he impressed most of the foreign journalists who generally recognized him as "the moving spirit of the Congress" may account for the origin of the notion that he is the "father" of Pan-Africanism. Whatever the origins of that belief may be, most contemporary observers expected him to win significant concessions for the movement in the very near future. This speculation seemed to be borne out by the revival of the Pan-African Association at the end of the 1921 congress.

Based in Paris, the Pan-African Association held periodical meetings for four years and was run by three French-speaking West Indians and an African American. These were Gratien Candace, Isaac Béton (secretary), Camile Mortenol (treasurer), about whom not much is known, and the black American Rayford Logan (assistant secretary), then resident in Paris, who later became a professor of history at Howard University (Washington, D.C.).[160]

The first major assignment of the Pan-African Association was the summoning of a Pan-African conference in 1923. The London sessions lasted two days, from 7 to 8 November, and were held in Denison House. Among the participants were John Alcindor, Chief Amoah III of the Gold Coast, Rayford Logan, and Kamba Simango, an Angolan educated in the United States. Also present were some distinguished members of the British Labour party, namely, Harold Laski, Sidney Olivier, and H. G. Wells.

In his opening speech, Du Bois, the chairman, said that it had not been possible to meet in Lisbon on the date originally announced. The reason was the unilateral postponement of it by Isaac Béton on financial grounds.[161] This unauthorized action had to be reversed since it was considered more beneficial to hold a congress, even if only a handful attended, than to have none at all. Because the conference was originally intended to meet in Lisbon, they must keep faith with the world by having a further session there.[162]

Decisions taken included the establishment, at the earliest opportunity, of Pan-African committees in England, British West Africa, British Caribbean, Brazil, Haiti, Liberia, South Africa, Portugal, and the United States; the Pan-African Association located in Paris was to continue but as a Pan-African committee for France and its colonies.[163] The committees were charged with the duty of spreading information about the black world and of organizing a Pan-African convocation in 1925.

— On 9 November, the delegates issued a statement setting out what they believed to be the "eight general and irreducible needs" of Africans and their descendants. The first was a voice in their own government; the second, access to the land and its resources; the third, trial by jury; the fourth, free elementary education for all, broad training in modern industrial technique, and higher training of selected talent; the fifth, the development of Africa for the benefit of Africans, and not merely for the profit of Europeans; the sixth, the abolition of the slave trade and the traffic in liquor; the seventh, world disarmament; and the eighth, the organization of commerce and industry so as to make the main objects of capital and labor the welfare of the many, rather than the enrichment of the few.[164]

The socialist economic policy advocated by the delegates was robbed of considerable force when they proceeded to demand specifically for "the civilised British subjects in West Africa and in the West Indies the institution of home rule and responsible government."[165]

The "uncivilised" colonial subjects of northern Nigeria, Uganda, and Basutoland (now Lesotho) should be prepared for "home rule and economic independence, and for eventual participation in the general government of the land."[166] Citizenship rights of voting and representation in the French Parliament enjoyed by Senegal and the French Caribbean should be extended to other sections of the French Empire. The white settler minorities in Kenya, Rhodesia, and South Africa were admonished to surrender "native" land alienated to them; there was no "other road to peace and progress."[167] In each of these places there should be an end to "the pretension of a white minority to dominate a black majority"; nothing could be more ironical than the spectacle of "the official head of a great South African State [General Smuts]" striving blindly to build peace and goodwill in Europe by "standing on the necks and hearts of million[s] of black Africans."[168]

For the black Americans, the document demanded full civil rights and the suppression of lynching. With regard to the autonomous nations of Liberia, Ethiopia, and Haiti, the delegates urged not only respect for their political integrity but also "their emancipation from the grip of economic monopoly and usury at the hands of the moneymasters of the world."[169] Britain was asked to hand over the Egyptian Sudan to Egypt, now independent. Finally, persons of African ancestry in Brazil and Central America were told to be no longer satisfied with a solution of the Negro problem involving their assimilation by another race without fully recognizing their "manhood."

These resolutions were adopted without amendments at the Lisbon session jointly organized by José de Magalhaes and Rayford Logan. Eleven nations and colonial territories were represented, the largest contingent being that of Portuguese Africa; also in attendance were two former Portuguese colonial administrators.[170]

The decision to set up Pan-African committees in different parts of the world, first taken at the 1900 congress, never materialized. Nor was the proposed 1925 Pan-African Conference held. Arrangements to hold it in the West Indies had to be abandoned "on account of the difficulty of transport"; a meeting did take place in New York in August 1927 and it called for reforms demanded in previous gatherings.[171] After the New York congress the initiative passed from black Americans in the New World to Africans and West Indians in England and France.

With the death of John Alcindor in the mid-1920s, the APU lapsed into obscurity, clearing the way for the appearance of more dynamic pressure groups. The first such organization to emerge was the West African Students' Union. We must, however, not suppose that the WASU owed its existence solely to the ineffectiveness of the APU. A more important factor was the color prejudice that marked British society of the time. Most men of African blood went to England with an idealized concept of the country with its reputation for justice and fair play. But daily life there often fell short of these ideals. Their admiration of England and their pride in membership of the British Empire proved to be empty and hollow if not misguided.

Kobina Sekyi, a Gold Coast philosophy student at University College, London, conveyed his impressions in a series of articles entitled "The Anglo-Fanti."[172] It did not take the African long, Sekyi observed, to discover that he was regarded as a savage even by the starving unemployed who begged him for alms. Amusing questions were frequently put to him about whether he wore clothes before his voyage to England, whether it was safe for Europeans to visit his country since the climate was unsuitable for civilized people, and whether wild animals roamed about in his village.

Among Africans who went to Britain in 1922 to study law was Ladipo Solanke, a Nigerian from Abeokuta and graduate of Fourah Bay College, Freetown. Like Kobina Sekyi and Peter Thomas, he found race relations in the imperial capital deplorable. As a result he was seized with a determination to unite Africans and fight the color bar.[173] Discussions with other West Africans culminated in a meeting held in London on 7 August 1925. Speakers regretted that after seven years of existence the APU could not boast of a single concrete achievement; finally, it was resolved to launch the WASU.[174]

At a subsequent meeting officers were elected as follows: president, W. Davidson Carrol, a Gambian lawyer educated at Oxford; vice president, J. B. Danquah of the United Gold Coast Convention fame; honorary secretary, Ladipo Solanke; treasurer and financial secretary, a Nigerian medical student called Joseph Akanni Doherty.[175] An important member of the WASU worth noting is the Sierra Leonean London University undergraduate who subsequently became a vice president of the union and governor-general of his country, H. J. Lightfoot-Boston. Another is J. C. de Graft Johnson from the Gold Coast, also a London University student.

— The WASU had nine aims, namely, to establish a hostel; to foster the spirit of national consciousness and racial pride among all African peoples; to serve "as a Bureau of Information on African history, customs and institutions"; to "act as a centre for Research on all subjects appertaining to Africa and its development"; to "present to the world a true picture of African life and philosophy, thereby making a definitely African contribution towards the progress of civilisation"; to foster cooperation and the spirit of true leadership among its members; to "promote, through regular contacts, the spirit of goodwill, better understanding and brotherhood between all persons of African descent and other races of mankind"; to publish a monthly called *Wasu*; and finally, to "raise necessary funds for the carrying out of the above-named objects [sic]."[176]

None of these aspirations is new in the history of Pan-Africanism. Four years before the inauguration of the WASU, the APU had discussed the necessity for a hostel.[177] The case for a new interpretation by Africans of their past to replace the unreliable accounts of racist anthropologists, missionaries, and travelers had been eloquently made by Edward W. Blyden. Not only did Solanke endorse the arguments of Blyden on this matter, he also showered praises on patriots like Mensah Sarbah and Casely-Hayford, who produced *Fanti Customary Laws* (London, 1897) and *Gold Coast Native Institutions* (London, 1903) respectively.[178] Speculating on the future of West Africa, J. H. Lightfoot-Boston stressed that it "was in consequence of the recognition of the need for co-operation that the West African Congress NCBWA was formed."[179] He confirmed that "the same spirit was responsible for the formation of the West African Students' Union."[180] Similarly the attempt to use a journal to publicize the history, culture, and aspirations of the African world goes back to the turn of the twentieth century, if not earlier, when Henry Sylvester Williams's Pan-African Association started *The Pan-African*.

The first object of the WASU to materialize was the launching in March 1926 of *Wasu* with a Sierra Leonean student, Melville Marke, as editor. Its subeditors were J. C. de Graft Johnson and Julius Ojo-Cole, a Nigerian undergraduate at King's College, London. From the beginning, *Wasu* secured a circulation that extended beyond the United Kingdom, Africa, and continental Europe to the New World and even Asia.[181] Except on a few occasions, the magazine was issued as a quarterly, instead of as a monthly, owing to financial difficulties. A society known as the Rising Ethiopian Development Association (Chicago) and the African Patriotic Students' Club (New York) served as agents for its distribution in America.

Far from constituting a new and distinct Pan-African movement led by men with unorthodox ideas, the WASU represents a continuation of existing Pan-African traditions and goals. It was neither

West African nor a students' union. It was not West African be-
cause, according to its constitution,[182] membership was open to any
African and African descendants. In fact, the East African Jomo
Kenyatta, as well as the West Indian H. Bereford Wooding,[183] were
among its members, and in 1935 the black American singer Paul
Robeson succeeded Casely-Hayford as one of the union's patrons.

— The WASU was not primarily a students' union because its aims
reflected not the academic and personal problems of African students in England but a concern for the predicament of the Negro
race and the future of Africa. It is significant that the Freetown
branch had five lawyers, a medical practitioner, and a lecturer at
Fourah Bay College.[184] Similarly, most of the branches in Nigeria
had as members barristers, doctors, chiefs, clergymen, and teachers.[185] In Kano, the chief of Sabon Gari assisted by two Yoruba
clerics led the branch; the prince, later the *Oni* of Ife, was an active
member of the Ile-Ife branch while the paramount chief, Oba Alai-
yeluwa Ademola II, the *Alake* of Abeokuta, served as a patron.[186]

Note should be taken of the impact that the exertions and ideas
of Casely-Hayford, J. E. Kwegyir Aggrey, and Marcus Garvey had
on the WASU during its formative period. Addressing its members
on 5 November 1926, scarcely three months after its inauguration,
Casely-Hayford described the aspiration of the African as the "attainment of nationality, the possibility of raising his head among
the other peoples of the world, and of commanding his national
and racial opportunity."[187] Unless the African did his own thinking
and produced his own leaders in all walks of life, "he would always
remain a hewer of wood and drawer of water."[188] The members of
the union were portrayed as the flower of African intelligence. It
was their duty to continue the work of correcting wrong impressions
about people of African extraction and to assume the burden of
"looking after [the] West African's prosperity in the coming generation."[189] The audience now took their leadership role as confirmed
by Casely-Hayford more seriously and saw themselves as the means
of enhancing the status and prestige of West Africans in particular
and persons of African ancestry in general.

The sayings of J. E. Kwegyir Aggrey also exercised considerable
influence on the WASU. Indeed, they did much to raise the opinion
of many persons of African descent of their race and potentialities
and to rehabilitate the word *black*, which had been devalued, espe-

cially by nineteenth-century racists. An early convert to Christianity, he went to the United States in 1898, where he obtained many degrees and honors within the next quarter of a century. Aggrey's work on the two Phelps-Stokes Education Commissions to Africa[190] earned him recognition in his native Gold Coast; but it was love for his own black race as expressed in his aphorisms that won him international fame. Among his famous sayings are:

> I am proud of my colour; whoever is not proud of his colour is not fit to live.
>
> If I went to heaven and God said, "Aggrey, I am going to send you back, would you like to go as a white man?" I should reply, "No, send me back as a black man, yes completely black. . . . Because I have [sic] work to do as [a] black man that no white man can do. Please send me back as black as you can make me."[191]

The WASU's desire to promote understanding and brotherhood between Africans and the other branches of humanity may have derived partly from Aggrey's famous simile of the need for both black and white keys on the piano for the production of musical harmony. "His sudden death in New York in 1927 . . . robbed the Gold Coast of a valuable son and the world of a work that would have been founded on experience of the African in many environments."[192] The editorial comment on his death in *Wasu* and the memorial service held in his honor by the union are a measure of the man's influence on the organization.[193]

A third celebrity of African origin whose racial and political philosophy affected the WASU was Marcus Garvey. He was released from Atlanta Prison in 1927, the year Aggrey died, and emigrated to England the following year. On his arrival, Garvey acquired an office designated "European Headquarters" at 57 Castleton Road, West Kensington, London. The facilities of this office were for some time also used by the WASU. Though the Black Star Line and the back-to-Africa schemes were wrecked by his imprisonment, his massive propaganda for pride in black skin left an indelible mark on African nationalism everywhere despite the criticisms made against him by whites and influential persons of African stock, notably W. E. B. Du Bois.

From his London base, Marcus Garvey attempted to revive the campaign for justice and respect for Africans and their descendants

and for their resettlement in the fatherland. On 6 June 1928 he
delivered at Royal Albert Hall, London, a long and passionate
speech with the title, "The Case of the Negro for International
Racial Adjustment, Before the English People."[194] He had been
jailed, he explained, because an auxiliary of the UNIA "posted a
letter to somebody; in the evidence an envelope was presented to
the witness which he identified as addressed to him, but he could
not identify any letter contained in the envelope, and the prosecut-
ing attorney presented it in evidence as a fair assumption that the
envelope bore mailed matter from the Black Star Line, of which I
was President, and because of that—an empty envelope—I was sent
to prison in America for five years."[195]

Arguing that "being imprisoned in the United States of America
is not like being imprisoned in England, where you have morality
and principle and justice and law before you can take away the name
of a man and deprive him of his character," he appealed to the
British public not to jump to any hasty conclusion about his character, challenging any man in the world to say that he had ever
defrauded him of even a single penny.[196] Garvey then recalled how
the British West India Regiment was used to incorporate most of
West Africa into the British Empire and how, during the Great War,
the valor of black-skinned soldiers ensured the defeat of Germany,
thereby making it possible for France and Britain to take over the
imperial acquisitions of the vanquished.

Not only had Africans and their descendants fought to extend
the boundaries of the British Empire, they had also fought for the
American nation. The first man who shed his blood in America for
the independence of the American Colonies was a black man named
Crispus Attucks on Boston Common. During the Civil War, black
soldiers saved the day many a time. The great Theodore Roosevelt
was saved to serve his country and humanity not by his own Rough
Riders but by black men.[197] Did his audience, he asked:

> know that we have gladly borne your burdens for four hundreds of
> years? The cotton mills of Lancashire, the great shipping port of Liv-
> erpool, tell the tale of what we have done as black men for the British
> Empire. The cotton that you consume and use in keeping your mills
> going has for centuries come from the Southern States of United States;
> it is the product of negro labour. Upon that cotton your industry has
> prospered and you have been able to build a great Empire to-day.[198]

Although black men had received unfair treatment in the colonies, they did not hate whites, since God intended humanity to live in common brotherhood. What blacks were demanding was a fair chance, a fair opportunity to live in peace and develop their talents.

Marcus Garvey followed up this speech with a letter of 5 September 1928 addressed to Reginald Bridgeman,[199] a former British diplomat and now international secretary of the League Against Imperialism launched in Brussels the previous year. Garvey outlined in the form of questions, twenty-two in number, the grievances and aspirations of the peoples of the African world. Did Bridgeman accept Africa to be the "proper, moral and legal home of the black race?" Did he think the Negro was entitled to all the rights of other human beings? Was he satisfied that the Negro had been given in modern times a fair chance to develop himself? Did he believe that the Negro could best develop himself under the tutelage and direction of the other races? Did he think that the black republics of Haiti and Liberia had been given a fair chance to develop as proof of the ability of the Negro for self-government? When the time came for the repatriation of the African diaspora to their ancestral home, would he help to make the venture a success? Did he believe that because of the "higher cultural attainments" of the Negroes of the Western world and those of West Africa, "they should be the real and only missionaries to their own people in Africa?" In the concluding section of the letter, Garvey reaffirmed the aims and objectives of his organization, the UNIA.

Also in 1928, Garvey submitted a petition to the League of Nations on behalf of the UNIA. Incorporating the earlier petition (1922), the document was published in London the same year as a thirty-page booklet.[200] It enumerated the disabilities imposed on blacks since the Atlantic slave trade and condemned South Africa's native policy, the horrors of the Belgian Congo, and the mandate system. Also severely attacked were the alienation of lands belonging to Africans to white settlers and the agreement negotiated between the Liberian government and the American Firestone Rubber Company in 1926. Points raised in his speech at Royal Albert Hall, in his Petitions to the League of Nations, and in his letter to Bridgeman, all were kept alive by a journal started in the early 1930s by Garvey and called the *Black Man*.

Despite his exertions, he found it impossible to recapture his former following. In the opinion of George Padmore, the black population in Britain proved too scanty to provide any substantial organizational strength and too poor to contribute the funds needed if the UNIA was to be resuscitated on a global scale.[201] As a result, Padmore further explains, the Black Redeemer "spent his declining years addressing small crowds of English people in Hyde Park, boasting of his former glory."[202]

The declining fortunes of Garveyism enabled the WASU to flourish and other Pan-African pressure groups to emerge. From the beginning, the WASU operated from its secretary's lodgings, from where it moved in 1928 to premises offered by Garvey. The use of a whole house proved so effective in increasing both the union's activities and membership, that when the lease expired a year later, it was decided that funds should be raised to secure another house. Consequently, the WASU authorized Ladipo Solanke to go to West Africa and appeal for funds. From October 1929 to September 1932 he visited several West African cities and towns. Chiefs and other influential leaders were approached. The tour yielded about £1,381, enabling a hostel to be opened in January 1933 in Camden Town in the Saint Pancras District of London.[203]

Besides furnishing money for the hostel scheme, the tour provided an opportunity for the formation of branch unions where none existed. Among the branches started as a direct consequence of the tour were those of Cape Coast, Elmina, Nsawam, and Sekondi in the Gold Coast; Aba, Abeokuta, Ebute Metta, Enugu, Jos, Port Harcourt, and Zaria in Nigeria. The first branch to be established was in Accra, followed in 1928 by another in the Belgian Congo. The Freetown, Accra, and Lagos branches included many foundation members of the parent union and, in several cases, as in Lagos, the branches were inaugurated by former members of the parent union themselves.

Meanwhile there appeared in London in December 1931 an organization styled the League of Africans, whose aim was "to promote mutual understanding and to maintain sincere, friendly relationships among the Native races of South, East and West Africa, Egyptians and other Native races of North Africa."[204] Officers were elected as follows: president, A. H. Koi, a Gold Coast medical student who subsequently became a member of Kwame Nkrumah's first administration; vice president, T. Deressa from Abyssinia; treasurer, Jomo Kenyatta; general-secretary, Miss M. Faro of Transvaal (South Africa); assistant secretary, the Gold Coaster Julius S. Adoo.[205] The League of Africans seems barely to have survived its inaugural meeting for there is scarcely any evidence of its activities in British journals such as *West Africa* and *The African World*. Nor is it mentioned by the WASU or the League of Coloured Peoples, another Pan-African pressure group launched earlier the same year. The League of Africans was probably an offshoot of the League of Coloured Peoples, whose name would logically make Asians eligible for membership.

The League of Coloured Peoples was started chiefly due to the efforts of the Jamaican Harold Arundel Moody (1882–1947), a devout Christian trained at King's College, London, where he obtained the degree of doctor of medicine in 1919. His scientific studies could not suppress his religious disposition, for Christianity continued to loom large in both his private and public life. During the 1930s he became president of the Christian Endeavour Union of Great Britain and Ireland as well as an executive member of the British and Foreign Bible Society.

However, he did not allow his deepening involvement in spiritual matters to overshadow the Negro question. Like Ladipo Solanke, Moody "also was very conscious of the need to bring together all the members of his own race resident in Great Britain for personal intercourse and consultation."[206] His chance came during the great depression, when Charles Wesley gave a talk to the Young Men's Christian Association, London. Moody naturally attended, and before the large gathering of persons of African descent he seized the opportunity to unfold his ideas. The ideas won the approval of Wesley, for he was himself not only a leading spirit of the New Negro Movement then in vogue but had also taken part in the New York Pan-African conference. A special meeting was summoned on 13 March 1931 in the YMCA Hall.

It was at this meeting that the League of Coloured Peoples was launched, with Moody as president. Among those present were Stephen Peter Thomas, a Nigerian law student, and his sister, Stella Thomas, who in 1933 became the first female African barrister. Their father, Peter Thomas, had attended the 1921 London congress. Also present at the inaugural meeting was the British Guyanese J. A. Barbour-James, also a participant at the 1921 London congress.

The objects of the LCP were:

> To promote and protect the Social, Educational, Economic and Political Interests of its members;
> To interest members in the Welfare of Coloured Peoples in all parts of the World;
> To improve relations between the Races;
> To co-operate and affiliate with organisations sympathetic to Coloured Peoples;
> To render such financial assistance to Coloured Peoples in distress as lies within its capacity.[207]

Compared with those of the WASU, the aims of the LCP were definitely more political.

For about two years the LCP possessed no official means of publicity. Money had been a problem right from the start since many of its members were students. But in July 1933 it launched an organ with the title *The Keys*, a name inspired by the aphorisms of J. E. Kwegyir Aggrey. Like *Wasu*, *The Keys* secured a wide readership; unlike *Wasu*, it frequently changed its name. After September 1939 it assumed the designation *News Notes*, finally adopting the title *League of Coloured Peoples Review*.

At first the LCP operated from Harold Moody's house in Peckman, but the volume of its membership soon underlined the urgent need for better arrangements. In October 1936 decisions were taken to establish permanent headquarters and to engage a full-time salaried secretary. Accordingly, the headquarters moved from the president's lodging to Farrington Street (London). A few months later, five committees were created, including a colonial questions committee, an editorial committee, and a finance committee.[208]

A feature of the association was its acceptance of white members, presumably as a way of fulfilling one of its objectives: the improvement of race relations. Although white members participated freely in debates and conferences, they were excluded from the executive committee. In an address delivered at an LCP conference on "The Negro in the World To-Day" held in Memorial Hall, London, from 13 to 15 July 1934, Moody argued that if the Negro was to be emancipated, the emancipator must come from within. Thus, during the year April 1933 to March 1934, officers of the society were three West Indians (excluding Moody) and three Africans, while in the executive committee there were eight West Indians, two Africans, two African Americans, and one Indian.[209] In the year 1936–37, Africans accounted for eight out of the thirteen executive members.[210] The next year four West Indians and two Africans formed the executive committee.[211]

That members were future leaders of their people and that the purpose of the league was to provide training in leadership were statements that the president often made and stressed. In a speech, "The Duty of the Educated African," given at the third annual conference of the LCP held from 3 to 5 April 1936, Moody declared that

> the task of building up a new Africa fell most appropriately on the young educated African. It was for him to equip himself thoroughly with knowledge, not merely in such subjects as medicine, chemistry or engineering, but also in the social sciences, sociology, economics, ethnology, etc. Secondly he should steep himself in the history of his own people so as to have that sense of racial pride and unity [, not] without personal sacrifice; the individual must be willing to subjugate his own interests to the good of the whole race.[212]

The League of Coloured Peoples was hardly four years old when disintegration threatened it. One cause of the misunderstanding is to be found in the interpretation of the phrase "coloured peoples." To the president it meant Africans and their descendants in the New World.[213] Indeed, the very first editorial in *The Keys* announced that the aim of the LCP was to state the cause of the black man. Nonetheless, some members felt that the Indians' interests ought also to be catered to. They cited the Indian presence in Africa and the fact that 40 percent of the population of British Guyana was Indian. Harold Moody's interpretation eventually prevailed, but there were still members who remained unconvinced.

Much more serious was the challenge to the president's leadership itself. Many of the members were young men fascinated by the revolutionary ideas of Karl Marx and Vladimir Lenin. Interested though he was in what was happening in the Soviet Union, the foundation for all things, Moody insisted, was Christianity.

But the most important cause of the opposition was the groundless suspicion that he was collaborating with the British Colonial Office to stifle the growing nationalism of African students.[214] As early as 1932, an anonymous appeal in *The Negro Worker*, a left-wing journal edited by George Padmore, was addressed to all colored students "to break with the sycophantic leadership of Dr. Harold Moody, a typical 'Uncle Tom.' "[215]

By the beginning of 1935, the situation had become so bad that Moody offered to resign. But the break never came. The offer was withdrawn and at the annual general meeting summoned in the same year he was reelected president, an office he held without interruption until his sudden death after World War II.

Between 1924 and 1936, African exiles in France formed pressure groups there, notably the Ligue Universelle Pour la Défense de la Race Noir, the Comité de la Défense de la Race Nègre, and the Ligue de la Défense de la Race Nègre led by the Dahomeyan Touvalou Houénou, the Senegalese Lamine Senghor, and the Sudanese Tiémoho Garan Kouyaté, respectively.[216]

The Ligue Universelle rejected "the idea of racial inferiority," stood for the solidarity of the African race, advocated the establishment of educational and economic institutions, and pledged itself to protect the territorial integrity and independence of Liberia, Haiti, Abyssinia, and San Domingo.[217]

Condemnations of the controversial Senegalese politician Blaise Diagne as a traitor to the black race proved fatal for the Ligue Universelle; weakened by the harassment of Diagne, the organization collapsed in 1926, barely two years after its inauguration, and was succeeded by the Comité. With the death of Lamine Senghor the following year, the Comité was in turn reconstituted as the Ligue de la Défense de la Race Nègre. By espousing the cause of the North African nationalist movement, L'Etoile Nord-Africaine, led by Messali Hadj, and by contemptuously alluding to men like Diagne and Gratien Candace from Martinique as agents of imperialism, the Ligue antagonized the French authorities, who suppressed it in 1937.

Unlike the Pan-African associations launched in England, notably the West African Students' Union, the League of Coloured Peoples, and the International African Service Bureau, those of France were short-lived and, as a consequence, could not make a sustained and meaningful impact. Launched in the heyday of Garveyism, from which they derived most of their inspiration, the French pressure groups collapsed before the death of Marcus Garvey himself in 1940. It appears that J. Ayodele Langley, who has examined their activities in considerable detail, has exaggerated their importance.[218] It was chiefly the Pan-African pressure groups in Britain that would keep alive the ideals of the movement from the mid-1930s to the end of World War II.

1. Frederick P. Noble, *The Chicago Congress on Africa, 1894*, a report in the Schomburg Collection, New York City Library, 280–81.

2. Ibid., 314.

3. Edwin S. Redkey, *Black Exodus, Black Nationalist and Back-to-Africa Movements, 1890–1910* (Hartford, Conn.: Yale University Press, 1969), 142, 182.

4. Quoted in ibid., 180. For details on Turner's back-to-Africa campaign, see chapters 2 and 8.

5. Noble, *Chicago Congress on Africa*, 313.

6. Smyth's paper is printed in J. W. E. Bowen, ed., *Africa and the American Negro: Addresses and Proceedings of the Congress on Africa* (Atlanta, 1896).

7. *Lagos Standard*, 27 July 1898, 2; *The Pan-African* 1 (October 1901): 4.

8. *Lagos Standard*, 27 July 1898, 2.

9. *Gold Coast Chronicle* (Accra), 12 August 1898, 3.

10. Henry Sylvester Williams to Booker T. Washington, 8 June 1899 (in Booker T. Washington Papers [hereafter BTW Papers], Principal's Office Correspondence, 1899, container no. 164, Library of Congress).

11. Ibid.

12. Alexander Walters, *My Life and Work: Vol. II* (New York, 1917), 253.

13. Williams to Washington, 8 June 1899, BTW Papers.

14. Ibid.

15. Williams to Sylvain, 17 July 1899, ibid.

16. Williams to Washington, 1 June 1900, BTW Papers, Principal's Office Correspondence, 1900, container no. 187, Library of Congress.

17. Walters, *My Life and Work*, 253.

18. The rest of the representatives as listed by Walters in ibid., 253–54, are C. W. French (Saint Kitts), Samuel Coleridge-Taylor (London), Pulcherie Pierre (Trinidad), Chaplain B. W. Arnett (Illinois), Prof. L. L. Love (Washington, D.C.), J. Buckle (London), Hon. Henry F. Downing (United States ex-consul, Loando, W.A.), T. J. Calloway (Washington, D.C.), the Reverend Henry B. Brown (Lower Canada), Counsellor Chas. P. Lee (New

York), J. F. Loudin (London), A. R. Hamilton (Jamaica), Miss Barrier (Washington, D.C.), Mrs. J. F. Loudin (London), and Ada Harris (Indiana).

19. *Manchester Guardian*, 25 July 1900, 7; *The Times* (London), 25 July 1900, 15.

20. *Daily News* (London), 24 July 1900, 6.

21. Ibid.

22. *Manchester Guardian*, 24 July 1900, 8; *The Times* (London), 24 July 1900, 7.

23. *The Times* (London), 24 July 1900, 7.

24. *Manchester Guardian*, 25 July 1900, 7.

25. *Daily News* (London), 25 July 1900, 3.

26. *Manchester Guardian*, 25 July 1900, 7.

27. Ibid.

28. Ibid.

29. *Manchester Guardian*, 26 July 1900, 8.

30. *Daily News* (London), 26 July 1900, 6.

31. Ibid.; Walters, *My Life and Work*, 260.

32. Ibid.

33. *Daily News* (London), 26 July 1900, 6.

34. *Manchester Guardian*, 26 July 1900, 8.

35. Imanuel Geiss, "Notes on the Development of Pan-Africanism," *Journal of the Historical Society of Nigeria* 3 (June 1967): 726.

36. Ibid.

37. *Manchester Guardian*, 26 July 1900, 8.

38. *The Times* (London), 26 July 1900, 11.

39. Walters, *My Life and Work*, 257–60.

40. Ibid., 258.

41. Ibid.

42. Ibid., 259.

43. Ibid.

44. Ibid.

45. Ibid., 259–60.

46. Ibid., 257.

47. *The Pan-African*, October 1901, 2–3.

48. Ibid.

49. See Kingsley's books *Travels in West Africa* (London, 1897) and *West Africa Studies* (London, 1897).

50. John E. Flint, "Miss Mary Kingsley—A Reassessment," *Journal of African History* 4 (1963): 100. Flint warns that to treat Kingsley's theories on a purely philosophical level is to miss their significance and argues that despite her claims, the African was not the focal point of her thinking. "Mary Kingsley," Flint goes on, "was the intellectual and philosophic

spokeswoman for the British traders to West Africa. She thought of herself as possessed of a mission to urge their views and defend their interests, resist attacks upon them, and undermine the influence of their enemies. Every argument she put forward, though usually developed logically from an analysis of African society and its needs, was directed to these ends" (p. 96).

51. Edward W. Blyden, *The African Society and Miss Mary H. Kingsley* (London, 1901), 9.

52. Miss Kingsley's letter was also published in the *Lagos Weekly Record*, 29 September 1900, 4–5.

53. Blyden, *African Society and Miss Mary H. Kingsley*, 7.

54. Edward W. Blyden, *African Life and Customs* (London: African Publication Society, 1908), 16 (page reference to 1969 edition).

55. *Inaugural Sermon Delivered at the Celebration of the First Anniversary of the "African Church,"* Lagos, West Africa, 21 December 1902. There is a copy in the Schomburg Collection, New York City Public Library.

56. Ibid., 7.

57. Blyden to Mojola Agbebi, printed in ibid., 17–20.

58. John Edward Bruce to Mojola Agbebi, 16 April 1903, reprinted in ibid., 27.

59. Blyden, *African Life and Customs*, 11.

60. Ibid., 39.

61. Ibid., 46.

62. Ibid., 11.

63. Ibid., 25.

64. Ibid., 21.

65. Ibid., 59.

66. Ibid., 56.

67. Ibid.

68. Ibid., 50.

69. Ibid.

70. Ibid., 46.

71. Ibid., 52–53.

72. Reprinted in ibid.

73. Ibid., 85.

74. The objects of the academy were the promotion of literature, science and arts, the culture of a form of intellectual taste, the fostering of higher education, the publication of scholarly works and the defense of the Negro against vicious assault. Occasional Papers no. 2, American Negro Academy, Washington, D.C., 1920.

75. Alain Locke, *The New Negro* (1925; reprint, New York: Atheneum, 1969).

76. The Harlem Renaissance, also known as the New Negro Movement, had no formal organization. It was essentially aesthetic, philosophical, and metaphysical rather than political. Not surprisingly, its leading spirits tended to be hostile to Marcus Garvey. See Locke, *The New Negro*.

77. For a full list of the foundation's members, see A. C. Hill and Martin Kilson, eds., *American Leaders on Africa From the 1880s to the 1950s* (London, 1969), 176–77.

78. Duse Mohamed Ali, *In the Land of the Pharaohs: A Short History of Egypt From the Fall of Ismail to the Assassination of Boutros Pasha*, 2d ed. (London: Frank Cass, 1968).

79. Imanuel Geiss, *The Pan-African Movement* (London: Methuen, 1974), 730.

80. G. Spiller, ed., *Papers on Inter-Racial Problems Communicated to the First Universal Races Congress Held at the University of London, July 26–29, 1911* (London: King and Son, 1911), v.

81. Claude McKay, *Harlem: Negro Metropolis* (New York: E. P. Dutton, 1940), 145; see also Theodore G. Vincent, *Black Power and the Garvey Movement* (Berkeley: Ramparts Press, 1971).

82. Amy Jacques Garvey, *Garvey and Garveyism* (London: Collier-Macmillan, 1970), 10.

83. Ibid.

84. *African Times and Orient Review*, October 1913.

85. Amy Jacques Garvey, *Garvey and Garveyism*.

86. Ibid.

87. Hucheshwar G. Mudgal, *Marcus Garvey: Is He the True Redeemer of the Negro?* (New York: African Publication Society, 1932), 5.

88. Ibid.

89. Ibid.

90. Ibid.

91. This is the title on the letterhead with which Garvey wrote Booker T. Washington on 12 April 1915. See BTW Papers, Miscellaneous Correspondence, 1915, container no. 939.

92. Ibid.

93. Ibid.

94. Mudgal, *Marcus Garvey*, 5–6.

95. Ibid.

96. Quoted in Amy Jacques Garvey, *Garvey and Garveyism*, 31–32.

97. Ibid., xiii.

98. Ibid.

99. Vincent, *Black Power and the Garvey Movement*, 128.

100. J. Ayodele Langley, *Pan-Africanism and Nationalism in West Africa, 1900–1945* (London: Oxford University Press, 1973), 36.

101. Ibid.

102. Amy Jacques Garvey, *Garvey and Garveyism*, 53.

103. Vincent, *Black Power and the Garvey Movement*, 120.

104. Ibid.

105. There is a copy of the petition in the Reginald Bridgeman Collection (in owner's possession).

106. Ibid. It should be noted that Tanganyika was not given to South Africa.

107. Ibid.

108. Archives du Sénégal (Dakar), file no. 4F14(31).

109. Ibid.

110. Ibid.

111. Enclosure to a letter dated 7 February 1923, ibid.

112. Governor A. R. Slater to Governor-General of French West Africa, 29 March 1923, Archives du Sénégal (Dakar), file no. 4F14(31).

113. Claude McKay, *Harlem*, 170.

114. Ibid., 168.

115. *West Africa*, 25 October 1924, 1178–80. Between 1921 and 1924 the membership of the Union for Students of African Descent rose from 25 to 120.

116. *Sierra Leone Weekly News*, 3 September 1921, 11.

117. For a full text of the memorandum, see *The Crisis*, March 1919, 224–25.

118. Ibid.

119. Ibid.

120. Ibid., 225.

121. *The Crisis*, April 1919, 271.

122. Ibid.

123. Ibid.

124. Ibid.

125. Ibid.

126. Ibid.

127. For a critical reassessment of French colonial policy, see Martin D. Lewis, "One Hundred Million Frenchmen: The 'Assimilation' Theory in French Colonial Policy," *Comparative Studies in Society and History* 4 (1961–62): 129–53.

128. W. E. B. Du Bois, *The World and Africa, An Inquiry Into the Part Which Africa Has Played in World History*, enlarged ed. (New York: International Publishers, 1965), 11.

129. Ibid., 11–12.

130. Locke, *The New Negro*, 386–87.

131. See Leys's books *Kenya* (London, 1925) and *The Colour Bar in East Africa* (London, 1941).

132. Locke, *The New Negro*, 390.

133. Ibid., 392.

134. *The Crisis*, December 1921, 69.

135. For a list of the delegates see ibid., 68–69.

136. *West Africa*, 3 September 1921, 988.

137. Ibid.

138. Ibid.

139. Ibid., 990.

140. Ibid.

141. Ibid.

142. *The Crisis*, November 1921, 13.

143. Ibid.; R. L. Buell, *The Native Problem in Africa*, vol. 2 (New York: Macmillan, 1928).

144. *The Crisis*, November 1921, 13.

145. Obadende's paper, "An African Programme," was published in *The Crisis*, May 1922, 33.

146. *The Crisis*, November 1921, 6.

147. Ibid., 8.

148. Ibid.

149. Ibid., 8–9.

150. *African World*, 3 September 1921, 177.

151. *African World*, 10 September 1921, 211.

152. Ibid.

153. Du Bois, *The World and Africa*, 240–41.

154. *A Man Called White: The Autobiography of Walter White* (New York: Viking Press, 1948), 61.

155. Reprinted in *The Crisis*, December 1921, 65.

156. *Public Opinion*, September 1921, 248.

157. *The Crisis*, December 1921, 63.

158. Reprinted in ibid.

159. Ibid., 67.

160. Rayford Logan, "The Historical Aspects of Pan-Africanism: A Personal Chronicle," *African Forum* 1 (1965): 97.

161. *The Crisis*, December 1923, 57.

162. *West Africa*, 10 November 1923, 1352.

163. *The Crisis*, January 1924, 122.

164. *West Africa*, 17 November 1923, 1377.

165. Ibid.

166. Ibid.

167. Ibid.

168. Ibid.

169. Ibid.

170. *The Crisis*, February 1924, 170.

171. *The Crisis*, October 1927, 263–65.

172. *West Africa*, 25 May–28 September 1918.

173. Ladipo Solanke, *A History of W.A.S.U.* (manuscript in British Museum [n.d.]), 1.

174. *West Africa*, 15 August 1925, 1002.

175. *West Africa*, 12 September 1925, 1176.

176. *Wasu*, March 1926; *Wasu*, May–July 1936.

177. *Sierra Leone Weekly News*, 3 September 1921, 11.

178. *Wasu*, March 1926, 11–15.

179. Ibid., 15–19.

180. Ibid.

181. Gammell to Editor, *Wasu*, 30 June 1933.

182. For a text of the WASU constitution, see *Wasu*, May–July 1936.

183. *Wasu*, March–June 1927, 7.

184. Philip Garigue, "The West African Students' Union: A Study in Culture Contact," *Africa* 23 (1953): 55–69.

185. Ibid.

186. Ibid.

187. *Wasu*, December 1926, 23–28.

188. Ibid.

189. Ibid.

190. For details, see Kenneth King, "The American Background of the Phelps-Stokes Commissions and Their Influence on Education in East Africa Especially in Kenya," Ph.D. diss., University of Edinburgh, 1968.

191. Quoted in E. W. Smith, *Aggrey of Africa* (London, 1930), 2, 4.

192. *West Africa*, 23 July 1932, 748.

193. *Wasu*, September 1927.

194. Printed by Poets' and Painters' Press, 146 Bridge Arch, Sutton Walk, London, 1968, with an introductory biographical sketch by G. K. Osei. Page references are to this edition.

195. Ibid., 12.

196. Ibid., 21.

197. Ibid., 16–17.

198. Ibid., 17.

199. Marcus Garvey to Reginald Bridgeman, 5 September 1928, Bridgeman Collection.

200. A copy can be found in the Bridgeman Collection.

201. George Padmore, *Pan-Africanism or Communism? The Coming Struggle for Africa* (London, 1956), 102.

202. Ibid.

203. See "The Official Report of the W.A.S.U. Mission, 1929–1932," *Wasu*, August–November 1935.

204. *West Africa*, 26 December 1931, 1606.

205. Ibid.

206. D. A. Vaughan, *Negro Victory: The Life Story of Dr. Harold Moody* (London, 1950), 52.

207. *The Keys*, July 1933, back cover. The last objective was a later addition.

208. *The Keys*, April–June 1937, 56.

209. *The Keys*, July 1933, back cover.

210. *The Keys*, July–September 1936, back cover.

211. *The Keys*, January–March 1938, back cover.

212. *The Keys*, July–September 1936, 14.

213. Vaughan, *Negro Victory*, 65.

214. *West Africa*, 3 February 1934, 109–10; *West Africa*, 7 April 1934, 350.

215. Reprinted in Nancy Cunard, ed., *Negro Anthology* (London, 1934), 555.

216. Langley, *Pan-Africanism and Nationalism in West Africa*, 287.

217. Ibid., 296.

218. Ibid., chap. 7, "The Movement and Thought of Francophone Pan-Negroism, 1924–1936."

3

The Impact of the Abyssinian Crisis and World War II

THE ABYSSINIAN QUESTION and World War II, which were to have a far-reaching influence on the development of Pan-Africanism, were preceded by the Liberian "scandal." The scandal itself served as a pointer of black feelings in a world dominated by whites.

Frustration caused by color prejudice and the persistence of racial myths partly account for the exiles' apparent connivance at the charges of slavery and forced labor leveled against Liberia during the Great Depression. In 1929 the League of Nations appointed a commission of inquiry headed by an Englishman, Cuthbert Christy, assisted by C. S. Johnson and Arthur Barclay, representing the United States and Liberia, respectively. The commission's report, published the next year, found that although "classic slavery" with slave markets and slave dealers no longer existed, a considerable measure of inter- and intratribal domestic slavery flourished.[1] It accused some American Liberians (i.e., African American settlers) of taking some indigenous inhabitants as pawns and of criminally abusing the system for their personal ends.[2] It also confirmed that members of the aboriginal population were being recruited and sent to Fernando Po and French Gabon under conditions of criminal compulsion scarcely distinguishable from slave raiding and slave trading. However, the commission was satisfied that domestic slavery received no encouragement from the Liberian government and that there was no evidence that leading citizens participated in it.

Despite the cautious tone of its findings, many white critics, among them several liberals, saw the report as a confirmation of the earlier allegations that the Liberian government had reduced the indigenous people to oppression and servitude. The result was that condemnations of Liberia increased in volume and bitterness. So widespread and sometimes sweeping were the accusations that several observers openly demanded that the country be placed under the control of a foreign commission; in other words, Liberia should become a mandated territory. The demand was repeated during the House of Lords debate in March 1932.[3]

No doubt, some of the critics of Liberia's domestic policy like John Harris of the Aborigines' Rights Protection Society (England) were motivated by humanitarianism. But conditions in South Africa, the Portuguese colonies, and the Belgian Congo, where whites were in charge, made their well-meaning attacks appear hypocritical if not racist. Hence, an incensed African, who signed himself "Africanus," could argue that Africa's lapses were not unique and that mismanagement prevailed everywhere, insisting that abuses in Liberia must not be "unduly magnified, because the delinquent happens to be a struggling African republic."[4]

The suspicion that the allegations of the European critics stemmed from racial prejudice was reinforced by the fear that a bad reputation for Liberia would be exploited by racists to further discredit peoples of African extraction and to prove their incapacity for self-government. This seems clear from an article, "The Future of Liberia: Proposed League Control," which Harold Moody as leader of the LCP wrote in an English daily. With the great scramble in mind, he accused whites of scheming to annex the only remaining spot (besides Abyssinia) that the black man could call his country.[5] The record of Portugal in Africa made anything but cheerful reading, but the League of Nations had made no efforts to expose the facts or to suggest that Portugal be advised about the way to govern African subjects humanely. Moody regretted that whereas a century ago, Wilberforce fought for the emancipation of slaves, his countrymen were today seeking to deprive the descendants of those slaves of the little vestige of freedom left to them. No man "is free who has not a country of his own which he may direct according to his will"; it was undesirable that "one branch of the human family however noble and however wonderful may have been its achievements should direct the destiny of every other branch of that family."[6] No race was strong enough, he believed, to lord it over the other indefinitely. Anticipating Kwame Nkrumah, Moody maintained that it was better to do wrong in liberty than to do right in chains. In his opinion, the full development and independence of the black man was essential for the moral and spiritual good of the white man and of humanity at large.[7] Moody revealed that he had had several talks with L. A. Grimes, Liberia's secretary of state, and had received from him documents presenting the case of the Liberian government.[8] Moody rejected the League of Nations' plan of assistance for Liberia as a proposition that no self-respecting nation would countenance. Among other things, the plan provided for a financial adviser to be nominated by the United States and approved by the president of Liberia.

Concluding, Moody expressed the hope that the white man would adopt "a more liberal attitude which must result in the discovery of 'new argosies of cultural exchange' for the universal good of man."[9] Coming from a man of conservative temperament, this article was a measure of the feelings of nationalism that the debate on the Liberian crisis engendered in the African diaspora. Such a public controversy could hardly fail to foster a corresponding feeling of solidarity among the exiles, for it was conducted on racial lines.

At the end of the second annual conference of the LCP held in High Leigh, Hoddesdon, from 23 to 25 March 1934, a resolution was passed and sent to the British colonial secretary. It condemned, as Moody had done the year before, the League of Nations' plan of assistance as a violation of the sovereign status of Liberia.[10] Convinced that the Liberian government was neither faultless nor thrifty enough, W. E. B. Du Bois approved of expert advice in principle. What he opposed was expert advice from whites; such advice accompanied by invested capital meant loss of political power. And Liberia was jealous of its independence.[11] Liberia's chief crime, he went on, "is to be black and poor in a rich, white world; and in precisely that portion of the world in which colour is ruthlessly exploited as a foundation for American and European wealth."[12]

Interest in Liberia was almost completely overshadowed from the middle of 1935 by Mussolini's preparations to attack Ethiopia, then better known as Abyssinia. At that time, the exiles, as Jomo Kenyatta put it, regarded Abyssinia as "the remaining relic of the greatness of an Africa that once was."[13] In anticipation of the Italian invasion, in August 1935 several persons of African origin formed an organization known as the International African Friends of Abyssinia with an office at 62 New Oxford Street, London.[14] A statement issued by Kenyatta said that the object of the IAFA was to assist by all means in their power in the maintenance of Abyssinia.[15] The release explained that the organization had on its committee and among its officers representatives of the Gold Coast, Somaliland, and East Africa. The names of the representatives, apart from Kenyatta, were, however, not given. But a letter of 14 August 1935 from Kenyatta to the suffragette Sylvia Pankhurst did contain them.[16] The officers were chairman, C. L. R. James; vice chairman, Dr. Peter Milliard, a medical practitioner from British Guyana; a second vice chairman, Albert Marryshaw, who attended the 1921 London Pan-African Congress; honorary secretary, Jomo Kenyatta; treasurer, Amy Ashwood Garvey, an ex-wife of Marcus Garvey; and secretary for propaganda, Samuel Manning of Trinidad.

The committee members were Muhammed Said from Somaliland; John Payne, an African American; and J. B. Danquah, G. E. Moore, and S. R. Wood. The last three were members of two political missions from the Gold Coast that came to Britain in 1934 to demand constitutional reform. One mission representing the traditional rulers and unofficial members of the Legislative Council was led by Nana Sir Ofori Atta with J. B. Danquah as secretary. The other mission was led by G. E. Moore and S. R. Wood, both of them officers of the Gold Coast Aborigines' Rights Protection Society (ARPS). When George Padmore came to England toward the end of 1935 to settle there permanently, he joined the International African Friends of Abyssinia. Though he did not form the IAFA, contrary to popular impression, he did eventually dominate it.

Also in anticipation of an Italian invasion, the LCP summoned a general meeting held in Memorial Hall on 4 September 1935. The crowded meeting unanimously passed a resolution that not only expressed an opinion about the imminent crisis but also laid down a policy concerning the future of Africa as a whole.[17] The LCP offered its utmost cooperation to the Abyssinians in the deep shadow of war hanging over their beloved country. Mussolini's policy was denounced as expressive of a deep-rooted conviction in the minds of most Europeans that Africans were ordained to be their serfs.[18] Europeans were urged to abandon this idea and invited to begin to recognize the African peoples as equal partners with them in the noble task of human advancement and to desist from looking upon Africa as a continent designed for ruthless exploitation. Finally, the resolution warned the metropolitan powers and the League of Nations that the time was "now ripe for them to consider a plan for the future of Africa which plan should be nothing less than the ultimate and complete freedom of Africa from any external domination whatsoever."[19]

The following month, October 1935, the Italians attacked Abyssinia. In their attempt to "raise Abyssinia to the level of other civilised nations," the fascist invaders violated a series of international agreements, notably the League of Nations Covenant (articles XII, XIII, and XV) and the Kellogg-Briand Pact (1928), both of which renounced war as an instrument of national policy, as well as the Italo-Ethiopian Treaty of Perpetual Friendship also signed in 1928. By bombing and spraying poisonous gas over the beleaguered population, Italy contravened yet another international convention, namely, the Geneva Protocol of 1925. At a time when pacifism had won the hearts of many, the unprovoked barbarities that marked the fascist campaign naturally engendered global sympathy for the Ethiopians.

For Africans and their descendants at home and abroad, the Italian adventure amounted to another rape of the fatherland. The reaction of Kwame Nkrumah, who was passing through England from the Gold Coast to the United States, was typical. When he saw the poster, "MUSSOLINI INVADES ETHIOPIA," he was overwhelmed by emotion. In his own words: "At that time, it was almost as if the whole of London had suddenly declared war on me personally."[20]

The West African press reacted in a similar manner. "We in West Africa," a Sierra Leonean weekly commented, "are not disinterested in this Italo-Abyssinian question, for our past experience has taught us that though out of the 'heats,' we cannot escape the 'finals.' "[21] A Gold Coast newspaper asserted that the conflict was revealing, especially to the African race, what was at the back of the minds of the European powers in their dealings with the weaker peoples of the world and was teaching the members of the African race never to rely "on the most solemn promise or in the most sacred treaty made by a European power with a subject race."[22] "What we would like to impress on the inhabitants of this country," the paper later declared, "is that war with Abyssinia is our war."[23]

Ethiopian Defense Committees were set up in various parts of West Africa. In London, the WASU also formed an Ethiopian Defense Committee. In France the Ligue de la Défense de la Race Nègre held joint meetings with l'Etoile Nord-Africaine "on behalf of Ethiopia and as a demonstration of racial solidarity."[24] Statements expressing support for Abyssinia were issued by L'Etoile Nord-Africaine and by black workers in Holland and the French Caribbean.[25]

When the Ethiopian emperor, His Majesty Haile Selassie, and the other members of the royal family arrived in England in 1936 to spend years of exile there, the IAFA gave a reception for them.[26] In an article, "Abyssinia and the Imperialist," apparently addressed to Europeanized blacks, C. L. R. James as chairman of the IAFA declared:

> Africans and people of African descent, especially those who have been poisoned by British Imperialist education, needed a lesson. They have got it. Every succeeding day shows exactly the real motives which move Imperialism in its contact with Africa, shows the incredible savagery and duplicity of European Imperialism in its quest for markets and raw materials.[27]

The IAFA disbanded when a number of European liberals, including admirers of the emperor, formed pressure groups to work on behalf of Ethiopia. In France a Comité International Pour la Défense du Peuple Ethiopien et de la Paix was inaugurated with headquarters in Paris. In Holland there appeared Nederlandsche Vereeniging Voor de Vrijmaking Abessynie (Dutch Society for the Liberation of Abyssinia) based at The Hague. Similarly the Venezuelans started a society known as the Friends of Abyssinia.

In Britain alone, over a dozen organizations worked on behalf of the besieged African monarchy of which the most effective were the Friends of Abyssinia (Ethiopia) League having as its patroness Princess Tsahai, daughter of the Ethiopian emperor, and the distinguished scholar Ernest Baker among its honorary members; the Circles for the Liberation of Ethiopia (Essex); and the Abyssinia Association. The Circles for the Liberation of Ethiopia, founded on the initiative of the suffragette Sylvia Pankhurst, published a weekly, *New Times and Ethiopia News*, with a worldwide circulation.

The Abyssinia Association began as a group of English persons particularly interested in Abyssinia, most of them having lived there or visited the country. The association aimed "to diffuse correct information about Ethiopia in lectures and the press; and to urge in every way action by the League of Nations to save the country from Italian conquest."[28] Among its founding members were Sir George Paish (chairman), Major Neil Hunter (honorary treasurer), and the economist H. Stanley Jevons (secretary). Others who later joined the society included the pacifist Norman Angell of *The Great Illusion*[29] fame, the Dean of Winchester, Eleanor Rathbone, M.P., Philip Noel-Baker, M.P., and Muriel Blundell, who subsequently replaced H. Stanley Jevons as secretary. Compared with the more recent unilateral declaration of independence by the white settler minority in the Rhodesia colony, the Italian invasion evoked an equal, if not greater, amount of concern in the white world for the African victims.

The vehement protest of the British populace against the policy of their government as reflected in the Hoare-Laval Plan resembled the vigorous opposition in the eighteenth and nineteenth centuries of the British abolitionists to the Atlantic slave trade. Drawn up by Sir Samuel Hoare, the British foreign secretary, and Pierre Laval, prime minister of France, the proposals were extremely favorable to Italy and would have compromised Ethiopia's independence had they been implemented, which they never were, thanks to the outcry of the British public.[30] It was suggested, among other things, that Italy should receive eastern Tigre (including Adwa but not Aksum) and the Donakil area except for the territory in the Ogaden. In a protest memorandum to the League of Nations, the Ethiopian administration rejected the proposals as an invitation to Abyssinia, the victim of an act of aggression, first to cede to its Italian aggressor, under the pretext of exchange of territories, about half of its national territory to enable the aggressor to settle part of its population there; and second, to agree that the League of Nations should confer upon the invader control over the other half of Ethiopian territory pending future annexation.[31]

The unexpected dogged resistance to the fascist adventurers offered boundless opportunities for the ventilation of patriotic sentiments and demonstration of solidarity with Abyssinia as well as the glorification of its history and culture. Besides furnishing the exiles with material that gave enormous scope for the propagation of Pan-African aspirations, the prolonged resistance showed that in the defense of the fatherland no sacrifice could be too great. It was more honorable to die free than move under a foreign yoke. In the popularization of the virtues of patriotism, the Abyssinia Association made a significant contribution. Not only did some of its pamphlets reprint from time to time quotations emphasizing the inalienable right of all human beings to liberty and justice, but the association itself frequently paid tribute to the memory of "Those Ethiopians Who Died for Freedom."

At a memorial service of the organization held in London on 18 March 1937, the preacher, the Dean of Winchester, reminded the congregation that what was at stake was "the issue between Right and Wrong, Freedom and Oppression."[32] Four months later a similar service was conducted in New Church, Owo (Nigeria) with the Reverend Africanus Mensah, founder of the church, as preacher. Though the text of his sermon was "Ethiopia shall soon stretch forth her hands unto God," his comments were more political than religious. He traced the history of the country from the reign of Queen Sheba to the eruption of the crisis. The exertions of Sylvia Pankhurst received high commendation and the League of Nations was severely rebuked for lifting oil sanctions on Italy barely a year after their imposition.[33]

Many observers the world over shared Africanus Mensah's views that the League had been partial in its handling of the conflict. Jawaharlal Nehru made it clear that the Congress party was not enamored of the League and that the people of India objected to "this suppression of the Abyssinian people or to any recognition of the aggressor nation."[34] A conference of the West African Youth League, an anti-imperialist movement launched and led by the Sierra Leonean agitator I. T. A. Wallace Johnson, also called upon the League to denounce the aggressor in a more practical form by enforcing an oil embargo.[35] An article, "Has the African a God?" written by Wallace Johnson for the *African Morning Post* (Accra)[36] deploring Italian atrocities, gave the British colonial authorities in the Gold Coast an opportunity to charge him with sedition. But he escaped to Britain where he helped to form more Pan-African pressure groups.

Though the League of Nations disapproved of Italy's intervention in Ethiopia, it failed to enforce economic sanctions on the culprit. The readiness with which European leaders accepted and even aided the Italian incursion drove many men of African blood to the conclusion that they were immoral and unscrupulous politicians united by instinct and interest against blacks. This view is well brought out in an editorial comment in the *Gold Coast Spectator*:

> Force, the white man's god, is again supreme. Addis Ababa is occupied. . . . Poison gas, British oil, and the white man's duplicity all combined to make the Italian advance victorious. . . . After the Great War [World War I] the League lent money to some of the small Central Powers to rehabilitate them. But these are white. The League refused funds to Ethiopia, even though Article XVI stipulates it. Ethiopia, being black, could not be supported, even in affliction, and her financial solicitations were treated with derision. This is the Christian nations at work![37]

As in West Africa so in the Caribbean, the much vaunted values of European civilization began to come under fire as is clear from the following outburst of the West Indian C. C. Belgrave:

> The cold, hard inhuman attitude, which the European Powers have assumed towards Ethiopia, has taught black men that somehow or other, there is a difference in justice; there is one kind of justice for the white folk, and another kind for black. We wonder if the European Powers still profess to be Christians.[38]

"Rest assured Ethiopia," a Gold Coast patriot consoled, "your territory will be freed once again, as was that of the Poles and Belgians. When that day comes, you will rebuild a strong Empire and negotiate international alliances with Liberia and Haiti."[39]

Erosion of confidence in the League of Nations and the moral integrity of European statesmen compelled the African race to draw closer together for more reliable means of defending their interests. Early in 1937 two Pan-African associations were established in the United States. One was the United Aid for Peoples of African Descent.[40] The organization sent a message of solidarity to the emperor as well as letters of protest to the American president Franklin D. Roosevelt, the Italian ambassador to the United States, the former British prime minister David Lloyd George, and the Pope (Pius XI).[41] The other pressure group was the Congress of the African Peoples of the World War, two of whose aims were "to make Liberia one of the Great Powers of the World" and "to help in the hard fight for

Ethiopian independence."[42] The congress announced that plans were "under way for a General Conference to be held in Africa" sometime in 1937, but there is no evidence that it took place.

In Britain, frustration engendered by the role of the League drove some members of the now defunct IAFA, assisted by newcomers, to inaugurate an organization called the International African Service Bureau. Among the newcomers were T. Ras Makonnen, a British Guyanese of Ethiopian extraction formerly known as Thomas Griffiths, and I. T. A. Wallace Johnson. The one was made treasurer, the other general secretary. The other officers were George Padmore (chairman); Jomo Kenyatta (assistant secretary); and the Barbadian trade unionist Chris Jones (organizing secretary).[43] "The executive committee included Chris Jones, J. J. Ocquaye (Gold Coast), L. Mbanefo (Nigeria), K. Sallie Tamba (Sierra Leone), Garan Kouyaté (Soudan), N. Azikiwe (Nigeria), Gilbert Coka (South Africa). Among its Patrons were Nancy Cunard, Dorothy Woodman, D. N. Pritt, Noel Baker, A. Creech Jones, Victor Gollenz, F. A. Ridley, Sylvia Pankhurst, and Max Yergan."[44]

Like the WASU and the LCP, the IASB provided itself with an organ. Called the *International African Opinion*,[45] the journal was launched in July 1938 under the editorship of C. L. R. James, assisted by the African American, William Harrison, a research student at the London School of Economics and Political Science. That the leaders of the IASB were bent on achieving concrete results is clear from the editorial in the maiden issue of the journal. The purpose of the groups was "to assist by all means in their power the unco-ordinated struggle of Africans and people of African descent against oppression which they suffer in every country." The members of the society recognized that their position in London made them more immediately aware of the problem of Negroes in British dependencies. Nevertheless, their appeal was directed to Negroes everywhere—in the colonial empires, South America, and the United States. Though the IASB also realized that problems differed from place to place, they were convinced that there existed a common bond of oppression, and as the Ethiopian struggle had shown, blacks everywhere were beginning to see the necessity for international organization and unification of their scattered efforts.

The nature of the struggle before them was becoming clearer, and they were determined to fight to the end "until economically, politically and socially, the black man was everywhere as free as other men were." The founders of IASB were realistic enough to appreciate that they could "not liberate the millions of Africans and peoples of African descent from their servitude and oppression. That task no one can do but the black people themselves. But we can help to stipulate [*sic*] the growing consciousness." In a release entitled "What Is the International African Service Bureau?" Wallace Johnson further explained that the IASB was a "non-party" organization that owed no allegiance or affiliation to any political party or group in Europe.[46] Active membership was confined to Africans and persons of African stock regardless of their political and religious persuasions. Such members were, however, required to accept the aims of the association. Non-Africans who sympathized with the aspirations of the bureau and desired to demonstrate their interest in Africans and their descendants in a practical way were permitted to be associate members.

In one respect, the IASB differed from the other exile pressure groups in Britain, for it sought

> to co-ordinate and centralize the activities of the various organisations be they Political, Trade Union, Co-operative, Fraternal, Cultural, etc. which at present exist in different parts of the black world, and in this way bring them into closer fraternal relation with one another, as well as sympathetic organizations in Great Britain and other countries, so as to arouse concerted action upon all questions affecting the common economic, political, social and educational well-being of the Africans and peoples of African descent.[47]

To see the Italo-Ethiopian conflict as the sole cause of the establishment of the IASB would, however, be an oversimplification of a complex situation. Other factors were also at work, notably the growth of articulate racialism even in Britain and the protracted debate on the German and Italian colonial demands. The significance for African nationalism of the Italo-German colonial ambitions in particular, and the debate in general, can be gleaned from a letter of October 1938 that Padmore wrote to the Gold Coast ARPS. In that letter he emphasized that the colonial question was coming up before the politicians of Europe as a result of the demands of Hitler and that it was necessary for men of African blood to be on their guard.[48] "In this respect," he concluded, "the closest collaboration

of our Bureau and the Aborigines' Rights Protection Society would
be of tremendous importance in making the voice of Africa heard
in the councils of the nations."[49]

One suggestion advanced to meet the German and Italian claims
advocated the return to Germany of its former dependencies and
the cession to dissatisfied powers of some others. A leading exponent of this idea was Lord Lothian who, as private secretary to
Lloyd George, helped in the wording of those clauses of the Treaty
of Versailles providing for the mandate system.

The most widely discussed proposal, which met with considerable support in liberal circles, was the remedy prescribed by Sir
J. A. Salter (later Baron), a former director of the Finance and Economic Section of the League of Nations. Salter's solution was first
put forward at a conference on "Peace and Colonial Problems" summoned by the National Peace Council (London) and held on 29
October 1935 in Livingstone Hall, Westminster.[50] J. A. Salter recommended first, that whether or not other countries took the same
step, Britain should return to its traditional policy of equal opportunity for all nations in its colonies; and second, that it should offer
to join with other imperial powers in placing its dependencies under
the mandate system and international control.[51] He also suggested
a reform of the mandate system itself to make it possible for representatives of the Permanent Mandates Commission to visit mandated territories in order to verify statements in the annual reports
of the mandatories. The terms of the mandate would remain the
same, but instead of applying exclusively to the territories taken
from Germany and Turkey after the Great War, the system would
cover all the colonies.

Arnold Ward, secretary of the Negro Welfare Association, was
present at the conference. Repudiating the trusteeship principle on
which the mandate system rested, he said that cooperation between
whites and blacks could only be put on a lasting basis by the emancipation of the colonial peoples. The interests of the subject inhabitants and of the dissatisfied powers, he concluded, were incom-
patible.[52]

Harold Moody echoed Arnold Ward's views, adding that it was
immoral for one race to seek to dominate another.[53] In a resolution
passed at an annual general meeting held in March 1938, the LCP
reminded the British government that when Britain was assigned

dependencies previously under German control, the purpose was that these territories should be developed primarily for the benefit of their indigenous inhabitants with a view to their self-government. Such development and the goal of freedom would be more readily attained if these colonies remained in the trust of democratic countries with a parliamentary form of government. On the other hand, the LCP felt that these objectives would be impossible to achieve if the territories concerned were handed over to countries ruled by despots.

Finally, the resolution called upon the British government and Parliament "to refuse to consider such transfer of these territories, the more strongly that the League is confident that if the indigenous population were consulted they would refuse to consent to such transfer."[54]

The IASB also opposed the transfer but for a different reason. In an editorial the bureau's organ explained that if Africans opposed transfer to Hitler, it was not because they envisaged any fundamental difference in treatment. It was because they refused any longer to be bandied about from one European power to another.[55]

Side by side with the debate on the German and Italian demand for colonial equality went another discussion on a request by the Union of South Africa for an early transfer to it of the protectorates of Basutoland, Bechuanaland, and Swaziland. When the self-governing territories of Cape Colony, Natal, Orange Free State, and Transvaal were merged by the Act of Union (1909), the three protectorates just enumerated remained under the control of the British. Their eventual incorporation into the Union of South Africa was, however, envisaged, and safeguards for the rights of blacks, though vague, were set out in the Preamble and Schedule to the act. It was also provided that the time of transfer was to be settled by agreement between the governments of Britain and South Africa. Early in the thirties, reports from South Africa hinted that the Union government was about to press for immediate transfer; this revelation caused Harold Moody to address a letter to J. H. Thomas, British secretary of state for dominion affairs, opposing the transfer plan on the ground that it would amount to an "extension of the present South African method of dealing with native races."[56]

In November 1934 General Jan Christiaan Smuts paid a visit to

England. At a dinner given in his honor at the Savoy Hotel (London) by the South African Club, Smuts threatened that if incorporation was unduly delayed the Union might decline to take over the protectorates, with consequent damage to their economic interests.[57] No doubt, the Union served them as a market for their agricultural products and livestock, but Smuts conveniently ignored the fact that the protectorates equally supplied the Union with much needed cheap labor for its mines and farms. The shortage of labor for the Union's mining and agricultural industries was intensified by the drying up of labor supplies from Portuguese Africa; hence the Union was anxious to have the protectorates under its control.

It was argued by some writers that the protectorates should be handed over because of the invaluable services rendered by South Africans, Generals Smuts and P. W. Botha in particular, during the Great War. Many, however, realized that the enactment of the Statute of Westminster in 1931 and of the Status of South Africa Act three years later meant that the safeguards set out in the South Africa Act of 1909 could in the event of incorporation be replaced or amended by the Union government without reference to the British Parliament. Such persons included Lord Lugard, who held that the time for transfer had not arrived and that when the time came transfer should be effected by a tripartite agreement or treaty which, while giving assurance to the natives against unilateral change, would associate them in the transaction.[58] The signatories on their behalf would really be representatives of the people and not merely the hereditary and generally conservative chiefs who then wielded enormous influence. Meanwhile the British government should undertake to improve the conditions of the black inhabitants by introducing administrative, educational, and economic reforms.

This proposal was rejected by both the IASB and the LCP for different reasons. In a petition to the secretary for dominion affairs, the IASB condemned the projected handing over of the protectorates to the South African govemment for three reasons. First, because Africans and Africa were not property to be bartered between one imperialist regime and another; second, because the policy of South Africa toward the indigenous population was objectionable; and third, because the African inhabitants concerned were not represented in the British Parliament, whose views must be heard before transfer could take place.[59] A booklet, *Hands off the Protectorates*, written by George Padmore but published in 1938 under the name of the IASB, opposed the proposal on the ground that the black Africans concerned did not approve of it.[60] A main objection of the LCP to the proposal was the anxiety of black South Africans that "their brothers of the High Commission Territories [i.e., the protectorates] should not share the unhappiness and misfortune of their situation in the Union."[61]

The debates on the South African, German, and Italian colonial ambitions served to bring the exiles closer together. This growing solidarity was demonstrated by the joint memorandum submitted in 1938 on the West Indies to the British colonial secretary by the League of Coloured Peoples, the International African Service Bureau, and the Negro Welfare Association. Disturbances had broken out in Trinidad and Barbados in July 1937 and continued with violent strikes in Jamaica and Saint Lucia, spreading to Antigua and British Guyana. Riots involving casualties had occurred in Jamaica, Saint Kitts, and Saint Vincent two years before, but the unrest of 1937 was clearly more serious if only because it appeared to affect every section of the British Caribbean. Toward the end of May 1938 riots broke out again in Jamaica; consequently, the LCP and the IASB took up the matter.

The following month both groups organized protest meetings in London condemning the brutality with which the strikers had been treated and demanding far-reaching reforms, including the immediate release of the strike leaders, land settlement schemes, improvement of housing conditions, a self-governing federation of the West Indies, and fully democratic institutions.[62] A Royal Commission of Enquiry was appointed the next month under the chairmanship of Lord Moyne. Despite its initial hostility to the commission, the IASB in collaboration with the LCP and the Negro Welfare Association seized the opportunity to present a joint memorandum laying down a minimum program of change and development to be adopted at once.[63]

The memorandum was in the main an elaboration of the June resolutions. It stressed the political requisite for better conditions as being the abandonment of the Crown colony system of government and urged that property qualifications for the right to vote and hold office be discarded as a first step toward democratic rule in these islands.[64] It demanded the rescinding of all sedition ordinances and emphasized the need to confer on the people the right to form trade unions. Among specific proposals suggested to the commission were the launching of a ten million dollar housing scheme; the introduction of compulsory free primary and secondary education as well as the establishment of a West Indian university; the removal of racial discrimination in the colonial civil service; and the provision of social welfare measures. Before the commission left for the West Indies, Harold Moody and Peter Blackman gave evidence before it.[65]

In a pamphlet with the title *The West Indies Today* (1938), the IASB advised West Indian dockers and oil and sugar plantation laborers to build up powerful trade unions. Though the IASB placed in the forefront of the immediate tasks the question of trade unionism as the primary weapon in the fight for economic emancipation, it urged the workers to realize that their economic struggles could not be divorced from their political aspirations; there was still need for independent working-class political action.

In December 1939 the Royal Commission submitted a report that emphasized the urgency for considerable extension in public social services, arguing a case for a general scheme for social reconstruction of the Caribbean. The most important recommendation was the establishment of a West Indies Welfare Fund from which the large expenditure envisaged on welfare services and development could be met.[66] The proposed fund was to be financed by an annual grant of one million dollars from the British Treasury for a period of twenty years.

The LCP was invited by the British colonial secretary to submit a memorandum setting out its views on the recommendations. But at a meeting on 22 May 1940, summoned by the LCP to discuss the recommendations as well as British colonial policy, George Padmore and Peter Blackman, representing the IASB and the Negro Welfare Association, respectively, were present.[67] The three organizations found themselves in substantial agreement with the commission on such matters as education, public health, housing, industrial legislation, and transport. They considered the treatment of the economic and political issues altogether unsatisfactory. In expressing their opinion, the organizations were handicapped by the refusal of the metropolitan government to publish the report on which the recommendations were based. Protesting against the secrecy, they maintained that if the Caribbean countries were to make any meaningful progress, it was their own people guided by their own leaders who would play the major part. To withhold from the people and their leaders a report in which the fundamentals of future policy were discussed by a commission of experts could only, in their view, be a blow to West Indian advancement.

Turning to the welfare fund, the pressure groups pointed out that West Indians did not wish to be permanent recipients of charity from England. The aim should be to make their countries economically self-supporting so that they could finance new welfare measures without external assistance. The sections of the recommendations concerning industrial development came under heavy fire. It was the view of the Pan-Africanists that if the West Indians were to prosper, they must acquire industrial skills. They possessed oil, raw materials, and easy access to the markets of North and South America. Advantage should be taken of the services of the highly skilled persons fleeing from the wrath of the Nazis. Though the organizations accepted the educational proposals, they regretted the lack of any reference to the contribution a university could make to the social, cultural, and economic life of the West Indies.

Attention was also drawn to the fact that the commission's recommendations failed to emphasize the need for economic equality. The student of West Indian affairs could not but be struck by the extent to which the social pattern of the old slave society still remained stamped on these islands. It was a pattern in which a handful of people owned most of the wealth while the vast majority of the population labored in poverty on the landed property of the rich white minority.[68] Problems that were essentially economic acquired racial overtones because the class structure tended to coincide with racial divisions. The LCP, IASB, and the Negro Welfare Association felt that the solution to the problem of economic inequality lay in the extension of social services and scholarships, the development of trade unionism, the control of monopolies in the sugar and fruit industries, the redistribution of wealth by taxing the richer classes more heavily, and land reform.

With regard to the political question, the Pan-Africanists advocated the establishment of an administrative federation of the islands. They also demanded fuller self-government with an extension of the franchise and other electoral reforms such as would place real power in the hands of the masses.

Subsequent events, among them the establishment of the University of the West Indies and the attempt, albeit abortive, to form a West Indian federation show that the suggestions of the LCP, IASB, and the Negro Welfare Association were in tune with the realities of the situation. In addition to the welfare fund set up for the West Indies, a more general scheme was envisaged for all the colonies in the metropolitan government's *Statement of Policy on Colonial Development and Welfare*,[69] issued during World War II, largely as a result of the recommendations of the Royal Commission of Enquiry.

What was the attitude of the exiles to World War II? There was no single concerted approach. The attitude adopted by the followers of Harold Moody in many respects differed from that for the Padmore group.

Disappointed by the role of European leaders in the Italo-Ethiopian crisis, the LCP was at first not inclined to support either the Allied or Axis powers. A meeting of 27 September 1939 sponsored by the LCP and held in Aggrey House (47 Doughty Street, London) took the view that "We must remember that we are Africans first and British subjects after."[70] This position was confirmed in March 1940 by W. Arthur Lewis, then a lecturer at the London School of Economics and former editor of *The Keys*. In his view, decent people everywhere "know that where one race sets out to exploit another there can be no peace in society; freedom and equality for all, whatever their race, colour or creed, is an essential pillar of civilisation."[71]

Going a step further, Padmore linked up the crusade against Hitlerism with colonial freedom. In an article, "To Defeat Nazism We Must Free Colonials," Padmore stated among other things that self-determination was an inalienable right of every people regardless of the stage of their social and cultural development.[72]

These statements by W. Arthur Lewis and George Padmore clearly anticipated the Atlantic Charter. But as the war got under way, the LCP modified its attitude and supported the Allied powers. At a general meeting of the organization convened on 22 May 1940 and attended by Padmore, W. Arthur Lewis, and Peter Blackman,

Harold Moody declared that men of African blood could have no interest in a German victory.[73] Such a victory, he went on, "could mean for us of the Colonial Empire the loss of justice, freedom and equality."[74] Moody's apparent volte face naturally leads one to expect from the LCP little or no harsh criticism of colonial rule, at least during the duration of hostilities. But the exact opposite turned out to be the case. This fact plainly contradicts the stereotype that Moody was an Uncle Tom whose sole ambition lay in a modest improvement of the relations between blacks and whites.

The war itself brought to a focus objects of long-standing agitation as well as new issues, some of which served to intensify the militancy of the exiles. It raised in sharp outline such questions as the nature of liberty, the powers of the state, the rights of the individual, and racial prejudice. With the eruption of hostilities, spokesmen for the British government made speeches denouncing the racial policies of Nazi Germany and claiming that the British Empire stood for racial equality. It seemed to the LCP that the time had come once more to draw that government's attention to its own racial policies and if possible to get these sanctimonious declarations crystalized into action.[75]

A target that immediately came under fresh fire was the policy on recruitment into the British colonial medical service. On 14 December 1939, a deputation armed with a memorandum as well as a copy of the current number of the *British Medical Journal* that contained an advertisement stating that applicants must be of European origin, called on Malcolm MacDonald, the colonial secretary.[76]

Among the members of the delegation were W. Arthur Lewis; J. H. Christian, a barrister from the Gold Coast; Charles E. Collet from Seychelles, then secretary of the LCP; and H. Dingwall of British Guyana, vice president of the LCP. MacDonald appreciated the opportunity to hear the grievances of the organization and promised to consider whether any general restatement of policy regarding the engagement of colored people in the unified services should be made.

MacDonald was soon succeeded by Lord Lloyd, who in turn was replaced by Lord Moyne. Yet nothing seemed to be happening. Indeed, a subsequent advertisement repeated the condition that applicants to the British medical colonial service must be of European stock. Consequently, Harold Moody wrote to Lord Moyne reminding him of the promise made by MacDonald. This letter opened a long correspondence between the two men.[77]

Moyne denied that there was any barrier to prevent the appointment of any inhabitant of a colony whether European or non-European, adding that a substantial number of the members of those services were non-European.[78] Moody referred the colonial secretary to an issue of an unnamed paper "just to hand" complaining that some of the advertisements coming from His Majesty's Dockyard and Admiralty were most offensive to colored people.[79] In a separate letter to Moyne, Moody further referred him to a passage in the *Nigerian Eastern Mail* for 22 April 1940 expressing the hope that "one or other of our elected Legco. [Legislative Council] Members will not fail to ask at the next session of the Council, why in view of the Government's promise re the appointment of Africans to higher posts, an African was not elevated to the Bench when this vacancy occurred."[80] The newspaper was referring to the transfer from Uganda of C. C. Francis to fill the post of lower judge in Nigeria. The colonial secretary explained that this post was among those normally filled by selecting the most suitable candidate from the colonial legal service.[81] Though direct appointments from the local bar to judicial posts in a dependency could be and were sometimes made when circumstances justified this course, Moyne argued, it would not be in the public interest to regard this as the normal procedure.

In his answer Moody said that early in the year the attention of the LCP had been drawn to a notice posted on a board at an unnamed British university inviting applications for the colonial civil service. On making further inquiries, the LCP discovered that the advertisement was based not on a circular but on an ordinary letter enclosing a memorandum entitled "General Information Regarding Colonial Appointments." This printed document was issued by the British Colonial Office in March 1939. Moody thought that page 64 of the document proved beyond doubt the unwillingness of the colonial secretary to consider applications from persons not of European extraction. In view of this document Moody neither saw how Moyne could deny the existence of the regulation nor understood what purpose such a denial would serve.[82]

Moyne countered with the quibble that under those regulations, he and his predecessors had specifically reserved to themselves the right to admit to the membership of any of the unified colonial services anyone born or ordinarily resident in any of the dependencies irrespective of color or race. Though the policy laid down by the regulations was well established, Moyne felt that they could be simplified to make their meaning clearer to persons unfamiliar with the organization of the colonial civil service. He had therefore approved revised language that applied to the unified colonial services as a whole. The revision, a copy of which was sent to Moody, stated that a candidate must be "a British subject or a British protected person, and (a) is of European descent, or (b) was born, or is ordinarily resident in a Colony, Protectorate, or Mandated Territory, or is a child of a person so born or resident."[83]

Though Moody agreed with the colonial secretary that the regulations needed to be changed, he considered the colonial secretary's amendments unsatisfactory. Since the position remained unclear, Moody demanded from the colonial secretary "a final letter announcing that all distinction between European and non-European is now to disappear."[84] To this Moyne replied that the regulation already provided for the admission to membership of the unified services of persons born or ordinarily resident in a colony and so on and that the regulations had been revised to remove any doubt that might have been thought to exist as to their effect. Moreover, in the revised regulations the opportunity had been seized to extend eligibility to the children of persons born or ordinarily resident in one of the territories concerned.[85]

Commenting on the correspondence between Moody and Moyne, W. Arthur Lewis stressed that whatever might be the shortcomings of the French imperial system, they did not include racial prejudice.[86] In the French Empire any man, including members of the subject population, might rise to the highest position merited by his ability. Hence, the appointment of a Negro governor was regarded as a matter of course. Lewis was here referring to the French Guyanese Félix Eboué[87] who was made governor-general of French Equatorial Africa during World War II. But in the British Empire, Lewis lamented, there could be no black governor because the maintenance of white prestige was considered to be an essential prop of the imperial regime. Men of African blood were not allowed to hold posts of distinction and responsibility. The LCP would not rest, Lewis warned, until such an iniquitous system was abolished.

The publication of the Moody-Moyne correspondence in the organ of the LCP provoked further comments in the British press and the *New Statement and Nation* sympathetically remarked that the amendment still separated Europeans from others.[88] The duty of the imperial administration, the journal contended, "is to obtain Africans for self-government and room must be found for educated and patriotic Africans." Similar encouraging comments were received from such well-known figures as Vernon Bartlett, the left-wing lawyer; D. N. Pritt, Arthur Creech Jones, and William Temple, archbishop of York.[89] These press and personal comments show that the publications of the LCP were not without effect and that a number of highly placed persons were following the activities of the exiles with keen interest.

More striking than the public interest the correspondence aroused was the fact that Moyne appeared to be going out of his way to thrash the matter out. Coming from a colonial secretary, the number of letters seems unusual, and it is clear that Moyne regarded this as an important political issue of a delicate nature.

Viewed in the context of the Pan-African movement, the number of letters exchanged represented a measure of the growing strength of the phenomenon. Indeed, a remarkable feature during the war of the Pan-African organizations in general and of the LCP in particular was the frequency with which they communicated with the British authorities. Scarcely had two months elapsed after the correspondence with Moyne than Moody initiated another in protest against the passage in August that year (1941) of the Southern Rhodesia Land Apportionment Act, under which most of the fertile lands were reserved for the white settler minority.[90] In 1942 alone, no less than six sets of correspondence were conducted with the metropolitan government on matters ranging from the Abyssinian question to constitutional problems in the Caribbean.[91]

Inundating the British Colonial Office with letters of protest and criticism was by no means the only way in which the LCP expressed its mounting opposition to the political subjugation of Africans and persons of African origin. Review of books on the colonial system formed another medium through which it aired its grievances. One example was W. Arthur Lewis's comments on *Africa and British Rule* (1941) written by Margery Perham. As Perham explained in the preface, she wrote the book with Africans in mind as an answer to their questions concerning the irregularities associated with British rule in their countries. Her contentions may be summarized as follows: Africans were "savages" as the English once were. The high state of "civilization" the English now enjoyed took several centuries to evolve and was attained mainly due to the efforts of conquerors like the ancient Romans and the Normans as well as the wise statesmanship of the Tudor dynasty (1485–1603). The four hundred years from the Norman conquest to the Tudor period witnessed the building of a strong central government and the forging of one nation out of a multiplicity of tribes and potentates. In the sixteenth century the Tudor monarchs destroyed what remained of the power of the feudal nobility. Africans were so backward at the time of their "discovery" by the British that the latter wondered whether the former were not really an inferior biological specimen incapable of advancement. "Subjection was the only way by which, on account of her [*sic*] backwardness, and the nature of Europe's nineteenth-century system, Africans could have been brought into the civilised world." It was natural that like Indians, Africans should desire the full British form of representative parliamentary democracy. "So did the Italians, Germans, Russians and many other people who have now found that it is quite unsuited to their traditions and character." Africans must therefore be content to improve their tribal organizations even though the English had to eliminate tribal governments and unify the country before progress was possible. She defended the color bar, especially in East and central Africa, with the specious argument that the handful of white settlers needed to be shielded from "barbarism."

In her concluding chapter, "Education and the Future," Perham, in accordance with the belief popular among the conservatives of the time, asserted that Africans "must have foreign rulers, and for a long time to come."[92] She did not and could not have foreseen the Suez Crisis of 1956, the granting of independence to the Gold Coast the following year, and the consequent wind of change that was to sweep over Africa and compel the imperialist powers to disburden themselves of colonies, some of which had become liabilities rather than assests.

Despite Perham's sparkling style, W. Arthur Lewis detected that she had in fact avoided answering the questions Africans were asking and that her book altogether amounted to an apologia for imperialism. Lewis, writing very much from the viewpoint of conditions in eastern and southern Africa or the West Indies, argued that, as a boy, an African discovered that his school was a shambles compared with that reserved for his white counterpart.[93] As he grew up he realized how inadequate were the lands on which his people depended for their livelihood and learned how they had been driven into infertile "native reserves" to make room for white settlers. He found his father a tenant on a European farm, compelled by law like a medieval serf, to work for at least three months on this farm in lieu of rent.

As a young man, he went away from his village to work in mines, and discovered that however competent he showed himself to be, a color bar, whether enforced by law as in South Africa or by custom as in the Rhodesias, prevented him from acquiring a skilled job. He discovered too that if he attempted to organize any protest he was branded a communist agitator and imprisoned. It did not take him long to see that if he had accidentally been born of white parents in Africa all doors would have been open to him.

Africans were seeking to know the reason for these irregularities, which plainly contradicted the avowed altruistic motives of the imperialists. Rejecting Perham's rationalization that European subjugation of Africa was a historical necessity destined to last "for a long time to come," W. Arthur Lewis pointed out that the exploitation of Africans could never be justified on the a priori ground that they were "inferior" and "barbarous." Accepting the existence of African "cultural backwardness," he argued that this went hand in hand with its economic backwardness. Confusing industrialization with "civilization," Lewis asserted that to civilize the continent, its human (black and white) and material resources must be utilized. Neither the present haphazard development in Africa by European shareholders, nor the measures envisaged in the *Statement of Policy on Colonial Development and Welfare* could bring "civilization" to "savage" Africa except as a slow and uncertain by-product of private profit. And if this was all the development the colonies were likely to get under British rule, then Perham must be right in saying that Africa was bound to remain backward for many generations.

In that case, Africans would still be more right to question whether this uncertain fringe benefit was worth the price they were paying. The time had come to critically examine not only the aims but also the methods of imperial rule. Before the colonial civil service could become an adequate instrument of a "civilizing mission," its aims and traditions would require a sweeping revision. Lewis maintained that instead of speculating on the supposed inferiority of Africans and condoning racial prejudice, Margery Perham should have addressed herself to the task of how to sweep away the abuses of imperial rule. Finally, he dismissed her book as mere propaganda for the British cause.[94]

Lewis's review provoked a reply from Miss M. M. Green of the School of Oriental and African Studies, University of London.[95] Green thought that those who shared Lewis's desire for a solution to the problems of Africans under British rule must be puzzled and unhappy about his assessment of Perham's book. Lewis, she went on, wrote as though "it were a time bomb dropped by an enemy rather than a constructive piece of work by one of the most sincere and able of the champions of African advancement."

An examination of the book, chapter by chapter, led Green to a different interpretation and to the surprising conclusion that Lewis had not read the book at all. In his answer, Lewis said that since Green apparently had never heard of the numerous disabilities the Africans were made to suffer, including the alienation of their lands, Green naturally admired a work that flattered her pride as a member of the governing race and ignored what to the subject peoples were the unpleasant facts they came up against every day.[96]

The tenor of Lewis's review article reflected the belief, widely held at the time, that the end of the war would usher in a new order in which liberty and equality would replace racism and imperialism. It was an expectation stimulated, at the onset of the war, by the declarations of the British authorities sanctioned by the famous Atlantic Charter and sustained by the anticolonial utterances of several of the leading American citizens of the day, notably Wendell Willkie.[97]

Signed on 12 August 1941 by President Roosevelt of America and the British premier, Winston Churchill, the terms of the Atlantic Charter were given in a broadcast to the world by Clement Attlee two days later. At the heart of the joint declaration was the principle that all people have the right "to choose the form of government under which they will live" and to determine their political destiny. Whatever were the intentions of the signatories, this principle implied a repudiation of colonialism. Since Churchill had not yet returned from the Atlantic meeting, the WASU invited Clement Attlee, his deputy, to confirm that the charter also covered the colonies. In a statement made on 15 August to the WASU, Attlee said:

> You will not find in the declarations which have been made on behalf of the Government of this country on the war any suggestion that the freedom and social security for which we fight should be denied to any of the races of mankind.
>
> We fight this war not just for ourselves alone, but for all peoples.[98]

There was nothing equivocal about Attlee's speech. As a result, the *Daily Herald* in reporting it gave it the front-page headline: "The Atlantic Charter: *it means dark races too.*"[99]

The high hopes that both the charter and the assurance of Attlee had raised in the minds of the exiles (as well as colonials elsewhere) soon suffered a shock—a shock that made the exiles as bitter as ever. When Churchill finally returned from the Atlantic meeting, he explained in the House of Commons that the third clause of the charter—"the right of all peoples to choose the form of government under which they will live"—applied only to the white peoples of Europe then living under the Nazi yoke. That was quite a separate problem, he went on, "from the progressive evolution of self-governing institutions in the regions and peoples who owe allegiance to the British Crown."[100]

Churchill's interpretation of the joint declaration inevitably sparked off a public debate on the ideas of equality and liberty. Commenting on Churchill's explanation, a Nigerian daily, *The West African Pilot*, for 5 November wondered how a British premier could utter such a statement "during an unparalleled destructive war which has cost colonial peoples their material resources and manpower."

This observation seemed borne out barely three months later by the surprising indifference displayed by most of the natives of Burma, Malaya, and Singapore in the face of Japanese aggression. The explanation offered by *The Times* Singapore correspondent for this indifference was repeated ad nauseam by most British and

American observers. In his despatch, the correspondent revealed that the colonial government had no roots in the life of the native population and that the British residents were completely out of touch with the people.[101] The result was that "British rule and culture and the small British community formed no more than a thin and brittle veneer."[102]

An editorial in *The Times* for 28 February 1942 is a good illustration of the popular desire, even shared by some conservative imperialists, for a "foreward colonial policy."[103] British dominion in the Far East, the editorial bluntly asserted, could never be restored in its former guise, and it was undesirable to do so even if it were possible. But defeats must serve, it counseled, "just as defeat in the American war of independence served, as the starting point to a fresh advance in which, adapting herself to changed needs, Great Britain may once more become a pioneer of new policies and a new outlook." Some of the articles seized the opportunity to demand immediate colonial reforms, some to question the wisdom of continued colonial rule, and others to challenge the rightness of colonial rule itself.

It was in the midst of public condemnations of British colonial methods as unrealistic, that the WASU in a resolution passed on 4 April 1942, demanded for British West Africa immediate internal self-government with a definite guarantee of complete independence within five years after the war.[104] The demand was made "in the interests of Freedom, Justice and true Democracy, and in view of the lessons of Malaya and Burma, as well as the obvious needs of giving the peoples of the Empire something to fight for."[105] The WASU was convinced that "constitutional advancement and economic progress must move forward hand in hand together before a FREE AFRICA, which is the goal of our ambition, could be achieved."[106]

George Padmore inevitably took advantage of Britain's difficulties in the Far East to denounce not only imperialism but also the British Labour movement, which he accused of defending British imperial interests whenever they were threatened.[107] "We desire to help the Englishman," declared Harold Moody, "to wake up to the true position as it is today. His day of domination has gone for ever. . . . We mean to govern ourselves and decide our own fate and our own future."[108]

Allegations of forced labor in Nigeria were promptly taken up by the LCP with the Colonial Office. In a letter of 30 June 1942 to Harold Macmillan, the colonial undersecretary, Moody deplored the use of forced labor in the West Indies and West Africa.[109] The letter desired "it to be recognised that the people of Africa cannot and must not be treated in any way less liberal than the people of Britain."

In a lengthy reply, Macmillan explained that it had become imperative since the loss of Malaya for the output of the Nigerian tin mines to be increased to the utmost as part of the war effort.[110] It had not been found practicable to do this effectively without recourse to some degree of compulsion. He enumerated provisions which had been made for the welfare of laborers so far called upon for work, among them prior medical examination and free transport to and from the minefields. Concluding, Macmillan assured Moody that "the matter will be very carefully considered before compulsion is applied in other cases, either in Nigeria or elsewhere in the Colonies and that wherever it has to be resorted to, every effort will be made to ensure adequate provisions for the welfare of the workers concerned."

The impact of the Atlantic Charter and the Far Eastern crisis also caused a conference summoned by the Fabian Colonial Bureau and held on 15 November 1942 to make far-reaching demands.[111] Those present at the gathering included the Labour members of Parliament Reginald Sorenson and Arthur Creech Jones;[112] Beoku Betts, president of the WASU; and the West Indian member of the LCP, Doris Morant. Harold Moody, who was chairman, stressed the need "for a united colonial agreement" to strengthen the Atlantic Charter, which, in common with other contemporary commentators, he criticized as vague.[113] Colonial status he again rejected as "a dead conception to be buried for ever," a thesis he further developed in two booklets, *Christianity and Race Relations* and *Freedom for All Men*, published in London in 1943. Reginald Sorenson feared that the statements of Churchill, as shown in his reply on the position of India in relation to the Atlantic Charter, might be endorsed by many working-class people who were more imperialist than was sometimes realized.[114] "We must proceed during the war to clarify our ideas and guarantee that in measurable time those areas subject to us should be free and independent," he concluded.

The conference finally adopted a resolution demanding that colored peoples should not be excluded from the terms of the Atlantic Charter and that a "Special Charter . . . be formulated, giving specific guarantees to British dependencies that Colonial status shall be immediately abolished."[115]

In his pamphlet *Freedom for All Men*, Harold Moody emphasized the need not only "to adjust ourselves to a world in which there is freedom and equality for all" but also "to remove from ourselves every vestige of race-superiority."[116] Relations between the various races were indeed among the issues brought to a focus by the war. During the war, the exiles showed themselves extremely sensitive to expressions that could be interpreted as offensive to black people, partly due to the presence of American soldiers in Britain. The attitude of the LCP to the word *nigger* was shown in a communication to the British Broadcasting Corporation complaining about its use by an announcer.[117] A reply acknowledged the mistake and expressed the hope that the league "would accept the BBC's apology for this slip, which is sincerely regretted."[118]

And in 1943 the WASU actually succeeded in having the script of a proposed film revised. In preparation for the shooting of the film *Men of Two Worlds*, Two Cities Film Limited had asked the WASU to recommend to them some African girls as extras. The WASU felt unable to do so without seeing the script, which was eventually submitted. After a careful study of it, the WASU decided that it should either be recast or dropped on the ground that it amounted to a misrepresentation of African life and aspirations. Meanwhile it was discovered that the Colonial Office had already approved the script. Thereupon, the WASU passed a resolution of protest, copies of which were delivered to the colonial secretary, Colonel Stanley, with comments and suggestions attached.[119] The resolution contended that the film represented a distortion of the African "social system"; that it cast a slur on the prestige of African peoples and the British Empire. In the attachments, the WASU among other things objected to the use of the term "witch-doctor." After the exchange of a series of letters between the WASU, the Colonial Office, and the film company, the script was substantially revised along the lines suggested by the WASU.[120]

Meanwhile the public discussion on the Atlantic Charter had continued unabated. The year 1943, which saw the publication of

Freedom for All Men by Moody, was also the year in which Nancy Cunard and George Padmore jointly produced in London a monograph with the title *The White Man's Duty: An Analysis of the Colonial Question in the Light of the Atlantic Charter*. The application of the third clause of the charter to all peoples regardless of the stage of their social development and the organization of colonial economies for the benefit of the native inhabitants were envisaged as the ideal postwar solution to the colonial problem. Suggestions about how this ideal solution could be carried out were given in a proposed "Charter for the Colonies," which formed the concluding chapter of the monograph. Notable among the measures recommended for the African dependencies were the introduction of economic, social, and political equality; the abolition of conscript labor and pass laws; the limitation of company profits; and the removal of restrictions on civil liberties with the exception of censorship of matters of strategic importance.

For the (British) West Indies, the booklet demanded the transfer of power "from the present Crown Colony bureaucracy to the elected representatives of the people, on the following basis: universal adult suffrage; removal of property qualification for membership of [legislative] Councils; people's control of expenditure." The measures did not amount to a demand for immediate and complete independence but for internal self-rule. Coming from writers imbued at that time with the revolutionary ideology of Marxism-Leninism, the demand for only internal self-government seems surprisingly modest.

A charter for the colored peoples was proposed at a conference of the LCP held from 21 to 23 July 1944.[121] Harold Moody and John Fletcher of the Friends' Service Council jointly presided. The chief speakers were H. W. Springer, a former treasurer of the LCP who subsequently became secretary of the Barbados Progressive League and member of the Legislative Council there; Malcolm Joseph-Mitchell from Trinidad, member of the LCP; C. W. C. Greenidge, a Barbadian member of the LCP; Peter Abrahams from South Africa, member of the IASB; John Carter, then secretary of the LCP; Rita Hinden of the Fabian Colonial Bureau; K. A. Korsah (Gold Coast); Rev. I. Ransome Kuti (Nigeria); and A. Taylor-Cummings (Sierra Leone). The last three were visiting members of the Royal Commission on Higher Education in West Africa.[122]

At the end of the conference, the charter for the colored peoples was proposed.[123] There were no fundamental differences between it and the earlier ones suggested by the Fabian Colonial Bureau and that jointly submitted by Nancy Cunard and George Padmore. What is worth noting was its submission to all the diplomatic missions in Britain, many of which promised to give it a sympathetic consideration.[124] His Majesty's Government, through the colonial secretary, stated in a reply dated 31 August that they were "not convinced that substitution of a uniform 'Charter' in place of the policy of individual treatment would help the present steady progress."[125]

Exiles in the United States also attempted to apply the principles of the Atlantic Charter to the African world. Among them was the Nigerian from Igboland, Akweke Abyssinia Nwafor Orizu. Since *Abyssinia* is not an Igbo word, the appelation was probably adopted during the Italian invasion as a gesture of support for the beleaguered Ethiopians. Educated at Columbia University (New York) where he obtained a master's degree in government and public law, he wrote a book entitled *Without Bitterness: Western Nations in Post-War Africa*, published in New York in 1944. Where Padmore and Moody sought reforms with self-determination as the ultimate goal, Orizu demanded immediate autonomy. Africa, he declared, "is indignant with European imperialism, as it has been, as it is, and as some planners still want it to be."[126] By warning the metropolitan powers that Africans wished "to be free now and forever," he anticipated Kwame Nkrumah.

A careful study of the indigenous African political systems led Orizu to reject the imperialist propaganda that Africans were inexperienced in the art of government and therefore incapable of ruling themselves. But his admiration of the African past was far from nostalgic. He was forward-looking enough to realize that in order to survive in the postwar era, Africa had to undergo a process of modernization. The new Africa would strive for economic independence, avoid the mistakes of the industrial West, show goodwill toward the rest of mankind, and above all

> advocate the true democracy—democracy without imperialism, without unequal treaties, without unfair exploitation, without mental slavery and without a racial superiority complex.[127]

The year Nwafor Orizu's book appeared also witnessed the submission of a memorandum on university education by the LCP to the visiting Royal Commission on Higher Education in West Africa. It was a document combining most of the educational ideas of Edward W. Blyden, J. A. B. Horton, and J. E. Casely-Hayford. More important, it reflected the cultural ideas of the Pan-Africanists. In character and purpose, the LCP's concept of higher education resembled concepts advocated in the second half of the nineteenth century by Horton and Blyden and that of Casely-Hayford outlined early in the twentieth century in his book *Ethiopia Unbound* (London, 1911). The LCP desired that the primary aim of training should be "for leadership, and for service to and love of country."[128] As much as possible, institutions of learning should be "mainly manned by Africans, whose objectives would be to bring out the very best possible in the life of the country and thus make West Africa an example to the whole of Africa."[129] Such institutions "while profiting by the experience gained in education in Britain, America and Russia [*sic*], should nevertheless evolve curricula of their own, calculated to meet the specific needs of the area to be served."[130] In such curricula, ample provision should be made for things that were characteristically African. "Every effort must be assiduously made to avoid merely Europeanising the African or to train him only to undertake the routine duties and less responsible work of the fully qualified European Officer."[131]

In recommending that university education should be free, the LCP anticipated developments in Nkrumah's Ghana. Like Blyden, the LCP emphasized the importance of languages. English must be taught in all schools and the multiplicity of African languages reduced to a few workable languages. Africans should be proficient in at least two. Production of literature in basic African languages should be actively supported by government and philanthropic bodies. Finally, the memorandum urged that the African must be encouraged to be truly himself. Implicit in this concluding plea is the now familiar concept of the African personality.

More important as a landmark in the Pan-African movement than the LCP's memorandum on university education was the formation in Manchester the same year (1944) of the Pan-African Federation (PAF), mainly due to the initiative of the IASB. The new organization was a merger of some exile and colonial nationalist movements in Britain and Africa. Among the constituent pressure groups were the African Union (Glasgow); the Friends of African

Freedom Society (Gold Coast); the IASB; the Kikuyu Central Association (Kenya); the Negro Association (Manchester); the United Committee of Coloured and Coloured People's Association (Cardiff); the WASU; and the West African Youth League.[132] The reader will observe that the LCP is conspicuously absent from the list. Whatever may be the reasons for this exclusion, they do not seem to include conflict of objectives as is evident from the rest of the chapter. Each member organization was allowed to maintain its separate existence and to retain its local autonomy, but was required to adhere strictly to the basic aims of the PAF. These were to secure equality of civil rights and independence for African peoples (and other subject races); to "promote the well-being and unity of African peoples and peoples of African descent throughout the world"; and to cooperate with peoples who share the aspirations of men of African blood.[133]

The PAF planned the establishment of institutes for the study of African history and culture, the publication of works by and about Africans, and "the convening of national and international conferences in order to further its aims and objects."[134] Manchester (58 Oxford Road) was chosen as headquarters because Peter Milliard and T. Ras Makonnen, the chairman and the general-secretary respectively of the group, were based there. Other officers included E. A. Cowan of the Negro Welfare Centre (assistant secretary) and J. E. Taylor, also of the Negro Welfare Centre (treasurer). Following his arrival from the United States in June 1945, Francis Kwame Nkrumah was made the regional secretary.

The aspirations of the PAF were reaffirmed and elaborated in an open letter of September 1945 to Clement Attlee who, as a result of the victory of the Labour party in the first postwar parliamentary election held in July was now prime minister of Britain.[135] The victory of the Labour party, it was claimed, was an event for which they as colonials had hoped and worked. At last the time had arrived for "Comrade Attlee" and his government to "give the Socialist answer to the Tory imperialism of Mr. Churchill's 'What we have we hold.' " It would be dishonest to condemn only the imperialism of Germany, Japan, and Italy; all imperialisms are bad. The PAF as a "responsible body representing vast sections of African and colonial thought, demands for the colonial peoples the immediate right to self-determination" and the following reforms: the speedy implementation of the educational reforms suggested in the West Indies reports on higher education;[136] the publication of the West Indian Royal Commissions Report "suppressed since 1940";[137] and the removal of the color bar, of disabilities based on race, and all restrictions on civil liberties. The Labour government was also urged to reaffirm "its determination to keep race-ridden South Africa out of the Protectorates (Bechuanaland, Basutoland, and Swaziland)." It was suggested that the Colonial Office should summon a conference of the African and other colonial leaders to discuss their problems. Such a conference, in the opinion of the PAF, would serve to usher in a period of cooperation and partnership, as against domination; it "would be a great stride towards the Century of the Common Man." A conference of some leaders of the people of African descent was held in Manchester the following month, but it was called not by the Colonial Office but by the PAF.

The recognition of the PAF as an effective platform for opposition to colonial rule can be seen from the tendency of West Indians and Africans to cable details of labor disputes to the secretary of the organization.[138] The PAF would then either organize a public demonstration or send a deputation to the colonial secretary or both. Thus, on the receipt in 1945 of a report on a general strike in Nigeria, the secretary of the PAF got in touch with the component unions and various action committees were set up.[139] In London, Kwame Nkrumah, the regional secretary of the PAF, summoned a public meeting, which took place in Conway Hall.[140] Resolutions were adopted expressing solidarity with the Nigerian workers and condemning the colonial administration. Donations were collected in aid of the strikers.[141]

Meanwhile, during the first half of 1945, the IASB put out five pamphlets, namely, *Kenya: Land of Conflict; African Empires and Civilizations; The Negro in the Caribbean; The White Man's Duty;* and *The Voice of Coloured Labour.*[142] The publications were edited by George Padmore with T. Ras Makonnen, Jomo Kenyatta, I. T. A. Wallace Johnson, C. L. R. James, and Peter Abrahams as advisory editors. The first pamphlet was written by Jomo Kenyatta. A survey of life and government in precolonial Kenyan society and the alienation of most of the natives' lands to white settlers led Kenyatta to the conclusion that indigenous Kenyans under colonial rule were oppressed, exploited, and deprived of civil liberties. He stressed that

Africans would never be satisfied until they enjoyed full self-government, and economic and social security, which could be achieved in a nonimperialist social order.[143]

The author of *African Empires and Civilizations* was a French historian, Raymond Michelet, who originally wrote it for Nancy Cunard's well-known anthology, *Negro*, from where it was reprinted by the IASB. The booklet, thirty-nine pages long, may be divided into three broad sections. The first part summarizes the main historical facts concerning the western Sudanese empires of Ghana, Mali, and Songhay. The second section examines various precolonial polities in central and South Africa, notably the kingdoms of Asande, Loanga, and Monomotapa (Mwene Mtapa). The third section of the pamphlet quotes freely from Leo Frobenius[144] and Maurice Delafosse[145] to illustrate the high level of civilization and artistic achievement reached in some of these political systems. Anticipating the conclusions of recent research, Michelet argued that before the European intervention, Africans had formed powerful states comparable to those of contemporary Europe. The African states "developed along far-reaching lines of unsuspected stability, whose civilisation, laws, customs and economic administration were perfectly balanced, and in which above all, the mode of life was simplified to an extent unknown to the white world."

In an editorial note, Padmore warmly commended the booklet as a refutation of the slanderous description of Africans as "savages without a past." He hoped that now that Africans stood on the threshold of a new day, they would take pride in the social achievements of their ancestors and "build their future collectivistic society on more lasting foundations, to the benefit not only of themselves but all humanity." This deployment of historical evidence using the best scholarly work then available was much more original than it now sounds.

The Negro in the Caribbean was contributed by Eric Williams, who later became prime minister of Trinidad and Tobago. It discussed the early economic system of the West Indies in its historical relation to slavery, showing the effects of sugar upon the entire social and political structure in the islands. He had worked out much of this argument in *Capitalism and Slavery*,[146] a major work of historical scholarship.

The White Man's Duty, jointly written by George Padmore and

Nancy Cunard, was an enlarged edition of the earlier one published in 1943.[147]

The last pamphlet published in 1945 by the IASB was *The Voice of Coloured Labour*. It contained the speeches and reports of the African and West Indian delegates to the World Federation of Trade Unions Conference held in London in February the same year.

Most of the above IASB publications were sympathetically reviewed in such periodicals as *Empire*, organ of the Fabian Colonial Bureau, *International Affairs* (Journal of the Royal Institute of International Affairs),[148] and *The Times Literary Supplement*. For instance, *The Negro in the Caribbean; African Empires and Civilizations; Kenya: Land of Conflict* were all reviewed in *The Times Literary Supplement* for 2 June 1945. In its review of *African Empires and Civilizations*, *Empire* remarked that it was "a melancholy comment on the parochial outlook of many Europeans that, despite the years of sociological study sympathetic to local cultures, such a pamphlet should still be necessary."[149] Reviews of the IASB publications in such respectable journals not only helped to publicize the grievances and aspirations of the exiles but were also a measure of the growing impact of their activities on enlightened opinion in Britain. These publications helped to prepare the ground for the historic Manchester Pan-African Congress, the subject of the following chapter.

1. League of Nations, *International Commission of Enquiry in Liberia* (Geneva, 1930), 83–84.

2. Under the system indigenous children were adopted into "civilized" Liberian families for purposes of education. Among other things, it facilitated intermarriage between the African American colonists and the aboriginal population and the participation of aboriginal elements in the government of the country. For further details, see H. L. Buell, *The Native Problem in Africa*, vol. 2 (New York: Macmillan, 1928).

3. United Kingdom, *Parliamentary Debates* (Lords), 5th ser., vol. 83 (1931–32): 912–38.

4. *West Africa*, 17 October 1931, 1259.

5. *Manchester Guardian*, 30 October 1933.

6. Ibid.

7. Ibid.

8. *West Africa*, 1 July 1933, 640.

9. *Manchester Guardian*, 30 October 1933.

10. *The Keys*, April–June 1934. For details of the League of Nations Plan of Assistance, see *African World*, 15 October 1938, 412. In November 1934, Charles Roden Buxton, a grandson of the great abolitionist and member of the LCP toured West Africa. At the request of the LCP he visited Liberia. His personal observations and discussions with high government officials led him to the conclusion that the alleged irregularities had been exaggerated. What many a critic did not know was that the Christy Commission took place in the midst of a presidential election campaign. As Buxton explains, "The President's opponents were well organised and produced Native witnesses to support charges which were, in fact, an important factor in the campaign" (Charles R. Buxton, *Impressions of Liberia, November 1934: A Report to the League of Coloured Peoples* [LCP Publications, n.d.]).

11. *Foreign Affairs*, July 1933, 682.

12. Ibid., 695.

13. *Labour Monthly*, September 1935, 536.

14. Ibid., 532; *New Times and Ethiopia News*, 30 January 1954, 3.

15. *Labour Monthly*, September 1935, 532.

16. Printed in *New Times and Ethiopia News*, 30 January 1954, 3.

17. *The Keys*, January–March 1936, 31; D. A. Vaughan, *Negro Victory: The Life Story of Dr. Harold Moody* (London, 1950).

18. Vaughan, *Negro Victory.*

19. Ibid.

20. *Ghana: The Autobiography of Kwame Nkrumah* (Edinburgh: Thomas Nelson, 1961), 22.

21. *Sierra Leone Weekly News*, 3 August 1935.

22. *Vox Populi*, 11 September 1935.

23. *Vox Populi*, 9 October 1935.

24. J. Ayodele Langley, *Pan-Africanism and Nationalism in West Africa, 1900–1945* (London: Oxford University Press, 1973), 324.

25. *New Times and Ethiopia News*, 30 May 1936, 3.

26. George Padmore, *Pan-Africanism or Communism? The Coming Struggle for Africa* (London: Dennis Dobson, 1956), 145.

27. *The Keys*, January–March 1936.

28. *New Times and Ethiopia News*, 16 May 1936, 4.

29. Norman Angell, *The Great Illusion* (London, 1910). See also his *The Fruits of Victory* (London, 1921) and *This Have and Have Not Business* (London, 1936).

30. A full text of the Hoare-Laval proposals was published in *The Times* (London), 14 December 1935, 12. For reaction of the British people, see *The Tragedy of Abyssinia* (London: League of Nations Union Publications, 1936).

31. *The Times* (London), 14 December 1935, 12.

32. *Nemesis* (Abyssinia Association Pamphlet) (London, 1939). On the front page of the pamphlet are the following excerpts:

> We believe in liberty. . . . We assert the right of all nations to live their own lives. [Mr. Arthur Greenwood, M.P., 3.9.39]

> The British Government and the British people are profoundly convinced that every nation has its contribution to make to the common civilisation of humanity, but that no nation, great or small, can do itself justice unless it be free. [*The Times* (London), 5 September 1939]

33. *New Times and Ethiopia News*, 3 July 1937, 2.

34. *New Times and Ethiopia News*, 9 October 1937, 5.

35. Wallace Johnson Collection, Institute of African Studies Library, Legon (University of Ghana).

36. *African Morning Post*, 15 May 1936.

37. *Gold Coast Spectator*, 9 May 1936.

38. *New Times and Ethiopia News*, 16 January 1937, 3.

39. *New Times and Ethiopia News*, 14 August 1937, 6.

40. *New Times and Ethiopia News*, 6 March 1937, 8.

41. *New Times and Ethiopia News*, 19 June 1937, 8.

42. *New Times and Ethiopia News*, 7 April 1937, 7.

43. Padmore, *Pan-Africanism or Communism?*

44. Langley, *Pan-Africanism and Nationalism in West Africa*, 338.

45. There is a complete file in the Schomburg Collection.

46. Quoted material in this paragraph reprinted on the inside pages of the cover of George Padmore, *Hands Off the Protectorates* (London: I.A.S.B. Publication, 1938).

47. Ibid.

48. Padmore to W. Essuman-Gwira Sekyi, 4 October 1938, in Gold Coast ARPS Papers, acc. no. 156/1965.

49. Ibid.

50. *Peace and Colonial Problem* (London, 1935).

51. *Economic Policies and Peace* (Metterns Lecture) (London, 1936), 30–31.

52. *Peace and Colonial Problem*, 51.

53. *Peace* (London), December 1935, 144.

54. *The Keys*, April–June 1938, 85–86.

55. *International African Opinion*, 7 November 1938.

56. *Sunday Times* (Johannesburg), 18 June 1933; *The Keys* (October 1933): 36, (April–June 1935): 86. See also the articles of Lionel Curtis, *The Times* (London), 13–15 May 1935.

57. *The Times* (London), 7 November 1934, 18.

58. *Manchester Guardian*, 28 May 1935, 11–12.

59. *International African Opinion*, July 1938, 4–5.

60. See, for example, *A Statement to the British Parliament and People* (London, 1935) by Tshekedi Khama, chief and regent of Bechuanaland, setting out his people's reasons for opposing incorporation.

61. *The Keys*, April–June 1938, 85–86.

62. *The People* (Trinidad), 30 July 1938; *International African Opinion*, August 1938, 16; *The Keys*, July–September 1938, 10.

63. At first the IASB denounced the commission as a bluff in view of the metropolitan government's failure to implement recommendations of previous commissions (Editorial, *International African Opinion*, August 1938).

64. *International African Opinion*, October 1938, 7.

65. LCP, *Eighth Annual Report*, March 1939, 4.

66. The recommendations of the Royal Commission were published separately as Cmd. 6174, 1940. The full report was published in October 1945 (Cmd. 6607).

67. *News Notes*, July 1940, 64–66. The reply of the three organizations is reproduced in extenso in Vaughan, *Negro Victory*, 107–11.

68. See, for example, David Lowenthal, *West Indian Societies* (London: Oxford University Press, 1972).

69. United Kingdom (Parliament), *Statement of Policy on Colonial Development and Welfare*, Cmd. 6175, 1940.

70. *News Notes*, November 1939, 4–5.

71. *News Notes*, March 1940, 1–2.

72. *New Leader* (London), July 1940, 5.

73. *News Notes*, July 1940, 64.

74. Ibid.

75. *News Notes*, August 1941, 99.

76. *News Notes*, January 1940, 3; August 1941, 100–101.

77. Published in *News Notes*, August 1941, 101–19.

78. Moyne to Moody, 4 April 1941, in ibid.

79. Moody to Moyne, 24 April 1941, in ibid.

80. Moody to Moyne, 26 April 1941, in ibid.

81. Moyne to Moody, 5 May 1941, in ibid.

82. Moody to Moyne, 21 May 1941, in ibid.

83. Moody to Moyne, 30 May 1941, in ibid.

84. Moody to Moyne, 12 June 1941, in ibid.

85. Moyne to Moody, 20 June 1941, in ibid.

86. *News Notes*, August 1941, 117–19.

87. For a biography of Félix Eboué, see Brian Weinstein, *Eboué* (London: Oxford University Press, 1972).

88. *New Statement and Nation*, 16 August 1941, 150. See also *Manchester*

Guardian, 1 August 1941, 2; *Western Mail* (Cardiff), 1 August 1941, 2; *Yorkshire and Leeds Mercury*, 1 August 1941, 3; and *West Africa*, 2 August 1941, 741.

89. *News Notes*, September 1941, 121–22.

90. *News Notes*, December 1941, 55–63. Moody to Moyne, 20 August 1941; Moyne to Moody, 22 August 1941; Cransborne (Dominions secretary) to Moody, 28 August 1941; Moody to Cransborne, 4 November 1941. See also LCP, *Eleventh Annual Report*, March 1942.

91. League of Coloured Peoples, *Twelfth Annual Reoprt*, March 1943, 6. The list of letters includes those written to Anthony Eden (foreign secretary) on the Abyssinian affair; Harold Macmillan (undersecretary of state of colonies) on forced labor in Nigeria and the West African medical services as well as to Lord Moyne on the Jamaica constitution.

92. She expressed a similar view in her article, "The British Problem in Africa," *Foreign Affairs* 29 (July 1951).

93. W. Arthur Lewis's review was printed in *News Notes*, September 1941, 125–30.

94. Ibid.

95. *News Notes*, October 1941, 7–8.

96. Ibid.

97. See Willkie's book *One World* (London: Cassel, 1943).

98. *Daily Herald*, 16 August 1941, 1.

99. Ibid.

100. United Kingdom, *Parliamentary Debates* (Commons), 5th ser., 9 September 1941.

101. *The Times* (London), 18 February 1942.

102. Ibid.

103. See, for example, Margery Perham's two articles, "The Colonial Empire," *The Times* (London), 13–14 March 1942, 5; the editorial "The Colonial Future," *The Times* (London), 14 March 1942); and Lord Samuel's "Parliament and the Colonies: Closer Contact," *The Times* (London), 8 August 1942, 5.

104. *West Africa*, 18 April 1942, 359; *News Notes*, May 1942, 37.

105. *West Africa*, 18 April 1942, 359.

106. *News Notes*, May 1942, 37.

107. *Forward*, May 1942, 5–7.

108. *News Letter*, May 1942, 25–32.

109. *News Notes*, September 1942, 145–46.

110. Harold Macmillan to Moody, 31 July 1942. Macmillan's letter is reproduced in full in ibid., 146–49.

111. *Manchester Guardian*, 16 November 1942, 6.

112. Reginald Sorenson and Arthur Creech Jones were also members of the LCP.

113. *Manchester Guardian*, 16 November 1942, 6.

114. See, for instance, *Manchester Guardian*, 10 September 1941, 2, where Churchill declared that the Atlantic Charter "did not qualify in any way the various statements of policy which have been made from time to time about the development of constitutional government in India."

115. *Manchester Guardian*, 16 November 1942, 6. For the text of the resolution see *News Notes*, February 1943, 148.

116. Harold Moody, *Freedom for All Men* (London, 1943), 15.

117. *News Notes*, June 1940, 39.

118. Ibid.

119. Solanke to Colonial Secretary, 27 July 1943; printed in *Wasu*, June 1944, 11.

120. The correspondence between the WASU, the Colonial Office, and the company published in *Wasu*, June 1944, 11–15.

121. LCP, *Fourteenth Annual Report*, March 1945, 11.

122. Ibid.

123. Ibid.

124. Ibid.

125. Ibid.

126. A. A. Nwafor Orizu, *Without Bitterness: Western Nations in Post-War Africa* (New York: Creative Age Press, 1944), xiv.

127. Ibid., 19.

128. *News Notes*, February 1944, 73–74; LCP, *Thirteenth Annual Report*, March 1944.

129. Ibid.

130. Ibid.

131. Ibid.

132. Padmore, *Pan-Africanism or Communism?* 149.

133. Ibid.

134. Ibid.

135. There are minor differences between the text of the open letter as published in leaflet form by the PAF probably in October 1945 and as extensively reproduced by George Padmore in *Pan-Africanism or Communism?* 156–58. In this study, the earlier leaflet version has been used. Earlier in July the WASU had sent a similar letter to Harold Laski, chairman of the Labour party (*Wasu*, March 1946, 42).

136. United Kingdom, Parliament, Cmd. 6655, 1945.

137. Ibid., 166–69.

138. E. B. Ndem, "Negro Immigrants in Manchester: An Analysis of Social Relations Within and Between the Various Coloured Groups and of Their Relations to the White Community," M.A. thesis, London University, 1954, 119.

139. Ibid.

140. Ibid.

141. Ibid.

142. Padmore, *Pan-Africanism or Communism?* 150, erroneously attributes the pamphlets to the PAF.

143. Jomo Kenyatta, *Kenya, Land of Conflict* (London: Mercury Books, 1945), 23.

144. *The Voice of Africa, Being an Account of the Travels of the German Inner African Exploration Expedition in the Years 1910–1912*, trans. Rudolf Blind (London, 1913). For a recent scholarly analysis of the methods and observations of Frobenius as against his general ideas, see J. M. Ita, "Frobenius in West African History," *Journal of African History* 13 (1972): 673–88.

145. *Les Nègres* (Reider); see also *Les Noirs de l'Afrique* (Paris, 1922).

146. Eric Williams, *Capitalism and Slavery* (Chapel Hill: University of North Carolina Press, 1945).

147. Ibid., 201–2.

148. *International Affairs*, October 1945.

149. *Empire*, May–June 1945. For further reviews see *The Tribune* (London), 18 March 1945.

4

The Manchester Congress
and Its Aftermath

EARLY IN 1944 Harold Moody and Amy Jacques Garvey separately approached Du Bois on the necessity for a postwar Pan-African meeting.[1] The three, together with Paul Robeson, announced in April the same year their readiness to assist in convening a "Pan-African Congress to be held in London as soon after the war as possible."[2] Eventually, they lost the initiative to the PAF, who not only changed the venue but also arranged every aspect of the conference.

The idea of a convocation in Manchester was first mooted during a conference of the World Federation of Trade Unions (WFTU) that met in London in February 1945. To this conference came representatives of black colonial labor from Africa and the Caribbean. Seizing the opportunity, the PAF invited the colonial delegation to a discussion in Manchester at which the necessity for another Pan-African congress was considered. A provisional agenda was drawn up. "The delegates took it back to their countries and discussed it with their people."[3] Most of the colonial organizations approved the agenda with minor amendments, pledging themselves to send delegates.

Exploiting this enthusiasm, the PAF timed the proposed congress to coincide with the second conference of the WFTU to be held in Paris from 25 September to 9 October that year.[4] Associations too poor to send delegates "gave mandates to the natives of the territories concerned who were travelling to Paris to attend the World Federation of Trade Unions Conference."[5] Some organizations that did not send delegates to the WFTU conference mandated individuals already in Britain to represent them.[6]

The task of making the necessary arrangements fell on a special committee comprising Peter Milliard (chairman); George Padmore and Kwame Nkrumah (joint political secretaries); Jomo Kenyatta (assistant secretary); and Peter Abrahams (publicity secretary).[7]

Though officially opened on 15 October by the lord mayor of Manchester, Alderman Jackson, the Manchester Pan-African meeting was jointly presided over by W. E. B. Du Bois and Peter Milliard, president of the PAF. The Charlton Town Hall, where the conference took place, was decorated with the flags of Ethiopia, Haiti, and Liberia. Taking part, as in the previous Pan-African meetings, were students, men and women from varied walks of life with a sprinkling of fraternal delegates and observers. But unlike the preceding Pan-African congress, Africa was for the first time adequately represented. Many of these Africans were soon to become important in one capacity or the other in their own countries. Notable among the Nigerian participants were Obafemi Awolowo, who subsequently became a premier of western Nigeria; H. O. Davies, later to be a chairman of Nigeria's state-sponsored newspapers; and Jaja Nwachuku, Nigeria's foreign minister in the Balewa administration. The poet Raphael Armattoe, Hastings Banda, and Garba Jahumpa represented Togoland, Nyasaland (now Malawi), and Gambia, respectively. Garba Jahumpa later became minister of agriculture and natural resources in the government of Gambia. Also in attendance was I. T. A. Wallace Johnson. The Gold Coast contingent included Kwame Nkrumah, J. S. Annan, Kankam Boadu, Edwin J. Duplan, and Ako Adjei, all of whom served in the Nkrumah administration;[8] the historian, J. C. de Graft Johnson, as well as Joe Appiah and Karankyi Taylor, both of whom subsequently became bitter opponents of the Nkrumah government.

All the constituent societies of the PAF were represented.[9] Of the eighteen colonial trade unions and the twenty-five cultural and political organizations represented, the following may be mentioned: the Federal Worker's Trade Union, Trinidad and Tobago; the Workers' Association, Bermuda; St. Kitts-Nevis Trades and Labour Union; the Trade Union Congress, Sierra Leone; the National Council of Nigeria and the Cameroons; the Aborigines' Rights Protection Society, Gold Coast; the National Council of Gambia; the Progressive League, Liberia; the African National Congress, South Africa; the Progressive League, Barbados; the People's National Party, Jamaica; the Labour Party, Grenada; the African Development Association, British Guyana; the Universal Negro Improvement Association, Jamaica; and the Negro Welfare and Cultural Association, Trinidad and Tobago.[10] Fraternal delegates included those from the Federation of Indian Organizations in Britain and the Independent Labour party of Britain.

The impressive list of trade unions, political parties, and cultural organizations represented naturally leads one to regard the conference as the most representative in the series. But in reality, it was not. What was gained from the participation, for the first time, of Gambia and the adherents of Garveyism was offset by the nonrepresentation of Haiti, the French Caribbean, French black Africa, Ethiopia, Portuguese Africa, and the Belgian Congo. There were no delegates from Arab North Africa, which for all practical purposes still remained outside the pale of the Pan-African movement. And apart from W. E. B. Du Bois, black America was similarly unrepresented.

If the Manchester meeting could scarcely be said to be more representative than any of the preceding Pan-African congresses, the character of its representation differed from the earlier ones in some respects. For the first time, the African participants came not as individuals, as hitherto had been the case, but as accredited delegates from organizations. Equally worth noting is the fact that either in terms of sheer numbers of delegates or organizations participating, Africa was for the first time adequately represented.

Bitter condemnations of the colonial system marked the proceedings of the congress for two main reasons. One was the preponderance of professional politicians and trade unionists imbued with socialist ideas. The other reason lay in the fact that the conference took place at a time when the incompatibility between foreign domination and the principles of the Atlantic Charter had everywhere become glaringly self-evident. Discussions centered on the familiar issues of racial discrimination, the shortcomings of the social, economic, and constitutional policies of the metropolitan powers, and independence as the ultimate objective. Specifically, the following formed the topics of debate: "The Colour Problem in Britain"; "Imperialism in North and West Africa"; "Oppression in South Africa"; "The East African Picture"; "Ethiopia and the Black Republics"; and "The Problem in the Caribbean."

The first day of the conference was devoted to an examination of "The Colour Problem in Britain."[11] The main reports were delivered by the Gold Coaster Edwin J. Duplan and E. Aki-Emi of the Negro Welfare Centre, Liverpool, and the Coloured Workers' Association, London, respectively. They complained mainly of discrimination in employment. Supporting statements were made by Peter Abrahams and the Nigerian F. O. B. Blaize, a WASU delegate.

"Imperialism in North and West Africa" was discussed in the first session of the second day of the meeting. The principal rapporteur was Kwame Nkrumah, joint political secretary of the congress. He outlined the political and economic trends in these regions, blaming colonialism as one of the major causes of wars. At the same time he called for strong and vigorous action to eradicate it. Nkrumah's statement was supplemented by a number of reports notably from J. S. Annan, secretary of the Gold Coast Railway Civil Servants' and Technical Workers' Union; I. T. A. Wallace Johnson, secretary of the Sierra Leone Youth League; Soyemi Coker of the Nigerian Trade Union Congress; Joe Appiah and Kankam Boadu of the WASU; J. Downes Thomas of the Bathurst Citizens' Committee (Gambia); Magnus Williams representing the National Council of Nigeria and the Cameroons; and H. O. Davies of the Nigerian Youth Movement.

Special attention was given to the South and central African problems with Marko Hlubi and Peter Abrahams as the principal speakers. The former opened the debate with an examination of the social, economic, and political disabilities suffered by colored people in the Union of South Africa. South Africa's native policy, he explained, was based on the segregation of Africans, while discrimination underlay all legislation. Though the Africans were denied the vote, they were forced to pay poll and hut taxes whether they were employed or not. Those who went to the towns to work were herded in "allocations," which were nothing more than ghettoes. These conditions could not be changed, for Africans had no union recognized by the employers. Furthermore, the Riotous Assembly Act made protest meetings illegal. Concluding, Marko Hlubi appealed to African descendants elsewhere to help their "brothers" in South Africa to break the bonds that shackled them to the white herrenvolk.

Peter Abrahams, the other principal speaker, continued the enumeration of the grievances of the indigenous population of South Africa. Attention was drawn to the pass laws, which everywhere in the Union hedged the Africans in. In addition to the poll and hut tax receipts that served as passes, there were ten others that Africans were obliged to carry at one time or another. Passes were needed to leave the reserve to go to town, to travel on the railway, to seek employment, to visit another location, to stay out after the nine o'clock curfew hour. Africans were also obliged to obtain passes to live within a municipal location to carry on trade. Teachers or preachers had to secure a special pass to show that they were exempted from carrying all the others.

Jomo Kenyatta acted as the official reporter on "The East African Picture." His statement covered six territories, namely, Kenya, Somaliland, Uganda, Tanganyika (now Tanzania), Nyasaland (now Malawi), and the Rhodesias. The East African peoples, he explained, fell into three divisions: farmers, cattle rearers, and hunters. "Each group had its own territories, which it considered its own property and on which it could move as it pleased, cultivating here today and there tomorrow, building its villages here and there as it wanted, or hunting as it wished. Many of these people lived happily and contented."[12]

The advent of white settlers and the consequent allocation of the natives' land to them had changed the picture. In a supporting statement, Garba Jahumpa of the Trades Union Council of Gambia, urged the conference "to demand, first and foremost, the complete freedom of our South African brothers." He believed that the duty of the conference delegates was "to learn about all our peoples from all over the world, and if we went back to our different countries and remained dormant, the Congress will have been a failure."[13] The congress should resolve to establish somewhere in the world a central council that would keep in touch with the whole of the African world and developments there.

A report on "Ethiopia and the Black Republics" was given by T. Ras Makonnen, secretary of the PAF. He accused Britain of planning to join Ogaden Province, a section of ancient Ethiopia, to British and Italian Somaliland in order to enlarge the British Empire.[14] As compensation the British Government, he alleged, was prepared to return to Ethiopia part of Eritrea, which formed an integral part of Ethiopia before it was grabbed by Italy. Supporting Makonnen,

Peter Abrahams reiterated that there were only three states in the world run and controlled by black men. They were Haiti, Liberia, and Ethiopia. It was important that Africans and their descendants should be most vigilant in the interests of these three states.

The main reports of the West Indian territories were delivered by George Padmore and Ken Hill of the People's National party, Jamaica. Padmore traced the history of the West Indies from the arrival of Columbus there late in the fifteenth century to the Emancipation Act of 1833. He said that the West Indies could briefly be described as the "sugar section of British imperialism, for in the West Indies you have a Government of sugar for sugar by sugar."[15] In his statement, Hill assured the conference that the West Indians had never forgotten their racial origins and that they looked upon Africa with pride. They pledged themselves to work for its redemption and to support the fight of African peoples for complete freedom and independence. A supplementary statement by Claude Lushington, representing the West Indian National party, declared self-government as the object of his party. He was convinced that as long as West Indians remained under alien domination they would continue to be exploited by absentee owners. "Let us govern ourselves, if even badly at first rather than be well governed by others," he concluded.[16] This concluding remark is significant as suggesting the probable source of Kwame Nkrumah's well-known declaration that independence in danger was preferable to foreign subjugation.

After five days of discussion, the conference adopted far-reaching resolutions that may be examined under the headings of specific and general demands.[17] Immediate independence was demanded for British and French West Africa, the British Sudan, the French North African colonies of Algeria, Tunisia, and Morocco, as well as the Italian dependency of Libya. Comprehensive constitutional, economic, and social reform was urged for British central and East Africa, the French Congo, the Belgian Congo, the British West Indies, and British Guyana (now Guyana). These reforms, to be implemented at once, included the enfranchisement of every native adult, the removal of restrictions upon civil rights, the abolition of all racial and discriminatory laws, the revision of the civil and criminal codes as well as the system of taxation, the reallocation of land especially in East and central Africa, the establishment of new industries, and the development of the existing ones. Also demanded were the "introduction of all forms of modern social legislation in existence in metropolitan areas, e.g., old-age pensions, family allowances, national health and unemployment insurances" and compulsory free education at elementary- and secondary-school levels.

The resolutions supported the demand of Egypt for "the removal of British armed forces," regarded the "struggle of our brothers in South Africa as an integral part of the common struggle for national liberation throughout Africa," and opposed the South African request for the incorporation, into the union, of the High Commission territories of Bechuanaland, Basutoland, and Swaziland on the ground that the natives concerned did not wish such a transfer.

The governments and peoples of Ethiopia, Liberia, and Haiti were assured that any manifestation of imperialist encroachment that threatened their independence would be resisted. At the same time, the metropolitan powers were informed that these states symbolized the political hopes and aspirations of African peoples still under imperialist domination. The congress supported in the interest of justice and economic geography the claims of the Somalis and Eritreans to be returned to their home (i.e., Ethiopia), instead of being parceled out to foreign powers. It also demanded the withdrawal of the British military administration from Ethiopian soil and the extension by the United Nations Relief Organization to the Abyssinians the same aid as was being afforded to the other victims of aggression.

The congress identified itself with the heroic struggles of the thirteen million people of African descent in the United States in their fight to secure the rights of full citizenship, political, economic, and social. Africans and peoples of African descent throughout the world would continue to support their African American "brothers" in the fight for their rights by intelligent organized planning, legal contention, and political pressure. The successful realization of the political, economic, and social aspirations of the African Americans was bound up with the emancipation of all African peoples, as well as other dependent peoples and the working class everywhere.

The other part of the resolutions—the general demands—consisted of a declaration to the colonial peoples and a challenge to the imperial powers to honor the principles of the Atlantic Charter. In their "Declaration to the Colonial Workers, Farmers and Intellectuals," the delegates expressed their belief in the right of all peoples to govern themselves and control their own destiny. All dependencies must be free from alien control, political and economic. The struggle for political power by the colonial peoples was the "first step towards, and the necessary prerequisite to, complete social, economic and political emancipation."

Concluding, the declaration called on the workers and farmers of the colonies to organize effectively. Colonial workers must be in the front of the battle against imperialism. "Your weapons—the Strike and the Boycott—are invincible."

The congress ended its deliberations by inviting the metropolitan governments to implement the principles of the Atlantic Charter in their dependencies. Africans and their descendants were determined to be free and desired "the right to earn a decent living; the right to express our thoughts and emotions, to adopt and create forms of beauty." They were not ashamed to have been an age-old patient people. But they were unwilling "to starve any longer while doing the world's drudgery, in order to support by their poverty and ignorance a false aristocracy and a discredited imperialism." And if the Western world showed itself still determined to rule humankind by force, then Africans, as a last resort, might have to appeal to force in order to achieve self-determination even if force destroyed them and the world. That the metropolitan powers might not timidly hand over freedom on a platter of gold was for the first time in the history of the Pan-African movement recognized. This recognition meant a shift from the earlier strategy of peaceful and constitutional opposition to one of active resistance and "positive action."

The Manchester Pan-African Congress truly marks a turning point in the history of the Pan-African movement. The turning point consists neither in the unequivocal manner in which the delegates expressed their desire for independence nor in the hostile tone in which the desire was voiced. As we have seen in the preceding chapter, unequivocal demands for freedom and harsh criticisms received further impetus from the Atlantic Charter, the temporary collapse of the British Empire in the Far East, and the anticolonial utterances of several of the leading American citizens of the day, notably Wendell Willkie.

There was therefore nothing new or revolutionary in the militancy and resolutions of the delegates to the Manchester meeting. Hence, Arthur Creech Jones, the first postwar Labour colonial secretary, could say that it "did not require the impetus of the [Manchester] Pan-African Congress or the demand for Indian freedom to induce the Labour Ministers at the Colonial Office in 1945 to drive ahead with political, social and economic changes in the colonies."[18]

It was the strategy rather than the resolutions adopted at this meeting that made it a turning point in the history of the Pan-African movement. Before the Manchester meeting, Pan-Africanism was, in the main, a protest movement of middle-class African American intellectuals resident outside Africa and in which little or nothing of real interest to the African and West Indian masses had been said. Not surprisingly, it received practically no support from the nationalist organizations in Africa, or the masses there and in the Caribbean.

The Manchester congress reversed this situation. The old belief that the struggle for freedom could be fought and won in Europe was laid aside. Henceforward, the struggle must be conducted in the homelands as the Indians were already doing. Though Du Bois was present and active, the new approach reflected the socialist influence of George Padmore and Kwame Nkrumah. The African and West Indian workers as represented by their trade unions and political parties became associated, for the first time, with the Pan-African movement. The winning of popular support for the movement constituted only one aspect of the new strategy. Another aspect consisted in the call to the intellectuals and the masses to join forces in the campaign for political emancipation.

In this new strategy, the African trade unions subsequently played a significant role. Imanuel Geiss has aptly described them as "the labour-wing of the nationalist movement" and shown how by strikes, mass demonstrations, and boycotts they played a considerable part.[19] But in attributing the militancy that marked the postwar activities of these trade unions to a new impetus to industrialization engendered by the war, he missed the point. The explanation for both the militancy and the deep involvement of the trade unions in the postwar African nationalist movements lies more in the newly acquired nationalist ideas of the returned soldiers and the Manchester deliberations than in any other factor. Was it not at this gathering that the trade unions were told that they "must be in the front of the battle against imperialism?" The recognition that freedom has to be fought for, the decision to shift the battlefront to African soil and enlist the support of the masses, and the adoption of a strategy of "positive action," all these ushered in a new phase in the history of the Pan-African movement. From then on the ideals formulated in America and Europe would begin to be heard increasingly in Africa itself as African liberation movements grew from strength to strength.

To effect the program drawn up, the congress charged the executive of the LCP to take steps to "publicise the resolutions and other directives adopted by the delegates, and to establish suitable machinery through which advice and assistance could be extended to the organisations represented in the Congress."[20] Consequently, the PAF set up a working committee with Du Bois and Kwame Nkrumah as president and secretary-general respectively.[21] At a meeting of the committee held in London, it was decided that the headquarters of the Pan-African congress should be established in London "to act as a kind of clearing house for the various political movements that would take shape in the colonies."[22] In a letter to the Gold Coast ARPS, Nkrumah announced that an international secretariat had been set up in London to maintain contact between all colonial organizations.[23] Nkrumah further explained that all the organizations represented at the Manchester meeting were expected to affiliate to the PAF, stressing that affiliation would not involve the surrender of local autonomy.[24]

While arrangements were being made to establish in London the proposed headquarters of the Pan-African congress, some West Africans approached Nkrumah on the necessity to form a West African National Secretariat (WANS).[25] Among the West Africans were I. T. A. Wallace Johnson, G. Ashie-Nikoi, who represented the Gold Coast ARPS and the Gold Coast Farmers' Association at the Manchester conference,[26] and Kojo Botsio, who subsequently served in the Nkrumah administration. The WANS was eventually established in London at a meeting held on 14 December 1945.[27] Nkrumah was appointed secretary, assisted by the Nigerian Bankole Akpata. The objectives of the organization were:

1. To maintain contact with, co-ordinate, educate and supply general information on current matters to the ·various political bodies, trade unions, farmers, educational, cultural and other progressive organisations in West Africa with a view to realizing a West African Front For a United West African National Independence.

2. To serve as clearing house for informations [sic] on matters affecting the destiny of West Africa; and to educate the peoples and the working class in particular, of the imperialist countries concerning the problems of West Africa.

3. To foster the spirit of national unity and solidarity among the various territories of West Africa for the purposes of combating the menace of artificial territorial divisions now in existence.

4. To work for unity and harmony among all West Africans who stand against imperialism.

5. To publish a series of pamphlets on West African affairs to be known as the West African National Secretariat series, and a monthly paper, THE NEW AFRICAN, to be published in London.[28]

There seems to be no evidence that the proposed WANS pamphlets were published. But in March 1946, the first issue of *The New African* appeared with the subtitle "The Voice of the Awakened African" and the motto For Unity and Absolute Independence. Eight months later, publication of the magazine ceased owing to financial difficultes of the WANS.[29]

The WANS found a substantial measure of acceptance in West Africa, where, by the end of March 1946, the organizations supporting the secretariat included the Gold Coast ARPS, the Farmers' Committee of the Gold Coast and Nigeria, the Trade Union Congress of Sierra Leone, and the West African Youth League, Sierra Leone branch.[30] In Britain, the WANS received even greater support among the exiles, and during the one and a half years beginning in February 1946 the Pan-African initiative seemed to have passed over to it.

At a meeting of Africans held in London on 27 March 1946 and summoned by the WANS, a resolution was adopted for immediate transmission to the United Nations then meeting New York.[31] The exiles were quick to see the new possibilities offered by the United Nations, which, unlike the defunct League of Nations, was not dominated by the colonial powers. The resolution expressed dissatisfaction with the United Nations organization for excluding from direct representation millions of "freedom-loving" peoples of Africa and other parts of the colonial world.[32] The Trusteeship Council of the United Nations was invited "to take such steps as may affect the speedy realisation of complete independence for the peoples of the colonies."[33]

In the summer of 1946, the WANS and the WASU jointly summoned a meeting held in London from 30 August to 1 September and attended by representatives of British and French West Africa. French West Africa was represented by Sourous Apithy and Léopold Senghor, both of whom were at that time members of the French National Assembly.[34] The theme of the conference was "Unity and Independence of All West Africa," the purpose, "to discuss the present political, economic and social conditions in West Africa, and to determine in that light a plan for creating a united and independent West Africa."[35] The conference unanimously called for the creation of an all–West African national congress in the belief that united and independent West Africa could and would act as the lever with which the entire African continent would be liberated for all time from foreign domination and exploitation.[36] In calling for an all–West African national congress, the conference attempted, unsuccessfully, to revive with a broader basis the National Congress of British West Africa, which soon collapsed after the death of J. E. Casely-Hayford, one of its founders.[37]

In November 1946 representatives of the WANS, the PAF, the LCP, and the Transvaal Council of Non-European Trade Unions despatched a resolution to the United Nations Trusteeship Council.[38]

The resolution urged the Trusteeship Council to reject South Africa's demand to incorporate the mandated territory of South West Africa. The council was further asked to take over the administration of the mandate and to require of the Union of South Africa an undertaking to respect and abide by the principle of the United Nations Charter in the treatment of all peoples within its jurisdiction on pain of expulsion from membership of the United Nations organization.[39] An investigation of the social, economic, and political conditions of the colored community in the Union was demanded. The resolution emphasized that the policy pursued by the South African government toward its subjects of non-European origin was "a direct negation of the principles of racial tolerance, justice and freedom."

Since the year 1920, when the Union became the mandatory of South West Africa, the native policy of the Union had steadily deteriorated. The passage in 1936 of the Native Franchise Act, the Native Land Act, and the Urban Areas Act deprived the native of the Cape Province

> of the right to buy, hire or occupy land wherever they chose and confined them to restricted areas; the right to be on the Common Voters Roll, their representation being limited to three appointed European members in a House of Assembly consisting of one hundred and fifty-three members; their right to sell their labour where they chose by restricting their movements.[40]

There was little doubt that in its attitude to the territory of South West Africa, the Union government had assumed a position unbecoming of a trustee and true of a conqueror bent upon territorial aggrandizement and the spoliation and humiliation of the vanquished.[41] Such a government, the resolution argued, could not reasonably be entrusted with the care of subject and helpless peoples. The racial policy of that government was a direct affront to the avowed determination of the United Nations to reaffirm faith in fundamental human rights, in the dignity and worth of the human being, in the equal rights of men and women of nations large and small.[42] The resolution admitted that Africans were not the only victims of this racialism, for the Indians, about a quarter of a million in number, suffered a similar discriminatory treatment. Concluding, the resolution demanded justice and social equality for the Indian community in South Africa.[43]

In addition to sponsoring resolutions and conferences on matters considered to be of crucial importance to peoples of African descent, the WANS attempted to stimulate opposition to colonial rule in West Africa. As early as June 1946, Nkrumah had despatched one hundred copies each of the March, April, and May issues of *The New African* to the Gold Coast ARPS and presumably to the other West African organizations that had expressed support for the objects of the WANS.[44] The PAF also made a similar effort to quicken the pace in the colonies of the campaign against imperialism when in January 1947 it launched *Pan-Africa*, a monthly journal of African life, history, and thought. It was edited by T. Ras Makonnen, assisted by Dinah Stock.

Unlike *The New African*, *Pan-Africa* had an impressive staff of associate and contributing editors from different parts of the British Empire and the world. In June the list of such contributors included David Talbot, about whom little or nothing is known (Ethiopia); Kwame Nkrumah and Samson Morris from Grenada, who in 1950 became the secretary of the LCP (England);[45] H. W. Springer, a former treasurer of the LCP who returned to Barbados to become secretary of the Progressive League and member of the Legislative Council there (Barbados); W. Esuman-Gwira Sekyi, a well-known Gold Coast lawyer and onetime secretary of the Gold Coast ARPS (Gold Coast); Magnus Williams, a Nigerian politician who represented Nnamdi Azikiwe and the National Council of Nigeria and the Cameroons at the Manchester congress (Nigeria); Yagoub Osman, who later became Sudan's ambassador to Moscow (Sudan); Jomo Kenyatta, later president of Kenya.[46] *Pan-Africa* excited alarm in official quarters and was banned by East African colonial governments as "seditious."[47]

Earlier in January 1946 the IASB started a monthly with the title *Colonial Parliamentary Bulletin*. Edited by Padmore, the *Bulletin* was devoted entirely to questions, discussions, and debates in the British Parliament concerning colonial and dependent peoples. For instance, the March–April (1946) issue reproduced parliamentary questions and answers on West, East, and South Africa, the West Indies, the Middle East as well as Southeast Asia. To overseas readers interested in imperial affairs, the *Bulletin* offered a unique opportunity of following the way the Labour government was tackling colonial administration in the British Empire.

The *Bulletin* was supplemented by books penned by a number of the exiles. Their aim was to further expose the evils of foreign domination and to speed up the African revolution. One entitled *My Africa* appeared in New York in 1946 and was produced by Mbonu Ojike, a Nigerian and graduate of the University of Chicago. The first part of the book is autobiographical, the rest a clear exposition of African customs and traditions. Like Edward W. Blyden, Orishatuke Faduma, and Mojola Agbebi, Ojike opposed the de-Africanizing policy of the European colonial officials and Christian missionaries. Ojike's pride in African culture is evident from the following excerpt:

Let each girl, of each color, be proud of what she is, she cannot be another. It is ridiculous and degrading to invent chemicals and urge ones face to sear its skin and become lighter or darker.

For the African to seek modernisation in shameful foreign names is equally disgraceful. His language is one vital mode of expressing his culture and remaining honorably African. Christian missionaries and not Christianity have no one else to blame for this uncultural practice. A man can be as good as anyone else intellectually, financially, politically and religiously whether he is called James or Ikoli or Churchill or Stalin.[48]

Not surprisingly he urged Africans to boycott what was boycottable in foreign culture, an exhortation that earned him in his own country the nickname Boycott King.

Of the exiles' publications that appeared after the Manchester conference, none aroused as much controversy as George Padmore's *How Russia Transformed Her Colonial Empire*. Published late in 1946 and written with the help of Dorothy Pizer, the work was a comparative study of Soviet methods of solving colonial and racial minorities problems with British and other Western metropolitan administrations in Africa and Asia. The book was widely reviewed in the British press and even in places as far afield as India,[49] Jamaica,[50] and Nigeria.[51] It met a mixed reception among the British reviewers. F. A. Ridley, a member of the Independent Labour party, commended it as an important book, which could become a classic on the colonial question.[52] But *The Times Literary Supplement* considered it unbalanced and accused Padmore of writing with unqualified admiration for the Soviet scheme of things.[53]

Another publication that admired the Marxist-Leninist attitude to the colonial problem was a booklet by Kwame Nkrumah entitled *Towards Colonial Freedom* and published in London in 1947. Nkrumah rejected the imperial doctrines of "civilizing mission" and "trusteeship."[54] Imperialism was denounced as calculated exploitation[55] and the teachings of Marx and Lenin upheld as "the most searching and penetrating analysis of economic imperialism."[56]

Meanwhile the controversy over the merits and demerits of Padmore's new book continued. It was in the midst of this debate that Harold Moody, who had been leader of the LCP since its inception in 1931, suddenly died. With his death in 1947, the presidency of the LCP was assumed by the famous West Indian cricketeer, Learie Constantine, with Malcolm Joseph-Mitchell, an economist from Trinidad, as general secretary.

New leaders also appeared in the WASU; of these, many of whom were soon to become important in their countries, the following may be named: Ako Adjei, Kankam Boadu, Kojo Botsio, all of whom later served in the Nkrumah administration; Dennis C. Osadebay who was later made a premier of Mid-Western Nigeria; Okoi Arikpo, later Nigeria's commissioner for foreign affairs; and Albert Margai, who subsequently became a prime minister of Sierra Leone. The role some of these young nationalists were soon to play in West African politics was foreshadowed by the keen interest they showed in, and the assistance they gave to, the National Council of Nigeria and the Cameroons (NCNC) delegation which arrived in London on 10 July 1947.

The purpose of the NCNC mission was to present a memorandum to the new colonial secretary, Arthur Creech Jones, setting out the grievances of the Nigerian people with particular reference to the Richards Constitution introduced in 1945.[57] The members of the delegation included Nnamdi Azikiwe, editor of a daily, the *West African Pilot*; Mallam Bukar Dipcharima, who later joined the Northern People's Congress (Nigeria) and became a member of Balewa's administration; and Mrs. Ransome Kuti, wife of the Reverend I. Ransome Kuti, who was a member of the Commission on Higher Education in West Africa appointed in 1944.[58] The WASU not only gave a reception in honor of the delegates but also "sponsored for them a public meeting at the Conway Hall and in co-operation with other [exile] organisations, another at Euston Hall."[59] George Padmore himself served as press secretary to the mission.[60] Such were the links established between the delegation and the exiles that before the mission returned to Nigeria early in August, Nnamdi Azikiwe endorsed the decision of the Manchester congress and the WANS to work for "immediate self-government and the realization of a United West African Federation."[61]

A few months after the departure of the NCNC mission, Kwame Nkrumah was offered the general secretaryship of the United Gold Coast Convention, formed on 4 August 1947.[62] On the advice of the WANS, Nkrumah accepted the offer, and on 14 November he left London for the Gold Coast.[63]

The year 1948 witnessed an intensification of the political consciousness of the members of the WASU in particular, largely as a result of the labor unrest that broke out in the Gold Coast early that year. European traders were boycotted while ex-servicemen demanded some compensation for fighting the Empire's wars. Demonstrations by ex-servicemen culminated in disturbances in several major cities including Accra and were put down with loss of life. Some political leaders were arrested, among them, Kwame Nkrumah. On 29 February the WASU despatched resolutions of protest to the British prime minister, Clement Attlee, Governor Creasy of the Gold Coast, and the secretary-general of the United Nations.[64] At the same time a "patriotic message" was sent to Agyeman Prempeh II, the Ashantehene of Ashanti.[65] Three days later, the WASU, the WANS, and the Gold Coast Students' Union sent a joint deputation to the Colonial Office in further protest.[66] In Manchester, the African Students' Union formed there in 1946, with the Nigerian Eyo Bassey Ndem as secretary, held a public protest meeting in the Charlton Town Hall.[67] Ndem attended the Manchester conference as the delegate of the Calabar Improvement League.[68]

In the summer 1948 issue of their organ, the WASU called upon the British government to "take a brave and statesmanlike decision to free the rest of her 'Colonial Empire.' "[69] It was this call for independence for the colonial empire, particularly in Africa, that marked the activities of the exiles for the rest of 1948. This keynote is well illustrated in "The African's Prayer" adapted by the WASU:

> Our Country, which art on Earth,
>   Honoured be thy Name;
>   Thy Freedom come, Thy work be done
>   Abroad, as it is done at home.
>
> Give us each day the vision clear
>   And forgive us our foolishness,
>   As we forgive them that daily try to fool us.
>
> And lead us not into submission,
>   But deliver us from trickery.
>   For thine will be Freedom,
>   Due Power, and due glory,
>   For ever and ever—Amen.[70]

This concern for the destiny of the African peoples led Lord

Milverton (later Sir A. Richards) to accuse Ladipo Solanke of aiming to make WASU first and foremost a political organization for the promotion of certain political aims.[71] Milverton's fears might have been partly prompted by the way in which branches of the WASU in West Africa attracted both the intelligentsia and traditional rulers and the fact that members of the parent union, upon returning home, invariably entered politics. It was significant that the principal organizers of the United Gold Coast Convention on 4 August 1947 were J. W. de Graft Johnson, R. S. Blay, J. B. Danquah, and Ako Adjei, some of them pioneer and all of them former executive members of the WASU.[72] It was also significant that the convention invited Kwame Nkrumah, a vice president of the WASU in 1946 to become its first secretary.[73]

With the return of Kwame Nkrumah to the Gold Coast and the development of national consciousness in the four British West African territories, interest in a West African federation, which, since the time of Edward W. Blyden, had been a chief objective of some West African intellectuals, began to decline. There emerged in London such organizations with a national basis as the Nigerian Union, the Gold Coast Students' Union, the Sierra Leone Students' Union, and the Gambia Union. These unions maintained a considerable attitude of independence toward one another and to the WASU, directing most of their attention to problems concerning the corresponding country. The LCP also began to decline shortly after 1947 when its founder-leader Harold Moody died. The association maintained a precarious existence for another four years, after which it finally collapsed. Nor did the PAF fare any better than the LCP and the WASU after the departure of Jomo Kenyatta and Kwame Nkrumah. The departure of these two men seemed to have robbed the PAF of much of its former impetus and dynamism. The last issues of *Pan-Africa* and the *Colonial Parliamentary Bulletin* appeared in 1948, and for over a decade there was no common Pan-African journal based in Europe. Indeed, during the decade after the Manchester gathering, national self-government became the most urgent question in African politics.

This preoccupation is aptly illustrated by *Aids to African Autonomy: A Review of Education and Politics in the Gold Coast*, contributed by S. D. Cudjoe, a Gold Coast medical practitioner trained at Edinburgh University and the Royal College of Physicians and Surgeons. Though published in London in 1949 and reprinted the next year, that is, some six years before Padmore's famous *Pan-Africanism or Communism?* the booklet is scarcely mentioned even by serious scholars. Yet the author's ideas are no less revolutionary than Padmore's, his concern for the fortunes of Africa and the Africans equally passionate, his style probably more sophisticated and elegant. For these reasons Cudjoe's tract receives extensive coverage here.

The author addressed the volume to those educated men and women of Africa directly or indirectly involved in politics who might be under the mistaken impression that individual achievements would "establish the respect we desire for our race as a whole, while we remain a subject people."[74] Castigating the methods and impact of European missionary enterprise, he regretted that the missionaries themselves seemed to lack adequate educational values by which they could select what was good in African culture. "They undermined the whole of the African framework, because they could neither understand nor appreciate it. Though they tried hard to make the Africans ashamed of their past, their new converts were unwilling to dissociate themselves from ties which had given their people a measure of security for generations.[75] The attempt to uproot what was essentially African and introduce another entirely Western in outlook produced receptive converts who could not differentiate between humility and humiliation, because the freedom of doubt and question had been denied them.[76]

As a group, Cudjoe went on, the gospel preachers neglected to challenge the rightness of the European conquest even though they knew that the empire was built and sustained by force of arms to serve the interest of the invaders. He deplored the readiness with which the missionaries resorted to charitable collections in the metropolitan country when it was clearly the duty of imperial administrations to provide adequately for African education.

Turning to the methods of missionary education, the Pan-Africanist remarked that the missionary schools did not adapt their textbooks to the environment of African life; Cudjoe contended that difficulties arose not only from the meaning of foreign words but also from the whole train of associations those words possessed in their country of origin. Similarly, books translated into the local languages retained an almost literal rendering of thought patterns the African mind found alien.

Cudjoe's attacks on the metropolitan powers and their African collaborators were equally biting. Foreign domination was a fact progressive Africans ought to be ashamed of. "The condition of African progress is not foreign rule, but emancipation in the widest possible sense."[77] Where a government failed to translate its avowed belief in freedom and equality into practice, it was the duty of the people to take steps to secure those rights.[78] Educated Africans must initiate an exchange of views with the masses immediately in order to "create that psychological period of incubation so necessary for the inauguration of concerted action. Nothing could be more positive than their visionary grasp of those things which will be needed to recreate a virile and united Africa, or their determination to harness all the basic elements of nationalism, which are already there in the tribal consciousness."[79]

Cudjoe regretted that while every nation in the world fought a civil war or staged a revolution as a step toward unity, imperial historians have made such antecedents appear barbarous only in the case of non-European peoples, and thus succeeded in presenting European domination of Africa as an instrument for peace.[80] Margery Perham was rebuked for pleading with Europeans not to consider the black man inferior until he had been placed in good conditions under the influence of civilization for at least five hundred years.[81] "It is a great wonder that she postpones for five hundred years a decision which is so glaringly self-evident."[82]

The author condemned the seizure of African territories as fundamentally unjust, stressing that none of the British African possessions belonged to the Crown either by natural right or by the willing sanction of African traditional law.[83] Those who defended the subjection of Africans on the ground of native misrule were reminded of the insistence of E. D. Morel[84] that the misgovernment of modern European politicians had "brought Europe to a state of misery and wretchedness unequalled in the history of the world."[85] In Morel's opinion the chief forces destroying European civilization whether in Europe itself, Africa, Asia, or the United States lay precisely in a limited conception of liberty. The imperial powers would jeopardize world peace again if they insisted on maintaining the prewar conditions in their dependencies. Colonial and world justice must rest on enlightened majority decisions, not might.[86] He agreed with Bertrand Russell that there was "no hope for the world unless power can be tamed and brought into the service, not of this or that group of fanatical tyrants, but of the whole human race, white, yellow or black, for science has made it inevitable that all must live or all must die."[87]

Finally, Cudjoe warned that neither the empire nor the Commonwealth would survive for long unless

> all are free. This is the noble death for the more efficiently the Empire maintains the bondage of Africa, the more it poisons itself in the process of inevitable suicide.[88]

As a case for the immediate removal of the foreign yoke, Cudjoe's tract is persuasive and may be compared with Thomas Paine's *Common Sense*. Underlying the Gold Coaster's argument are the political doctrines that there are no people unfit for liberty or incapable of creating a democracy of their own; that self-determination was not a prize to be awarded to Africans only after they had attained a prescribed maturity; and that no real progress was possible without freedom from the start.

To what extent Cudjoe's pamphlet influenced the exiles and events in the fatherland is difficult to say. But it is certain that Padmore read the fuller manuscript from which the volume was extracted.[89] Given the nationality of the author and Padmore's special relation with Nkrumah, we may assume that Nkrumah must have seen it and perhaps showed it to the other leaders of the Gold Coast liberation movement. The work was also known in WASU circles and the appointment of the author to the union's board of directors in the early fifties may have been a gesture of appreciation.[90]

All the same, the desire to end colonial bondage was not universal in Africa and the Caribbean during the immediate postwar years. Such French-speaking African politicans as Léopold Senghor of Senegal preferred greater participation in the political process within the French union to self-government. Despite its Communist orientation, even the Rassemblement Démocratique Africain, led by Félix Houphouët-Boigny from the Ivory Coast and formed in 1946 by prominent African politicians to fight the elections to the French

National Assembly, clashed with the colonial authorities not for demanding independence but because they were pressing for further social, political, and economic reforms. It was significant that the disturbances which swept over Madagascar in March 1947 were blamed on the Mouvement Démocratique de Rénovation Malgache because the party "had asked for more freedom within the French Union."[91]

As time passed, French-speaking Africans became increasingly dissatisfied with an arrangement that treated them as Frenchmen. "They now wished to be recognised for what they were, and not to be patronised."[92] In July 1952 a military coup d'état, spearheaded by General Mohammad Neguib and Colonel Gamal Abdel Nasser, overthrew the regime of King Farouk, who had become a stooge of the British government. The same year witnessed the outbreak of the Mau Mau movement, a desperate attempt by a desperate people to change a system of economic and social injustice that had been a marked feature of Kenyan history.[93] Two years later the Algerians launched the Front de Libération Nationale in revolt against the French overlords.

Then came the Bandung Conference of 1955 at which Africans and Asians affirmed their solidarity in their effort to dislodge imperialism. They even went further to formulate methods whereby unity among the independent nations of Africa and Asia could be quickened. For the Africans, the conference proved to be of great psychological and political significance. It was the first time, at least in modern history, that Africans spoke as equal participants in an international forum on issues concerning the continent as a whole and its relations with the world at large. After Bandung the pressures for change grew stronger everywhere.

Men like the medical doctor R. N. Duchein of Liberia realized that self-government represented only a means to the ultimate Pan-African aims of political unity, cultural emancipation, and economic independence. To keep the wider aspirations afloat, he launched a society in 1954 in Liberia styled the Pan-African Unification Organization. Its members were Africans drawn from various colonies who found common ground in the idea of African unity. With the intensification of the struggle for self-determination, some members went back to their respective countries, thereby weakening the association. In 1957 Duchein published a document, *The Pan-African*

Manifesto, in Accra. His purpose was to revive interest in continental unity.

The Liberian stressed that his group harbored goodwill toward all the races. Nonetheless, he attributed the relative backwardness of Africa to European intrusion and condemned "all attempts at adopting new ways brought by another race claiming to be superior.["94] In his view, "everything African which is not inconsistent with modern science and with the progress of Africa must be considered superior and maintained to be improved in the line of African tradition. We believe in an African Personality."[95]

Of the reasons he advanced why Africans must unite, two may be mentioned: first, because "foreign races have determined to take Africa for themselves for ever";[96] second, without a powerful nation capable of defending "ourselves, we are doomed to disappear as a race or live in insignificance like the Indians of the Americans."[97] To ensure African unity and survival, Duchein advocated the formation of a Pan-African federation extending over the whole of Africa south of the Sahara "where Africans will rule themselves and enjoy fully in liberty, respected, the inalienable rights of man."[98] It should be noted that the proposed federation embraced African descendants "scattered abroad who want to come back to their motherland and integrate in African life."[99] By also including Egypt in the United States of Africa he envisaged, "because of the great civilisation our forefathers built there,"[100] Duchein foreshadowed the bringing of Arab North Africa into the mainstream of Pan-Africanism in 1958.

Concluding, Duchein warned that no nation would welcome the emergence of a strong Africa capable of playing an important role in world affairs. "Most will dread it, while a few which pretend to be friends of Africa wish a free Africa checkered into a multitude of small nations constantly at loggerheads with one another, so as to have a better chance to exploit them."[101]

These arguments and other sentiments were later used by Nkrumah, who probably read the manifesto since it was published in Accra. As if in response to Duchein's appeal for a continental outlook, there emerged in March 1958 the Committee of African Organizations (CAO) with headquarters at 200 Gower Street, London.

The CAO started as a federation of African student unions in England. Subsequently, membership was extended to student bodies in other parts of Europe as well as the United States, Canada, the Soviet Union, and Eastern Europe. The aim of the CAO was "unity for Africa and freedom for all African countries."[102] Its organ was called *United Africa*, for which a Ghanaian student, Antwi Akuako, was one of the editors. Prominent members of the organization included Simon Kapwepwe, who later became Zambia's foreign minister, Oliver Tambo of the African National Congress of South Africa, William Abrahams, a well-known Ghanaian professor of philosophy and associate of Kwame Nkrumah, and Oscar Kambona, who later served in Julius Nyerere's administration as minister of foreign affairs.[103]

Under the auspices of the CAO, such important African leaders as Kwame Nkrumah, Jomo Kenyatta, Milton Obote, Chief Albert Luthuli, Kenneth Kaunda, Hastings Banda, Nnamdi Azikiwe, and the West Indian lawyer, David Pitt, gave public lectures.[104] In January 1959, after his release from detention in connection with the Mau Mau affair, Jomo Kenyatta led a delegation of the Kenya African National Union to London for constitutional talks. While in London, he addressed a public meeting organized by the CAO at the Africa Unity House.[105] His topic was "African Freedom and Unity." He paid a warm tribute to Kwame Nkrumah, saying that the independence of Ghana marked the end of the European domination of Africa.

Indeed, the emancipation of Ghana served to pave the way for closer cooperation among African peoples. Between 1958 and 1963 African leaders began to meet at frequent intervals. Some of these meetings were conferences of states already independent. Others were nongovernmental gatherings of leaders of independence movements and trade unions.

1. Imanuel Geiss, *The Pan-African Movement* (London: Methuen, 1974).
2. Ibid.
3. PAF press release, no. 4 (1945): 2.
4. Ibid., in GCARPS Papers, acc. no. 77/64, correspondence file no. 5; George Padmore, *Pan-Africanism or Communism? The Coming Struggle for Africa* (London: Dennis Dobson, 1956), 155. The date of the meeting sum-

moned by the PAF is given by the press release as February and by Padmore as March. February should be preferred in view of the fact that Padmore wrote nearly eleven years after the event.

5. Padmore, *Pan-Africanism or Communism?* 155.

6. Ibid., 156.

7. Ibid., 155.

8. J. S. Annan served as secretary of defense; E. Duplan was a key figure in the Bureau of African Affairs, Accra, while Ako Adjei filled the post of foreign minister but soon quarreled with Nkrumah.

9. The LCP sent delegates.

10. For a full list of the delegates that attended the Manchester meeting, see George Padmore, ed., *History of the Pan-African Congress*, 2d ed. (London: Susan Tulley, 1963), 71–74.

11. Details of the proceedings of the conference are published in George Padmore, ed., *Colonial and . . . Coloured Unity: A Programme of Action* (Manchester: Pan-African Service, 1947), 27–54. See also PAF press release nos. 5, 7–11 (1945), in GCARPS Papers, acc. 77/64, correspondence file no. 5.

12. Ibid., 40.

13. Ibid., 42.

14. Ibid., 44.

15. Ibid., 46.

16. Ibid., 48.

17. The resolutions are published in Padmore, ed., *Colonial and . . . Coloured Unity*, 55–67. The "Resolution to U.N.O. on South West Africa," ibid., 64–65 was not adopted at the Manchester conference but later in 1946. See *News Letter*, December 1946, 40–41.

18. *Guardian* (London), 3 September 1963, 8.

19. "Some Remarks on the Development of African Trade Unions," *Journal of the Historical Society of Nigeria* 3 (December 1965): 367.

20. Padmore, *Pan-Africanism or Communism?* 172.

21. *Ghana: The Autobiography of Kwame Nkrumah* (Edinburgh: Thomas Nelson, 1961), 45.

22. Ibid.

23. Nkrumah to J. P. Allottey-Hammond, 25 November 1945, in GCARPS Papers, acc. no. 77/64, correspondence file no. 5.

24. Ibid.

25. Nkrumah, *Ghana*, 45.

26. Ibid.; Padmore, *Colonial and . . . Colored Unity*, 1947.

27. Nkrumah to Allottey-Hammond, 8 February 1946, GCARPS Papers, acc. no. 78/64, correspondence file no. 6.

28. Ibid.

29. Nkrumah to Allottey-Hammond, 29 September 1947, GCARPS Papers, acc. no. 78/64, correspondence file no. 6.

30. Nkrumah to Allottey-Hammond, 8 February 1946; Allottey-Hammond to Nkrumah, 14 March 1946, GCARPS Papers, acc. no. 78/64, correspondence file no. 6.

31. *New African*, May 1946, 23.

32. Ibid.

33. Ibid.

34. Nkrumah, *Ghana*, 47.

35. *Wasu* 12 (Summer 1947): 13–15.

36. Ibid.

37. Ibid.

38. *News Letter*, December 1946, 40–41. The resolutions were also published in Padmore, *Colonial and . . . Coloured Unity*, 64–66.

39. Padmore, *Colonial and . . . Coloured Unity*, 64.

40. Ibid., 65.

41. Ibid.

42. Ibid., 65–66.

43. Ibid., 66.

44. Nkrumah to Allottey-Hammond, 11 June 1946, GCARPS Papers, acc. no. 78/64, correspondence file no. 6.

45. *League of Coloured Peoples' Review*, January 1951.

46. *Pan-Africa*, June 1947.

47. Padmore, *Pan-Africanism or Communism?* 174.

48. Mbonu Ojike, *My Africa* (New York: John Day, 1948), 108.

49. *A Nationalist Review of Indian Affairs*, January 1947.

50. *Public Opinion*, 11 January 1947; 3 May 1947.

51. *West African Pilot* (Lagos), 5 May 1947.

52. *Socialist Leader*, 14 December 1946.

53. *The Times Literary Supplement*, 11 January 1947.

54. Kwame Nkrumah, *Towards Colonial Freedom* (London: Heinemann, 1963), 1.

55. Ibid., 1, 11.

56. Ibid., 11.

57. For the provisions of the Richards Constitution, see James Coleman, *Nigeria: Background to Nationalism* (Berkeley and Los Angeles: University of California Press, 1958), 271–95.

58. See chapter 3.

59. *Wasu* 12 (Summer 1948): 37.

60. Padmore, *Pan-Africanism or Communism?* 174–75.

61. Ibid., 175.

62. Dennis Austin, *Politics in Ghana, 1946–1960* (London: Oxford University Press, 1964), 54.

63. Ibid.

64. *Wasu* 12 (Summer 1948): 3–9.

65. Ibid.

66. Ibid.

67. E. B. Ndem, "Negro Immigrants in Manchester: An Analysis of Social Relations Within and Between the Various Coloured Groups and of Their Relations to the White Community," M.A. thesis, London University, 1954, 99. Ndem, who was secretary of the African Students' Union from 1946 to 1948, does not give the date of the meeting or the names of any of the participants. The public meeting is the only activity of the ASU during 1946 to 1948 discussed. But he explains that "it [ASU] has a wide and all embracing objective viz. political, social and literary interests. Aside from political activities which occupy its attention more than anything else, it provides a forum for debates, lectures and all matters of educational interest."

68. Padmore, *Colonial and . . . Coloured Unity*, 71.

69. *Wasu* 12 (Summer 1948): 3.

70. Ibid., 4.

71. *West Africa*, 2 October 1948, 1004.

72. Austin, *Politics in Ghana*, 52–53.

73. Ibid., 54.

74. S. D. Cudjoe, *Aids to African Autonomy: A Review of Education and Politics in the Gold Coast* (London: College Press, 1950), Preface.

75. Ibid., 3.

76. Ibid., 4.

77. Ibid., 20.

78. Ibid., 19.

79. Ibid., 20.

80. Ibid., 22.

81. Ibid., 24.

82. Ibid.

83. Ibid., 28.

84. E. D. Morel, *The Black Man's Burden. The White Man in Africa from the Fifteenth Century to World War I* (New York, 1920), reprinted in 1969 by Monthly Review Press, New York.

85. Quoted in Cudjoe, *Aids to African Autonomy*, 28.

86. Ibid., 41.

87. Bertrand Russell, *Power: A New Social Analysis* (London: George Allen and Unwin, 1938).

88. Cudjoe, *Aids to African Autonomy*, 42.

89. Ibid., Acknowledgements.

90. *West Africa*, 28 August 1954, 808.

91. Guy de Lusignan, *French-Speaking Africa Since Independence* (London: Pall Mall Press, 1969), 12.

92. Ibid., 11.

93. B. A. Ogot and J. A. Kieran, eds., *Zamani: A Survey of East African History* (Kenya: East African Publishing House and Longman, 1968), 283.

94. R. N. Duchein, *The Pan-African Manifesto* (Accra: Guinea Press, 1957), 12.

95. Ibid.

96. Ibid., 9.

97. Ibid.

98. Ibid.

99. Ibid., 12.

100. Ibid.

101. Ibid.

102. Kwesi Armah, *Africa's Golden Road* (London: Heinemann, 1965).

103. Ibid.

104. Ibid., 9.

105. Ibid., 10.

5

From Accra to Addis Ababa

THE IMPACT of the Bandung conference, the Loi-Cadre of 1956 conceding internal autonomy to the French overseas territories, the independence of Morocco and Tunisia the same year followed by that of Ghana the next, as well as promises of freedom for other British possessions, all served to pave the way for closer cooperation among African peoples. Was it not in 1957 that Kwame Nkrumah, the prime minister of Ghana, told the world that the independence of his country would be meaningless unless it was linked with the total liberation of the continent of Africa? No wonder he invited George Padmore and W. E. B. Du Bois to the new nation.

While the independence celebrations were still going on, Nkrumah announced his intention of summoning a meeting of the self-governing states of Africa, which actually met in Accra from 15 to 22 April 1958.[1] Eight countries were represented, namely, Egypt, Ethiopia, Ghana, Liberia, Libya, Morocco, Sudan, and Tunisia. Of these, five were from North Africa. South Africa declined the invitation to attend unless other "responsible powers" came.

In his opening speech, the Ghanaian prime minister said: "We, the delegates of this conference, in promoting our foreign relations, must endeavour to seek the friendship of all and the enmity of none. We stand for international peace and security in conformity with the United Nations Charter. This will enable us to assert our own African personality and to develop according to our ways of life, our own customs, traditions and cultures."[2]

Wide-ranging resolutions were adopted on political, economic, social, and cultural matters.[3] The participating governments resolved to preserve the unity of purpose and action being forged as well as "the fundamental unity of outlook on foreign policy so that a distinctive African personality will play its part in co-operation with other peace-loving nations to further the cause of peace." They agreed to avoid any action that might endanger their freedom of interests and to resort to direct negotiations to settle differences among themselves and, if necessary, to conciliation or mediation by other free African states. They affirmed the right of African peoples to run their own affairs, promising direct assistance to the Algerian revolutionaries and the opponents of apartheid in South Africa. The delegates recognized the need to increase trade by improving communications between their countries and encouraging the investment of foreign capital and skills "provided they do not compromise the independence, sovereignty and territorial integrity of our state."

Anticipating many subsequent attempts at economic cooperation, the conference recommended the establishment of a joint economic research commission. Among other functions, the commission was intended to explore the possibility of coordinating the economic planning in each state toward the achievement of an all-African economic cooperation; to make proposals by which independent African nations could receive foreign capital, employ foreign experts, and encourage cooperation with other countries without destroying their unity or compromising their sovereign status. The commission was also expected to examine the possibility of holding economic conferences and creating an African common market and to ensure the establishment of equitable social and economic policies that would provide national prosperity and social security for all citizens.

Turning to relations between the races, the delegates condemned discrimination in all its forms and made elaborate recommendations for the improvement of cultural relations among the African peoples. Reciprocal visits of artists as well as annual inter-African sports meetings and youth festivals were approved. They decided to facilitate the exchange of teachers, professors, students, and educational materials. The revision of history and geography textbooks and syllabi used in schools was recommended "with the view to removing any incorrect information due to colonial and other foreign influences." Periodic and ad hoc conferences of African educators, scientists, scholars, and journalists were also proposed.

Also recommended was research on African culture and civilization, as well as the establishment of African publishing firms whose main function would be to introduce Africa's culture, civilization, and developments to the world and to the various African countries.

Finally, the participating governments set up a machinery for future consultation by ordering their permanent representatives at the United Nations to coordinate all matters of common concern; to take any steps necessary to implement conference decisions; and to make preparatory arrangements for future conferences. It was agreed that heads of the independent African states should meet at least once every two years and that meetings of foreign or other ministers should be held from time to time "to study and deal with particular problems of common concern to the African state." April 15, the date of the meeting, was declared African Freedom Day to be observed every year.

The Accra Conference of 1958 was the first time that African cooperation was discussed at a governmental level and the first time that African governments had in concert called on the colonial authorities to apply the principle of self-determination to their African possessions. Commenting on the gathering, the English journalist Colin Legum declared, quite rightly, that "the Accra Conference has opened a new chapter in the history of Africa, and in the relations between Africa and Europe."[4]

In December the same year (1958) an All-African Peoples' Conference (AAPC) was convened in Accra by Nkrumah in his capacity as chairman of the Ghana Convention Peoples' party.[5] The arrangements were, however, made by a preparatory committee composed of representatives of Ghana, Nigeria, Egypt, Somaliland, and Morocco. It was a meeting of African leaders from territories still under foreign domination. Two hundred delegates representing sixty-two nationalist organizations attended. Notable participants included Félix Moumie, leader of the Union of the Peoples of the Cameroons; Ntau Mkhehle of the Basutoland Congress party; and M. Roberto Holden from Angola. The NCNC contingent was led by N. S. McEwen, who, with the Ghanaian trade unionist John Tettegah, was elected joint secretary to the conference. Also present were Horace M. Bond, a former president of Lincoln University (United States) and Marguerite Cartwright, an African American author and journalist.[6] Among the fraternal delegates and observers may be mentioned a party of six Soviet writers led by the distinguished Russian historian, Professor Potekin. Both Nikita Khrushchev and Chou En-lai sent greetings. Only two of Africa's major parties—the Northern People's party of Northern Nigeria and the RDA—were not represented, though conference organizers said they had been invited.[7]

Tom Mboya, member of the Kenya Legislative Council and secretary-general of the Kenya Council of Labor, took the chair. Opening the conference, Nkrumah declared this to be the decade of African independence. He affirmed that the independence of Ghana would be meaningless unless it was linked up with the total emancipation of the continent. The delegates were urged to achieve first "the political kingdom: all else would follow." They were warned that imperialism could arise from regions outside Europe.[8] Accra was not an extension of Europe or any other continent.

In his address, the chairman contrasted the gathering with the Berlin Conference seventy-two years before, when foreign powers partitioned the continent. Africans were tired of being governed by other people and wanted everywhere to control their own destiny. Referring to the Cold War, he appealed to the big powers not to involve Africa, stressing, "we will not tolerate interference from any country, and I mean any."[9]

An address entitled "The Future of Africa" by W. E. B. Du Bois, then ninety-one years of age and unwell, was given on his behalf by his wife. Among other things, the veteran Pan-Africanist said: "If Africa unites, it will be because each part, each nation, each tribe gives up a part of the heritage for the good of the whole. That is what union means; that is what Pan-Africa means."[10] Concluding, he told the audience that they had nothing to lose but their chains; they had a continent to recover, freedom and human dignity to regain.[11]

At the end of their deliberations, the delegates announced that they had formed a permanent organization with headquarters and secretariat in Accra. The purpose of the new institution was to:

> Promote understanding and unity among peoples of Africa;
> Accelerate the end of imperialism and colonialism;
> Mobilise world opinion against denial to Africans of political and fundamental human rights;
> Develop feeling of one community to assist the emergence of a United States of Africa.[12]

Membership was opened to all African national political organizations and national federations of labor that subscribed to the aspirations of the gathering.

The enthusiasm generated among participants returning to their own countries influenced subsequent developments a great deal. Among the obscure delegates was the Congolese Patrice Lumumba, who went back to his native Belgian Congo to address a mass meeting in Leopoldville. This rally and other activities of his helped to precipitate Belgium's decision to end colonial rule in the country. At a seminar on contemporary Africa held at Northwestern University (United States) in 1951, a high-ranking Belgian colonial administrator believed that Belgium would remain in the Congo for another seventy-five years.[13] But in 1960 alone, seventeen African territories including the Belgian Congo won their freedom.

Two weeks before the AAPC of 1958, shortly after Guinea had won its independence outside the French Community as reorganized by General de Gaulle, Nkrumah and the Guinean president Sékou Touré announced the decision of their two countries to constitute themselves as the nucleus of a union of West African states.[14] They had been inspired "by the example of the 13 American colonies, the tendencies of the countries of Europe, Asia and Middle East to organise in a rational manner, and the declaration of the Accra Conference."[15]

Ghana also agreed, subject to parliamentary approval, to lend Guinea ten million dollars to stabilize the economy and provide administrative and technical aid. Guinea needed the money badly to prevent total collapse after France's withdrawal of its civil servants and equipment credits in retaliation against Guinea's refusal to remain in the French Community.

On his return to Conakry, the capital of Guinea, Sékou Touré claimed that his visit had blazed a trail for African independence and solidarity that he hoped would be translated "into a common co-operation and action in all fields to realise rapidly a United States of Africa."[16]

Accordingly, measures were taken in the following months to bring about closer cooperation, notably, the exchange of resident ministers who would attend cabinet meetings in the country to which they were accredited. On 1 May 1959, Sékou Touré and Nkrumah further stated that the union was open to all independent

African nations. The member states would "decide in common what portion of sovereignty shall be surrendered to the Union in the full interest of the African community."[17] There would be a union flag with red, gold, and green stripes, an anthem, and a motto. Each member country or federation was allowed to retain its local national flag, anthem, and motto. Independence and Unity was declared as the motto of the union, whose general policy would be to build up a free and prosperous African community. Its main objective would be "to help our African brothers subjected to domination with a view to ending their state of dependence, widening and consolidating with them a Union of Independent African States."[18] There would be union citizenship and no visas would be needed to travel from one member territory to another.

Heads of state in the union would determine common policy on matters of defense, but each constituent country would have its own army. Provision was made for an economic council charged with the task of formulating general economic policy and setting up a union bank capable of issuing and backing the currencies of the members of the union.[19] Finally, to bring Africans closer together, the union would take measures to coordinate historical research, the teaching of languages, and cultural activities designed to promote the harmonious development of African civilizations.[20]

The use of the term *union* as opposed to *federation* seemed to have alarmed President William Tubman of Liberia, who now took the initiative of inviting Nkrumah and Touré to a conference at Sanniquellie, a small Liberian village. The meeting produced the Sanniquellie Declaration of 19 July 1959.[21]

George Padmore attended in his capacity as Nkrumah's adviser on African affairs. The three governments agreed to speed up the revolutionary movement and bring about "unity, co-operation, harmony, coherence and mutual understanding" in Africa.[22] After reviewing the two communiqués on the Ghana-Guinea union as well as Tubman's proposals for an "Associated States of Africa," they proposed nine principles for consideration at the Second Conference of Independent African States to be held in Ethiopia the next year.

Among the principles were the name, Community of Independent African States, with Independence and Unity as its motto; the inherent right of Africans to self-determination; noninterference on the part of each member in the domestic affairs of any other; the extermination of colonialism; the right of dependent territories to join the community after obtaining their freedom; and the creation of an economic council, a culture council, and a scientific and research council.[23]

In a separate communiqué, Tubman, Touré, and Nkrumah demanded preindependence elections in French Cameroon to be conducted under the supervision of the United Nations. The reference is to Félix Moumie, who was now in exile, his party (UPC) having been banned. They supported the inclusion of the Algerian question on the agenda of the forthcoming session of the United Nations General Assembly and condemned apartheid. South West Africa, later Namibia, was considered to be a trust territory over which the United Nations could not relinquish responsibility. France came under severe attack for testing atomic devices in the Sahara. African culture was seen "as one of the essential elements of the struggle against colonialism." Finally, the three governments agreed to make the rehabilitation and diffusion of African culture an imperative national duty.

Following discussions on 24 December 1959 at Conakry between Kwame Nkrumah, Sékou Touré, and President Modibo Keita of Mali, a special committee met in Accra from 13 to 18 January 1960 to formulate proposals for a Ghana-Guinea-Mali union. The three heads of state had a further series of meetings in Accra from 27 to 29 April 1961 and agreed upon a charter. Regarded by its member states as the nucleus of a future United States of Africa, the charter was declared open to every country or federation of African countries that accepted its aspirations, namely,

> to strengthen and develop ties of friendship and fraternal co-operation between the member states politically, diplomatically, economically and culturally; to pool their resources in order to consolidate their independence and safeguard their territorial integrity; to work jointly to achieve the complete liquidation of imperialism, colonialism and neo-colonialism in Africa and the building of African Unity; to harmonize the domestic and foreign policy of its Members, so that their activities may prove more effective and contribute more worthily to safeguarding the peace of the world.[24]

The charter also provided for regular conferences between the heads of state of the union. Actually, the supreme executive organ of the Union of African States (UAS) was the Conference, which met once a quarter in Accra, Bomako, and Conakry respectively. The president of the host country served as chairman. At these conferences views were exchanged on African and world problems and the most effective way of strengthening and widening the union. Thus at the end of the second conference of the UAS held at Bamako on 26 June 1961, a joint communiqué was issued reaffirming the member states' determination to continue to support the anti-colonial struggle, particularly in Algeria, the Congo, and Angola. With regard to the problem of the European Common Market, they agreed on a common policy: to establish an African common market.

The UAS was an interesting experiment in African economic and political cooperation in the face of serious obstacles such as two official languages, three different currencies, poor communications between states, and widely differing levels of development. Embracing a market of more than fourteen million people, the association possessed exports that were hardly competitive: Ghana's cocoa, diamonds, gold, manganese, and timber; Guinea's aluminum, bananas, bauxite, coffee, diamonds, and iron; and Mali's cattle, cotton, groundnuts, rice, and river fish. In the long run, economic cooperation between the three states fell below expectations. Nevertheless, the UAS was politically significant, for it represented the first attempt to bridge the gap between French- and English-speaking territories in West Africa and by extension the entire continent.

The Sanniquellie Declaration represented a compromise between the radical provisions of the UAS charter and Tubman's views of African solidarity. On the one hand, Nkrumah, Touré, and Keita spoke for radical Pan-Africanists bent on rapid decolonization and speedy unification of the fatherland. On the other, Tubman stood for those who, though no less committed to African emancipation and unity, preferred a cautious and gradual approach. "The revolutionary core made the compromise, and would do so again later because of the urgent priority it gave to liberation issues."[25]

This polarization of the Pan-African movement also found expression at the All-African Peoples' Conference in Tunis, which met from 25 to 30 January 1960. About 180 delegates from thirty African territories attended the conference. In addition to violent anticolonial resolutions, the participants recommended the establishment of an organization to coordinate the aid and solidarity of all the independent countries and the sending of African volunteers to fight in Algeria.[26] Ghana's proposals for political union were rejected. But proposals for an African common market, bank, and technical research institute were approved. Also adopted were resolutions for closer economic and cultural cooperation. Differences of opinion occurred over the question of international affiliation by African trade unions. While the Tunisians and Nigerians, supported by central and East Africans, desired to maintain their existing connections, Morocco, Ghana, Guinea, and the UPC pressed for the severance of all trade union ties with international bodies. It was eventually agreed to refer the matter to a foundation conference of African trade unions planned for May 1960. Eventually it was resolved that the All-African Trade Unions Federations should not affiliate to any of the international bodies but that each local union could have the right to decide its own international relations.[27]

The division into two camps, the radical and the conservative, was confirmed at the Addis Ababa congress of the African nations, which took place from 14 to 26 June 1960. More than 250 delegates and observers from twenty African territories, eleven of them already independent, were present.[28] The Algerian provisional government, then in exile, also participated. In his inaugural speech the Ethiopian emperor Haile Selassie emphasized that the fate of Africa was no longer determined by foreigners. The traditions of Berlin and Algeciras, together with the entire system of colonialism, were being eliminated from the continent. Though Africans now had their destiny in their own hands, they must not slacken in their determination "never to allow new forms of colonialism, whatever their guise may be, to take hold of any of us, in threat to the hard-won independence and, indeed, to the stability and peace of the world."[29] African leaders, the emperor went on, "must, in self-abnegation, press forward the economic, political and spiritual welfare of their peoples in the interest, not merely of national gain but of that transcendent continental unity which alone can bring to a close the era of colonialism and Balkanization."[30]

His excellency Ato Yiema Deressa, the Ethiopian foreign minister and chairman of the conference, reviewed with satisfaction some practical applications of the resolutions passed at the Accra meeting. An economic commission for Africa had been launched, Ethiopia had made available two hundred scholarships for African students to attend Ethiopian educational institutions, and several profitable consultations had taken place, among them, "the Conference in Monrovia last year[31] to which Liberia made so statesman-like a contribution, and the recent conference in Accra on the matter of Atomic Tests in the Sahara."[32] Guinea, Togoland, and the Cameroons, which achieved self-government during the intervening two years, received a warm welcome. So, too, did the participants from Nigeria, Congo, and Somaliland, then on the verge of securing their own freedom. Africans must hold themselves in readiness to resist "every attempt by foreign interests to influence or compromise the independence of emerging states and by a solid front, deny to those interests the attainment of their selfish goals."[33] To maintain solidarity, the chairman urged African peoples to avoid every occasion for dissention among themselves and refrain from meddling in the domestic affairs of their brothers and neighbors. "Every form of propaganda, whether by press, by radio, or by word of mouth as between African states and peoples should be absolutely excluded."[34] Africans must never allow divided counsels to guide them whether at the United Nations or elsewhere. There was no reason, the chairman concluded, "why our unity and brotherhood should not only provide the settlement of all internal differences, but also ensure that no action can be taken on the international scene except that it be with mutual consent and with full understanding."[35]

In an indirect reference to Nkrumah's attempt to persuade the Ewe ethnic group in Togoland to join their kith and kin in Ghana, J. Rudolph Grimes, head of the Liberian delegation, thought that a way of avoiding friction and balkanization was to accept the present boundaries of African countries. With the Sanniquellie Declaration in mind, he said that "Liberia has proposed a program of West African Regional Co-operation whilst at the same time we have advocated consultation for a larger African Organisation in which regional efforts can be united under the title 'Community of Independent African States.' "[36] He expressed the hope that preliminary discussions would be started during the conference "for the summoning of a conference at a time and place to be agreed upon at the earliest possible time to develop the charter of this organisation."[37]

Recommending the Sanniquellie Declaration for adoption, Ako Adjei of the Ghana delegation claimed that

> [t]he unity, which the three leaders discussed and agreed upon, was intended to be a real political unity of independent African States, and not merely a system of economic co-operation. The three leaders signed a joint declaration in which they proclaimed to the whole world the principles upon which the Union of African States shall be based.[38]

Adjei suggested that a committee of experts be appointed to work out the details of the proposed union. The committee might consist of ministers, diplomats, and economists, and some of the subjects to be considered might include the formation of a customs union, the removal of trade barriers, and the establishment of an African development fund.[39] In the words of the Ghanaian delegate, "The problems confronting our peoples in Africa today are so important and so vital to our very existence, that we cannot afford to dissipate our energies in fruitless argument and academic polemical debate."[40] The conference was assured that the provisions of the Ghana Constitution included the readiness of the people of Ghana to surrender their sovereignty in whole or in part in the interest of a Union of African States.[41]

Though Yusuf Mataima Sule, representing Nigeria, agreed that Pan-Africanism was the only solution to all "our problems in Africa," he dismissed the idea of a union then as premature, preferring Tubman's approach through functional cooperation.[42] Sule placed the first priority on breaking all artificial economic, cultural, and social barriers. All these must be done before political unification. He weakened his otherwise reasoned argument when he resorted to personal attack. Ghana's demand for immediate union, he told the gathering, was merely a device to make Nkrumah ruler of the entire continent. In the Nigerian's opinion, "Individual ambition and greed for power may spoil everything[;] it will spoil the good work we have done and ruin the good work we are capable of doing in the future."[43] Sule believed that the conference of independent African states was the most effective mechanism for considering African problems and fostering African unity. He saw the conference developing into a permanent organization with a secretariat centered in Africa and a regular schedule of meetings as a step toward strengthening existing ties between African nations, encouraging cooperation and consultation in matters of common concern.[44] The permanent organization would also be a center of information on virtually every question affecting the interest and welfare of the continent. For administrative purposes, he recommended that it also be divided into several sections, including foreign commerce.

These suggestions were endorsed by the gathering, who now requested the president of the conference to ask heads of African states to initiate consultations through diplomatic channels with a view to promoting African unity, and to consider the matter at their next meeting in 1962.[45] It was clear that the Sanniquellie Declaration had been rejected.

Undaunted, President Nkrumah repeated the demand for a union of African states in a speech on African affairs given at the Ghana National Academy on 8 August, six weeks after the Addis Ababa conference.[46] "Political freedom is essential in order to win economic freedom, but political freedom is meaningless unless it is of a nature which enables the country which has obtained it to maintain its economic freedom."[47] The African struggle for liberty and unity must begin with political union. A loose confederation of economic cooperation was a waste of time. Only a political union would ensure uniformity in foreign policy, "projecting the African personality and presenting Africa as a force important to be reckoned with."[48] Nkrumah harmed his cause and made more enemies when he proceeded to denounce the supporters of a loose economic cooperation as imperialist protagonists and puppet leaders bent on blocking the path to African unity.[49] Political union, he emphasized, meant a common foreign and defense policy, as well as rapid social, economic, and industrial developments. The economic resources of Africa were immense—staggering. It was only through unity that those resources could be utilized for the progress of the continent and for the happiness of humankind. He saw three alternatives open to African states: "Firstly, to unite and save our continent; secondly, to disunite and disintegrate; or thirdly, to 'sell out' to foreign powers."[50]

The Ghanaian leader also reviewed events in the Congo, which regained independence only four days after the Addis Ababa conference. The violence, antiwhite feeling, and sectionalism that accompanied the proclamation of freedom were seen as the inevitable consequence of eighty years of colonial subjection. Nkrumah was convinced that prompt action by the African nations would prevent complete disintegration, if not advertise African solidarity.

As prime minister, Patrice Lumumba left no one in doubt about his endorsement of Nkrumah's approach to African unity and views on economic independence. "We have absolutely no intention," he declared,

> of letting ourselves to be guided by any ideology whatsoever. We have our own ideology, a strong, noble ideology which is the affirmation of the African personality. . . .
>
> Government policy will be none other than that of the people. It is the people who dictate our actions, and we operate according to the interests and aspirations of the people. Independence is the beginning of a real struggle.[51]

Though such pronouncements naturally alarmed the European multinational company Union Minière du Haute Katanga, the Congolese themselves lacked unity contrary to the implication of the prime minister's speeches. While his party, the Mouvement National Congolais (MNC), stood for a unitary state, the Parti Solidaire Africain led by Antoine Gizenga as well as Albert Kalonji's Kasai faction of the MNC wanted a federation.

By October 1960, when Nigeria attained self-rule, division had become rivalry. Actually, in the same month, a meeting of twelve states *d'expression française* was summoned by Félix Houphouët-Boigny in Abidjan to discuss the Franco-Algerian dispute. The need for such an initiative had become urgent in view of their approaching application for membership of the United Nations. At a second conference, which took place in Brazzaville from 15 to 19 December, the loosely knit states decided to form a more permanent association. This decision was implemented at a third meeting in Dakar held the following month. Out of these conferences grew a bloc known as the Brazzaville Group. Among the member states were Congo (Brazzaville), Ivory Coast, Senegal, Mauritania, Cameroon, and Madagascar. Togoland, Guinea, and Mali as well as the French-speaking countries of North Africa were excluded.

The Brazzaville Declaration issued on 19 December 1960[52] upheld the sovereignty of Mauritania, whose admission to the United Nations was vetoed by the Soviet Union. All "African States anxious for liberty and dignity of Africa, and anxious to avoid the cold war on our continent," were exhorted to secure the admission of Mauritania. Fearing that the Franco-Algerian conflict might degenerate into a world crisis in which Africa would bear the cost, the Brazzaville Group "resolved to ask France firmly to conclude the war in Algeria in 1961, and after frank negotiations to apply honestly the principle of self-determination."[53] The superpowers were accused of seeking "to recolonize Congo (Leopoldville) either directly or indirectly through the intermediary of certain Asiatic and African States."[54] A solution to the problem could "only be found at a Round Table Conference, which would group together the representatives of every party without exception."[55]

While opposing political union in the sense of integrated institutions, the Brazzaville Group agreed to appoint a commission with a view to establishing a plan of African and Madagascan economic cooperation on such matters as monetary and credit problems, crop price stabilization, and harmonization of the different national development plans, and guarantees to private investment.[56] The commission was intended to consider the creation of an Afro-Malagasy investment bank as well as the "problems posed by the adhesion, to come or already achieved, of Member States of the Conference to various organisations of the European community as well as to the various international organisations of a financial and economic character, in the hope of safeguarding their emergent national economies."[57]

The deliberate exclusion of certain African territories from the Brazzaville bloc created a dangerous precedent driving progressives and moderates further apart. In January 1961, King Muhammad V of Morocco summoned a meeting in Casablanca to which selected African countries and Ceylon—a strange member—were invited. The ostensible reason for convening the meeting was the Congo situation. For some time, African states in support of Lumumba had felt the need to coordinate their efforts. Since they had become a minority among the African group at the United Nations, they were anxious to regain their influence. Nonetheless, a more compelling motive that drove King Muhammad to summon the conference was the apparent isolation of Morocco following the rejection of its claim to Mauritania by the United Nations General Assembly the previous month. Because of their support for Mauritania, the

Brazzaville Group received no invitation. Apart from the king, Presidents Nasser, Nkrumah, Sékou Touré, and Modibo Keita of Mali attended. The Algerian provisional government was represented by Prime Minister Ferhat Abbas, Libya by its foreign minister, and Ceylon by its ambassador to Cairo.

Five major subjects dominated the proceedings: Mauritania, Congo, Israel, a union of African states, and a constitutional framework for the Casablanca powers.

Before the congress, Ghana, Libya, and the Algerian provisional administration did not recognize Morocco's claim that Mauritania formed part of its territory. Hence Ghana supported Mauritania's application to become a member of the United Nations. But for the sake of solidarity, the three governments changed their policy.

The debate on the Congo problem was reduced to an argument between Ghana and the rest. In the end, only Ghana refused to withdraw its troops from the United Nations Command in the Congo. With the same vehemence Ghana opposed the attempt to give direct military assistance to Antoine Gizenga's Stanleyville regime on the ground that such aid was logistically impossible.

The debate on Israel occasioned little disagreement probably because the Ghanaian delegates were unwilling to isolate themselves on yet another issue.

At the end of the deliberations, the conference approved an African Charter setting out the aims of its signatories: freedom, unity, nonalignment, decolonization, and cooperation among African nations.[58] To further these ends, the delegates agreed to form an "African consultative Assembly, as soon as conditions permit, composed of the representatives of every African State, having a permanent seat and holding periodical sessions."[59] A joint African high command was proposed. Its functions would be to ensure the common defense of Africa in case of aggression against any part of the continent.[60] The charter also provided for several committees, among them the African Political Committee, consisting of heads of states; the African Economic Committee, comprising ministers of economic affairs; and the African Cultural Committee made up of ministers of education. A liaison committee would be created to ensure cooperation between the various bodies.

By supporting the claim of Algeria to self-determination and denying the same right to Mauritania, the participants put themselves in a situation that was both inconsistent and untenable. Israel was denounced as an "imperialist base."

The broad principles outlined in the charter were incorporated in the protocol of the African Charter signed at a meeting of foreign ministers in Cairo held from 30 April to 5 May 1961.[61] Libya and Ceylon did not take part. The foreign ministers also approved the establishment of a secretariat at Bamako, the capital of Mali, with a Moroccan as secretary-general.

At two subsequent meetings of the Economic Committee, agreement was reached on proposals for an African common market, payments, union, a development bank, planning council, joint air and shipping lines, and a telegraph union. In August 1961 the Cultural and Defense Committees met in Tangier and Cairo respectively. At the latter gathering, it was decided to establish the African military high command proposed at Casablanca.

Just as the Brazzaville congress helped to precipitate the Casablanca convocation, so the Casablanca meeting helped to spark off the Monrovia meeting of May 1961.

Altogether twenty African states sent delegates who included sixteen heads of state. Among the participating governments were those of the Brazzaville bloc. Two of the original sponsors, Guinea and Mali, changed their mind at the last moment because of pressure from Ghana. Morocco and Egypt, the fourth and fifth Casablanca powers, were also unrepresented. Sudan withdrew its acceptance a few days before the meeting because Mauritania had been invited. Congo (Leopoldville) received no invitation because of the desire to avoid controversy with the Casablanca states over credentials. Thus, although the Monrovia congress was so far the largest single gathering of African leaders, it was actually less representative than the preceding Casablanca meeting. With the exception of Tunisia, North Africa was not represented.

In the absence of men like Nkrumah and Nasser, it was easy for the otherwise soft-spoken and gentle prime minister of Nigeria, Sir Tafawa Balewa, to emerge as the dominating figure. So pervasive was his influence that he was able to steer the discussion clear of controverisal issues, finally maneuvering the conference into accepting a gradual and functional approach to African unity. Such difficult issues as repeated atomic device testing in the Sahara by France and the Ethiopia-Somalia border dispute were swept under the carpet to create a facade of unanimity. The anticolonial and antiapartheid resolutions were made to lose much of their force by the failure of the delegates to recognize the Algerian provisional government. On the Congo question, the conferees condemned assassinations as a means of securing political power. The principles of absolute equality, inviolability of African frontiers, and noninterference (not applicable to colonial territories) in each other's affairs were affirmed. Deep regret was expressed at the absence of the Casablanca nations, which it was hoped would be present at subsequent conferences.

The delegates appointed a commission to meet in Dakar, the capital of Senegal, within three months to consider machinery for economic, technical, scientific, and educational cooperation and to submit recommendations to a later congress in Lagos.[62]

Though the Monrovia decisions were not fundamentally different from the provisions of the Casablanca African Charter, the Ghanaian press denounced the delegates as imperialist agents. Liberia, the host country, was described as being "in the economic-mess pot with her split, deformed and distorted personality."[63] President Tubman himself was called upon to admit that he was "an American first, African second."[64]

Infuriated by the tactless fulminations of Ghanaian journalists, the *West African Pilot*, a Nigerian daily, descended to the same level of abusive language. The newspaper recalled that Ghana was supposed to be united with Guinea; yet both countries possessed neither a common Parliament nor a common currency. Echoing Sule's accusation at the Addis Ababa conference of June 1960, the paper claimed that Nkrumah's "real aim is to swallow up little Togo and chew off parts of Ivory Coast. This talk of an African parliament and an Africa without boundaries is merely a cloak to conceal his aims."[65]

Politicians joined in the press war. In a press statement on African affairs issued on 28 June 1961,[66] Chief Obafemi Awolowo, leader of the opposition in Nigeria, advocated the division of the continent into zones as a first practical step toward the emergence of an all-Africa political union. Each zone would cooperate on economic, political, and cultural matters, culminating in a zonal political union. Unsure of his facts, the Nigerian politician ruled out political unification on a continental scale because, according to him, Africa lacked the "racial, cultural and linguistic homogeneity of the U.S.A., the centuries-old cultural and national unity of China and (to a great extent) of India, and the ideological orientation and cohesion of Russia [sic]."[67] Awolowo went on to urge the immediate formation of an organization for African community on the model of the American confederation. His solution combined functional cooperation at the confederal level and political unification at the regional or zonal level.

Nnamdi Azikiwe, then governor-general of Nigeria, contended that if both camps implemented the recommendations of their experts, "Pan-Africanism would have been realised without further fuss on the surrender of sovereignty and on the jockey for leadership entailed thereby."[68] It was naive, he believed, to expect that freedom fighters who passed through the crucible of persecution to win their independence would enthusiastically renounce their newly won power.

Azikiwe's notion of unification is not narrow, for it is not limited to black Africans. By a united continent he meant integrating African society from the Cape to Cairo. He envisaged a concert of African states similar in structure to the United Nations organization. Crucial decisions would be left to heads of state or heads of government or their representaives. He provided for a continent-wide parliament, court of international justice and secretariat to handle "the administration of the day-to-day affairs of this African leviathan."[69]

To achieve the possibilities held out by unification, Azikiwe proposed three conventions, one each on collective security, economic cooperation, and human rights. The convention on collective security provided for an African high command, a Pan-African declaration on neutralism, and

> a doctrine of non-intervention in Africa, on the same lines as the Monroe Doctrine in the western hemisphere. This doctrine should make it clear that the establishment or the continued existence of any colonial territory in the continent of Africa, by any European or American or Asian or Australian power shall be regarded not only as an unfriendly act, but as an act of aggression against the concert of African States. This is one concrete way of making it impossible for certain nations who have been forced to surrender their colonial swap in Africa, to seek by obvious methods to continue their isidious game.[70]

Among other things the convention on economic cooperation recommended the formation of a customs union, thereby breaking down all tariff walls, the establishment of an African common market, railway system, airways and telecommunications authority, and the introduction of a common currency. Movement of people and produce "in their respective countries would quicken and solidarity of views would be cemented." The convention on human rights was intended to elicit the confidence and support of the rank and file. Many of the provisions of the three conventions find an echo in the resolutions of the Casablanca and Monrovia blocs.

Like Azikiwe, President Sylvanus E. Olympio preferred functional cooperation with national sovereignties in tact. In an article published in the October 1961 issue of *Foreign Affairs*, Olympio commended the Monrovia conference for opening the way to international cooperation while preserving the sovereignty of African nations. He echoed Azikiwe's fear that few serious governments would be willing to relinquish their hard-won seats in international councils, seats that permitted them to be heard and that granted them the moral security provided by access to world opinion. Furthermore, experience showed that "in building a house one starts with a foundation, not a roof."

In an earlier article also published in *Foreign Affairs* (January 1961) Léopold Senghor had similarly warned that a United States of Africa could not be brought into being overnight. The history of the United States, the Soviet Union, and Germany proved that "a federation is really possible only between states that are at equal economic levels and have equal political maturity."[71] Disapproving of the call at the Tunis All-African Peoples' Conference for an African common market, he contended that African economies were more than complementary, as if the same situation were not true of the members of the European Common Market. It was paradoxical, Senghor went on,

> that at the very time some of the newly independent African States pretend to champion African unity they quarrel about frontiers and claim pieces of neighbouring territories, support emigres and phantom governments at great expense, see Fifth Columns everywhere.[72]

By a strange coincidence, the emergence of the East African Common Services Organization (EACSO) later in 1961 seemed to

vindicate the practicability of the views of Senghor, Olympio, Awo-
lowo, and Azikiwe. Actually, EACSO grew out of the East Africa
High Commission set up by the British authorities in January 1954.
From October 1961 to August 1962, rivalry among African peoples
and organizations continued unabated. Two African trade unions,
the All-African Trade Union Federation, and the African Trade
Union Confederation competed for recognition. The All-African
Trade Union received the support of the Casablanca powers; the
African Trade Union that of the Monrovia bloc.

Side by side with the squabbles among the various groups went
national disputes between some of the African states themselves.
These disputes had the effect of heightening the tension within the
movement for African unity. We have already noted Morocco's claim
that Mauritania constituted part of its territory. The Moroccans also
had a frontier dispute with the Algerians that resulted in warfare.
Similarly, Ethiopia, Kenya, and Somalia quarreled over their bor-
ders. Cameroon accused Guinea of harboring Félix Moumie. Cameroon also accused Nigeria of interfering in a plebiscite that led
to the incorporation of northern Cameroon into Nigeria. Tunisia
blamed Egypt for an attempt to assassinate President Habib Bourguiba. The Ewe problem ensured continued enmity between Togoland and Ghana, both of which harbored sections of the Ewe ethnic
community. "Many fellow nationalists resented the impression that
Nkrumah was staking a claim to lead the whole continent, particularly when his diplomacy seemed to be interfering in their internal
affairs and considerable groups of their younger generation looked
to him as their militant inspiration."[73]

The Monorovia conference closed with the agreement that the
conference resume in Lagos. Five days before the resumed Monrovia conference in Lagos on 25 January 1962, Nkrumah made a
statement on certain aspects of African unity before the Ghana
National Assembly. Without mentioning Awolowo, Olympio, and
Senghor by name, he rejected their arguments against continental
union. He remained convinced that

> local associations, regional commonwealth and territorial groupings
> will be just another form of balkanisation, unless they are conceived
> within the framework of a large union based on the model of the United
> States of America or the Union of Soviet Socialist Republics. When the

first thirteen states in the North American continent tried to promote the idea of a United States of America, this was ridiculed as an empty dream which was vigorously resisted by many. And who would have thought that seventy-five different nationalities at various levels of economic, social and political development in Russia [sic] could have been welded into the mighty force which the Soviet [Union] has become within this comparatively short space of time. I believe that Russia even began with three states.[74]

Nkrumah might have added that in the case of America, confederation or loose association nearly led to total collapse within the first decade of independence. It was the failure of a confederal system that prompted the Philadelphia Convention (1787), which gave birth to the United States of America. Concluding his speech, President Nkrumah said, "Our survival depends upon the political unity of Africa. The forces that unite us are far greater than the difficulties which divide us at present."

As the opening day of the Lagos conference approached, Africans and observers elsewhere hoped that the Casablanca group would attend so that their mutual hostility might at least be diminished. However, the exclusion of the Algerian provisional government by the sponsors angered the Casablanca powers. Consequently, they boycotted the meetings. Libya and Tunisia also refused to attend for the same reason; their absence was offset by the presence of two newcomers. Tanganyika and Congo (Leopoldville). Altogether no less than seventeen heads of state or government came. Despite the impressive number of countries participating, not a single North African nation sent delegates.

Welcoming the gathering, Governor-General Azikiwe deplored the absence of the Casablanca powers and tried to make up for the unrepresentative nature of the congress by emphasizing the combined population of the Monrovia group, estimated at 133.1 million as against 53.1 million for the Casablanca bloc.

Apparently displeased by Azikiwe's divisive arithmetic, Haile Selassie made it clear that Ethiopia belonged to one group only—the African group. He pointed out that a close and careful analysis of the policies adopted by the African nations today on a wider range of questions emphasized the large number of views shared in common, not the differences among them.[75] He therefore lamented the exclusion of the Algerian provisional government, whose absence had caused a number of other nations to decline invitations extended to them.[76] Ethiopia, Selassie stated unequivocally, was committed to the principle of political unity among African states. Indeed, he went on, "we believe that we all are, and that we differ only in our assessment of the speed with which [the] most desirable of goals can be attained."[77] The task before Pan-Africanists was to devise the means whereby this basic agreement might be most rapidly advanced. "The furtherance of political unity, then, would be a fundamental objective of the Organisation of African States."[78]

The Dakar recommendations of the commission appointed at Monrovia as well as proposals for a functional approach to African unity submitted by Nigeria, Liberia, and Ethiopia were examined.[79] At the end of the discussion, the conference accepted in principle a draft charter for a permanent Inter-African and Malagasy organization, which was confirmed four months later, with a few amendments, at a meeting of foreign ministers also held in Lagos.

According to the charter, the purpose of the permanent body was to promote "a better life for the peoples of Africa and Malagasy by enlisting the efforts of Member States through cooperative and joint action."[80] The document enshrined the principles of sovereign equality of member nations irrespective of their wealth, size, or population; noninterference in the domestic affairs of member states; respect for the territorial integrity of each country; peaceful settlement of all disputes; unqualified condemnation of any subversive activity on the part of neighboring or other states; the constant promotion of cooperation in the fields of economics, health, nutrition, education, and culture; and dedication to the total emancipation of the remaining colonies in Africa.[81] Membership of the organization was open to every independernt state "in Africa and Malagasy under indigenous African rule." There were provisions for an assembly of heads of states and governments, a council of ministers and a general secretariat, as well as specialized agencies.[82] Finally, the gathering adopted the Dakar recommendations.

A careful examination of the provisions of the charter and the resolutions shows that Selassie was right when he remarked that not much difference existed between the programs of the various Pan-African groups. Though the resolutions derived from the principle of functional approach, subsequent events demonstrated that his opening address had paved the way for reconciling the two major groups: Casablanca and Monrovia.

At their Addis Ababa meeting held the following month in February 1962, the Pan-African Freedom Movement for East and Central Africa pledged "to establish a Federation of the component states of PAFMECA as a first real and logical step toward the full realisation of total African political unity and as the best method of speeding up the liberation of Africa."[83]

A communique issued in May 1962, after consultations between Touré and Senghor at Labe in Guinea, announced the decision of the two leaders to increase their joint efforts to bring together the Monrovia and Casablanca camps. On 28 June Touré and Selassie conferred at Asmara in Ethiopia. Events in Algeria and Congo (Leopoldville), both of which had been major points of disagreement between the radicals and the moderates, came to the aid of African unity. On 1 July 1962 Algeria became independent. At the same time, a new administration controlled neither by Gizenga nor Moise Tshombe emerged in Congo. Hence a June meeting of the Casablanca heads of state in Cairo was able to support a proposal by Guinea for a continental conference.

During a visit to Conakry in August, Félix Houphouët-Boigny said that he agreed with the necessity of bringing the two groups together as soon as possible to discuss African unity. In the same month, President Keita of Mali, visiting the Ivory Coast, expressed the hope that in a few months' time there would be nothing fundamental separating the two blocs. And in October, Houphouët-Boigny, Keita, and Touré met in Komodougou in Guinea to exchange views on African and international problems. It is important to note that the three presidents had not met together since 1958.

The growing desire for an end to the Casablanca-Monrovia conflict was abundantly reflected in the exertions of the London-based Committee of African Organizations. As soon as it became known that a congress of African states was being planned for May 1963 in Ethiopia, the CAO summoned a meeting of the All-African Students of Europe, which took place in Friends House, London, from 17 to 19 April. A four-point resolution was unanimously passed for transmission to all heads of African state and government:

1. The Youth of Africa expect the leaders of Africa meeting at Addis Ababa to perform one clear and honest duty—the duty of uniting all the States of Africa.

2. To this end, they should as individuals sink all their personal differences and as groups should disband the Casablanca, the Monrovia and the Brazzaville Groups, so-called.

3. They should draw up a charter of African Unity to which all the States should subscribe.

4. The Addis Ababa Conference should give a name to the Union and appoint a secretariat as well as the seat of its operation.[84]

In addition, the participants drew up a manifesto, also sent to all the African leaders.[85] Among other things, the students called for a Pan-African news agency, a Pan-African radio and television service, a Pan-African army under a joint high command, and an African common market.[86] They urged the inclusion of African history, music, culture, and languages in the syllabi of African universities.[87]

1. *West Africa*, 26 April 1958, 387.

2. Quoted in Teshome Adera, *Nationalist Leaders and African Unity* (Addis Ababa: Berhanena Selam Printing Press, 1963), 147.

3. *West Africa*, 10 May 1958, 449. For a full text of the resolutions, see Colin Legum, *Pan-Africanism: A Short Political Guide* (New York: Frederick A. Praeger, 1962), Appendix 4.

4. *Listener*, 1 May 1958, 722.

5. *West Africa*, 29 November 1958, 1143; 6 December 1958, 1167; 13 December 1958, 1191.

6. *West Africa*, 29 November 1958, 1143.

7. *West Africa*, 13 December 1958, 1191.

8. Ibid.

9. Ibid.

10. For a full text of the address, see W. E. B. Du Bois, *The World and Africa: An Inquiry Into the Part Which Africa Has Played in World History*, enlarged ed. (New York: International, 1965), 305–10.

11. Ibid., 310.

12. *West Africa*, 20 December 1958, 1215.

13. Hans Kohn and Wallace Sokolsky, eds., *African Nationalism in the Twentieth Century* (New York: Van Nostrand, 1965), 8.

14. *West Africa*, 29 November 1958, 1143.

15. Ibid.

16. Ibid.

17. *West Africa*, 9 May 1959, 447.

18. Ibid.

19. Ibid.

20. Ibid.

21. *West Africa*, 15 August 1959, 60.

22. Ibid.

23. Ibid.

24. Kwame Nkrumah, *Africa Must Unite* (London: PANAF Books, 1963), 142.

25. Immanual Wallerstein, *Africa, the Politics of Unity: An Analysis of a Contemporary Social Movement* (London: Pall Mall Press, 1968), 38.

26. For a full text of the resolutions, see Legum, *Pan-Africanism: A Short Political Guide*, 236–47.

27. A foundation conference of the All-African Trade Unions Federation did not take place in May 1961 as originally planned in May 1960.

28. *Second Conference of Independent African States, Addis Ababa, 14–26 June 1960* (Addis Ababa: Government of Ethiopia Publication, 1960), 1.

29. Ibid., 27.

30. Ibid.

31. The reference is to the African Foreign Ministers' Conference of August 1959; for details see *West Africa*, 15 August 1959, 609.

32. *Second Conference of Independent African States*, 28.

33. Ibid., 30.

34. Ibid.

35. Ibid.

36. Ibid., 33.

37. Ibid.

38. Ibid., 42.

39. Ibid., 43.

40. Ibid.

41. Ibid., 42.

42. Ibid., 66–67.

43. Ibid., 67.

44. Ibid., 70.

45. For a text of the resolutions, see ibid., 101–108.

46. Kwame Nkrumah, *Africa's Challenge. A Time of Danger and of Hope* (Accra: Government of Ghana, 1960).

47. Ibid., 9.

48. Ibid.

49. Ibid.

50. Ibid., 1.

51. Quoted in Wilfred Cartey and Martin Kilson, eds., *The African Reader: Independent Africa* (New York, 1970), 87–89.

52. For a text of the declaration, see Legum, *Pan-Africanism: A Short Political Guide*, Appendix 13.

53. Ibid., 180.

54. Ibid.

55. Ibid.

56. Ibid., 181.

57. Ibid., 182.

58. For a text of the charter, see Legum, *Pan-Africanism: A Short Political Guide*, Appendix 15.

59. Ibid., 187.

60. Ibid., 188.

61. For details of the protocol, see ibid., Appendix 16.

62. For resolutions of the Monrovia conference, see Legum, *Pan-Africanism: A Short Political Guide*, Appendix 17.

63. Quoted in Legum, *Pan-Africanism: A Short Political Guide*, 54.

64. Ibid.

65. *West African Pilot*, 18 May 1961, editorial.

66. Reprinted in extenso in Legum, *Pan-Africanism: A Short Political Guide*, Appendix 24.

67. Ibid., 269.

68. Nnamdi Azikiwe, *The Future of Pan-Africanism* (London: Nigeria High Commission, 1961), 18–19.

69. Ibid., 14.

70. Ibid., 15.

71. Ibid., 240.

72. Ibid., 244.

73. John Hatch, *A History of Postwar Africa* (New York and Washington, 1965), 400.

74. See minutes from Ghana Parliamentary debates, 20 January 1962.

75. Haile Selassie's speech is given in extenso in V. Bakpetu Thompson, *Africa and Unity: The Evolution of Pan-Africanism* (London: Longman, 1969), 175.

76. Ibid.

77. Ibid.

78. Ibid.

79. *West African Pilot*, 26 January 1962.

80. For a full text of the proposed charter of the Inter-African and

Malagasy States Organization, see Remi Foni-Kayode, *Blackism* (Lagos, 1965), Appendix 1.

81. Ibid., 76.

82. Ibid., 77, 80–81.

83. Africa Department, Foreign Office, *The Fourth PAFMECA Conference Held in Addis Ababa February 2nd to 10th 1962 (Speeches and Statements)* (Addis Ababa, n.d.), 81.

84. Kwesi Armah, *Africa's Golden Road* (London: Heinemann, 1965), 26.

85. For a text of the manifesto, see ibid., Appendix 3.

86. Ibid., 284–85.

87. Ibid., 285.

6

The OAU and Regional Groupings

ON 22 MAY 1963 the Casablanca and Monrovia factions assembled in the Ethiopian capital of Addis Ababa, where they agreed on a compromise formula for achieving African unity. Thirty-two African countries represented by heads of states or premiers or foreign ministers took part. Kwesi Armah, a member of the Committee of African Organizations (CAO), was also present. A notable absentee was President Sylvanus Olympio of Togo, who had been assassinated four months before the conference. Tesfaye Gegre-Egzy of Ethiopia served as secretary-general for the meeting. He later became the minister of Information in the Ethiopian government.

Emperor Haile Selassie's welcome address struck the keynotes of compromise and unity that guided the proceedings. It was the duty and privilege of the delegates "to rouse the slumbering giant of Africa, not to the nationalism of Europe of the nineteenth century, not to regional consciousness, but to the vision of a single African brotherhood bending its united efforts towards the achievement of a greater and nobler goal."[1] The emperor warned that "while we agree that the ultimate destiny of this continent lies in political union, we must at the same time recognise that the obstacles to be overcome in its achievement are at once numerous and formidable."[2]

Selassie's counsel of caution and gradualism did not prevent Kwame Nkrumah from using the occasion to restate the case for the total liberation and immediate political unification of Africa. Convinced that the nation-state is obsolete and that Africa's challenge is not that of building nation-states but that of regenerating a continent, the Ghanaian appropriately timed the launching of his latest book, *Africa Must Unite*, to coincide with the summit. In fact, copies of the publication were distributed to conference delegates. His argument may be summarized as follows. Africa is a rich continent, but its mineral and natural resources are unevenly distributed. So long as the African states remain separate political units, most of them will not only be poor but will have little or no prospect of escaping poverty. This is because most of them depend on the sale abroad of raw goods. As far as one can see into the future, the terms of trade will move against African states. Furthermore, as population increases and technological improvement is applied to the land, the number of the landless will multiply. African governments will then be unable to do more for their own people than the colonial regimes, and all "the resentment which overthrew colonialism will be mobilised against us." The only sensible solution is to develop heavy industry at the same pace as agriculture, but this can only be done on a continent-wide scale. Unless great industrial complexes are established in Africa—which can only be done in a united Africa—African peasants will find themselves at the mercy of foreign cash-crop markets and African governments will face the same unrest that dislodged the imperialists. Unless the African farmer is assured of a fair market, education and mechanization and even capital for development are no use to him. If African states fail to establish great industrial complexes, what have the urban workers and the peasants gained from political independence?

> Unite we must. Without necessarily sacrificing our sovereignties, big or small, we can here and now forge a political union based on Defence, Foreign Affairs and Diplomacy, and a Common citizenship, an African Currency, an African Monetary Zone and an African Central Bank. We must unite in order to achieve the full liberation of our continent. We need a Common Defence System with an African High Command to ensure the stability and security of Africa.[3]

Nkrumah's case for African union, by which he meant "the political and economic unification of the African continent," was well founded. Not only is Africa endowed with every known agricultural and mineral resource, it also possesses immense reserves of oil and coal as well as fantastic potential in hydroelectric power thanks to the great river systems of the Congo, Niger, Nile, and Zambezi. Furthermore, there exists arid and semiarid land capable of supporting additional millions of people if brought into cultivation by coordinated schemes of irrigation. Put simply, Africa abounds in the resources and energy needed for economic development on a continental scale.

No doubt Africans can still advance economically if they prefer to remain appendages of their former colonial masters. But their rate of economic progress will be at the mercy of the foreign senior partner, because no African country is strong enough to withstand external pressures or to operate as a viable economic unit in terms of modern economics. On the other hand, a Union African government will plan and develop the resources of the continent as a whole. It will develop internal communications and commerce. It will set up its own financial system and common market. In a relatively short time it will transform a hitherto colonially disarticulated continent into a coordinated, balanced economic and political unit.

Though pragmatic and persuasive, Nkrumah's argument failed to produce a positive response. Only a handful of the participants, notably Milton Obote, the prime minister of Uganda, supported him. Having previously antagonized most African leaders through his dynamism, excessive zeal, and indiscreet pronouncements, Nkrumah was hardly the best advocate of his case. Was he not accused of meddling in the internal affairs of Nigeria and Cameroons and even of instigating the assassination of fellow African President Olympio? No wonder the conference applauded Cameroonian President Ahidjo's suggestion that the summit should condemn the subversion of one African nation by another. Thus, hatred of a single personality and his administration reinforced by different colonial backgrounds and cultural diversity tilted the balance in favor of functional cooperation.

The case against Nkrumah's approach to African unity was admirably presented by President Philibert Tsiranana of Malagasy. "We intend," he declared,

> to conserve the total sovereignty of our states. . . . I should underline that our adhesion means by the same token a rejection of a formula for a Federation of African States because federation presupposes the surrender of a large part of national sovereignty. Similarly, we would reject

a confederal formula seeing that the authority we superimpose on the states might impose demands which would be unacceptable for certain of us.[4]

Habib Bourguiba pointed out that Africans hardly knew one another; they needed time to identify the things they had in common and those that divided them. Many delegates, including Julius Nyerere of Tanganyika (later Tanzania), felt that social and economic cooperation at a regional level could play an important role in the development of Africa and even lead to a single union government. A loose association with a dash of functional cooperation appeared to be the consensus.

A compromise charter that fell short of Nkrumah's Pan-African vision was adopted and ratified subsequently by the participating governments.[5] Under the charter a permanent body was launched, whose name—the Organization of African Unity—was suggested by President Hubert Maga of Dahomey. Its aims are to promote the unity and solidarity of the African states; to defend their sovereignty, their territorial integrity, and their independence; to coordinate and intensify cooperation and efforts to achieve a better life for the peoples of Africa; to eradicate all forms of colonialism from Africa; and to promote international cooperation, having due regard for the Charter of the United Nations and the Universal Declaration of Human Rights. To achieve these aims the member states pledged themselves to harmonize their policies, especially in the fields of diplomacy; economies—including transportation and communications; education; and culture; as well as health, nutrition, science, technology, defense, and security.

Despite the recognition of the need to defend the sovereignty and territorial integrity of member countries, the charter does not provide for a Pan-African army.

The document enshrined the following principles: (1) the sovereign equality of all member states; (2) noninterference in the internal affairs of states; (3) respect for the sovereignty, equality, and territorial integrity of each state, and for its inalienable right to independent existence; (4) peaceful settlement of disputes by negotiation, mediation, conciliation, or arbitration; (5) unreserved condemnation of political assassination in all its forms, as well as of subversive activities on the part of neighboring states or any other state; (6) absolute dedication to the total emancipation of the African territories that are still dependent; (7) affirmation of a policy of nonalignment with regard to all blacks.

Of the seven principles, five are in defense of the sovereign rights of the member states and the production of so-called colonially imposed boundaries. Given the frailty of the new nations, the novelty of recently won freedoms, and the wide disparity in the size of the component countries, it is understandable that the charter should seek to reassure members by adopting a cautious approach at the very beginning. Nkrumah's attempt to hasten the pace of total African unity failed but not because of its intent. What was being contested was the most realistic strategy for achieving that unity. Nkrumah's model was premature.

The tendency to see colonially delineated boundaries as an abomination probably derives from the assumption that European colonialism itself was an unmitigated evil. The European adventurers reduced to about forty the one-thousand-odd polities that characterized nineteenth-century Africa. In this way they created larger African political entities that alone can endure in the postwar world. Needless to add that Nkrumah's attempt to redraw the colonially imposed frontier between his native Ghana and Togoland brought him much of the opprobrium under which he labored at the OAU inaugural summit.

Though open only to self-governing African nations, membership in the OAU is not compulsory. Any member country may withdraw from the body after the expiry of a one-year notice.

Four major institutions were provided for by the charter. The Assembly of Heads of State and Government is the supreme organ, and the only body with decision-making powers. It meets in ordinary session once a year, two-thirds of the total membership being the quorum.

The Council of Ministers is another principal organ, though subordinate to the Assembly of Heads of State and Government. It is made up of foreign ministers of member states or such ministers as are designated in their place. The council serves as a cabinet to the assembly. According to article XIII of the OAU charter, its functions are to implement the assembly's decisions; to make arrangements for the annual conferences of the assembly; and to coordinate inter-African cooperation in the various fields already noted. The council approves the reports of the specialized commissions, the budget, and gifts made to the organization. It also has responsibility for drafting resolutions and declarations for consideration and adoption by the assembly.

The council holds two statutory meetings a year, one in February and another later in the year to prepare the agenda for that year's summit. At the request of two-thirds of the members of the organization, emergency sessions may be held. Each session is presided over by a chairperson assisted by two vice chairpersons and a rapporteur, all of whom are elected by secret ballot. The provisional agendas of the council meetings are prepared by the administrative secretary-general and communicated to member states a month in advance of the meeting. The agendas comprise the report of the administrative secretary-general and items decided by the assembly or the council, as well as those proposed by the specialized commissions and any member state.

This brings us to a third main institution of the OAU, namely, the General Secretariat. Its chief executive is the administrative secretary-general, so-called because the founding fathers of the OAU, alarmed by the bold initiatives taken by the United Nations secretary-general Dag Hammarskjöld during the Congo crisis, did not want the OAU scribe to assume the role of policymaker for the continent. The secretariat serves all the meetings of the Council of Ministers, the assembly, the specialized commissions, and ad hoc committees appointed by these bodies. It keeps the records of the proceedings of the meetings and helps the assembly and the council to implement their decisions. The secretariat also prepares both the annual report and the budget of the OAU. In addition to the secretariat in Addis Ababa, the OAU maintains regional offices in Lagos, Yaoundé, Dar es Salaam, Brussels, Geneva, and New York. There is also an OAU mission in Namibia, as well as an OAU permanent delegation to the League of Arab States in Tunis. Arabic, English, French, and Portuguese are the official languages of the organization.

A fourth major organ is the Commission of Mediation, Conciliation, and Arbitration. Made up of twenty-one members, its task is to settle disputes between states. In addition there are five specialized commissions: Economic and Social Commission; Education and Cultural Commission; Health, Sanitation, and Nutrition Commission; Defense Commission; Scientific, Technical, and Research

Commission. These bodies parallel United Nations agencies operating in Africa and they are expected to handle the technical aspects
of cooperation. On the surface there appears to be a duplication of
roles, but the intention is not to do away with the UN regional offices
in the continent. What Africans hoped for was cooperation, not
competition.

The OAU inaugural summit also adopted a series of important
resolutions. The Resolution on Africa and the United Nations demanded equitable representation of the continent in the principal
organs of the United Nations, especially the Security Council and
the Economic and Social Council and its specialized agencies. The
OAU also advised African representatives in the United Nations to
constitute a more effective African group with a permanent secretariat to bring about closer cooperation and better coordination in
matters of common concern. In the Resolution on Disarmament,
the delegates declared Africa a denuclearized zone and took strong
exception to all nuclear and thermonuclear tests as well as the man-
ufacture of nuclear weapons. The superpowers were urged to reduce conventional weapons, put an end to the arms race, and sign
a general and complete disarmament agreement under international
control. Among other things resolution VI recommended a meeting
of experts within three months pending the establishment of the
Economic and Social Commission provided for in article XX of the
charter. After examining the labor and social problems on the continent, the committee should suggest ways and means of raising
the social standard and strengthening inter-African cooperation
through the exchange of social and labor legislation, the organization of sporting activities, and the establishment of an African trade
union.

Another committee of experts was to meet within three months
pending the formation of the Education and Cultural Commission
also provided for in article XX of the charter. The committee should
submit a report to the above commission on educational and cultural issues bearing in mind the resolutions already adopted by the
Casablanca and Monrovia blocs. An institute of African studies
would be launched as a department of the African university proposed by Ethiopia. The establishment of an African news agency
and the introduction of programs in the major African languages
and the exchange of radio and television programs were urged.

Commenting on the inauguration of the OAU, Cyril Falls, a former Oxford University Chichele Professor of the History of War, wrote:

> By far the most significant event of the recent past is, however, the conference of Addis Ababa. Africa has achieved a "Summit" at a time when Europe and North America are merely hoping for one and by no means sure they will get it. It will certainly take a long time before, if ever, she reaches a general alliance such as N.A.T.O. or that dominated by the Soviet Union, but she has taken a long and sensational step on the road. Even a year ago it would have needed a very bold and percipient prophet to imagine anything of the land.[6]

At the first meeting of the OAU Council of Ministers at Dakar in August 1963, Addis Ababa was chosen as the permanent secretariat in deference to the antiquity of Ethiopia and in appreciation of Haile Selassie's contributions to African solidarity. During the summit of heads of state and government held in Cairo the next year, Ambassador Diallo Telli of Guinea was appointed as the first administrative secretary-general, a post he kept until 1972 when Nze Ekengaki, a Cameroonian minister of labor, succeeded him. Two years later Ekengaki was replaced by his compatriot William Eteki Mboumoua. At the Khartoum summit of 1978, Togoland's Edem Kodjo was appointed as the new head of the General Secretariat, remaining in office until 1983. Owing to an internal crisis, Peter U. Onu of Nigeria was appointed in an interim capacity from that year to 1985, when a new chief executive in the person of Ide Oumarou from Niger was elected.

We now turn to the efforts of the OAU to implement its prescriptions. What did it do or fail to do about the liquidation of the remaining enclaves of colonialism in southern Africa? How successful were its attempts to stem the rising tide of squabbles between and within African countries? What has been its attitude to economic cooperation and the commitment to raise the quality of life of African peoples?

First, we examine the role of the OAU with regard to the process of decolonization, then in full swing. As more and more African dependencies regained their freedom, the persistent refusal of Portugal to withdraw from Angola, Guinea-Bissau, and Mozambique became more and more unacceptable. Lisbon insisted that these

African territories were overseas provinces of metropolitan Portugal. Actually, Portugal needed them to boost national self-respect and its economy, one of the poorest in Europe. Equally provocative were the situations in Southern Rhodesia and South Africa, where white minority regimes usurped the functions of the imperial trustee with the apparent encouragement of the metropolitan power.

Once the Central African Federation caved in under the pressure of African nationalism in 1962, the white settlers in Southern Rhodesia began to press for full political autonomy. On the surface the demand seemed understandable in view of the granting of self-determination in 1964 to the two other members of the defunct federation, Northern Rhodesia and Nyasaland, which changed their names to Zambia and Malawi respectively. Actually, the trouble with Southern Rhodesia was much more complex than that of its erstwhile strange bedfellows. Since 1923 when Southern Rhodesia attained dominion status, the white colonists there began to behave like an imperial court, frustrating even otherwise reasonable proposals from the indigenous inhabitants for an orderly development of a nonracial community. As a result, the Africans who formed the bulk of the population and the white citizens found themselves moving along parallel lines in the same society.

A similar situation existed in South Africa. Apartheid, an Afrikaans word meaning "apartness" or "separateness," was a system by which the Pretoria regime regulated relations between white and nonwhite citizens. Officially adopted in 1948 and based on the myth that Europeans are the superior race, the system was designed to secure political supremacy and maximum economic prosperity for the small white minority. In 1961 South Africa was expelled from the Commonwealth because of its racist policies, although it still remained in the sterling area. Ostracism merely served to worsen matters, at least so it seemed at the time. In any case, it gave South Africa the chance to end its dominion status and to declare itself an antonomous republic.

It was Hendrick Verwoerd, a former professor of psychology and philosophy, newspaper editor, and senator, who proved an ingenious ideologue of apartheid. He was much concerned about South Africa's image abroad and feared the impact of the winds of change sweeping over the rest of the continent. Verwoerd also wanted to

keep Africans and Europeans apart economically and geographi-
cally. As he expressed it in 1961, "The development of the Bantu
races will buy the white South African his freedom and right to
retain domination in his own country, settled for him by his forefathers." In 1963 Pretoria began to establish Bantustans, semi-
autonomous African homelands within South Africa. Transkei was
the first Bantustan to emerge. The hope was that this policy would
not only win apartheid respectability abroad but also provide a safe
outlet for African frustrations at home.

Thus, while Portugal clung tenaciously to its colonial possessions
on the continent, South Africa and Southern Rhodesia adopted the
posture of ruthless colonial masters. While Western liberals found
the behavior of the three governments repugnant, the last two in
particular caused Britain great embarrassment, "South Africa because British trade had created commercial ties which could not be
broken without considerable loss, Southern Rhodesia because it
remained nominally subject to British sovereignty but was plainly
not subject to British direction."[7]

It was against this background that the Addis Ababa summit
passed resolutions on decolonization as well as on apartheid and
racial discrimination.[8] The conference appointed a delegation of
ministers of foreign affairs to speak on behalf of all African states
at the meeting of the Security Council, which would be called to
examine the report of the United Nations Committee of Twenty-six
on the situation in African territories under Portuguese domination.
The summit demanded the breaking-off of diplomatic and consular
relations between African states and the governments of Portugal
and South Africa if they remained intransigent. The paticipants
decided to mount a boycott of the foreign trade of the two regimes
by (a) prohibiting the import of their goods; (b) closing African sea-
and airports to their ships and planes; and (c) forbidding their air-
craft to overfly the territories of all African states.

The Resolution on Decolonization reaffirmed that "South-West
Africa is an African territory under international mandate and that
any attempt by the Republic of South Africa to annex it would be
regarded as an act of aggression."[9] It urged the Great Powers to
cease lending directly or indirectly any support to those colonialist
administrations that might use such assistance to suppress African
liberation movements "particularly the Portuguese government,

which is conducting a real war of genocide in Africa. Allies of the imperialists must choose between their friendship for the African peoples and their support of powers that oppress African peoples."[10]

The rest of the world in general and the West in particular called OAU's bluff, for they continued to trade with and sell arms to South Africa and to keep Southern Rhodesia afloat through sanction-busting companies. Many a member of the OAU found it hard to abide by recommended sanctions. The geographical location of Zambia for instance made it almost impossible for that country to boycott South Africa without at the same time committing economic suicide. Lesotho, Botswana, and Swaziland found themselves in an even more vulnerable position. Restrictions on South African air and sea transport were robbed of much of their intended force by the halfhearted and piecemeal manner in which they were imposed. "The lead in defying OAU policy was taken by President Hastings Kamuzu Banda of Malawi, who in 1967 went so far as to establish diplomatic relations with South Africa."[11]

Anticipating subsequent developments, the resolution on decolonization urged "the colonial powers, particularly the United Kingdom, with regard to Southern Rhodesia, not to transfer the powers and attributes of sovereignty to foreign minority governments imposed on African peoples by the use of force and under cover of racial legislation."[12] After reaffirming their support of African nationalists in Southern Rhodesia, the independent African states declared their readiness to receive on their territories nationalists from liberation movements, in order to give them training in all sectors and afford young people all the assistance they needed for their education and vocational training.

May 25 was designated African Liberation Day. On that day popular demonstrations would be organized. The opportunity would be seized to disseminate the recommendations of the summit and collect sums over and above the national contributions for a special fund being launched in aid of African emancipation.

The Resolution on Decolonization established a nine-member coordinating committee, better known as the Liberation Committee, with headquarters in Dar es Salaam and regional offices in Lusaka and (until 1974) Conakry. The members were Algeria, Congo-Leopoldville (Zaire), Ethiopia, Guinea, Nigeria, Senegal,

Tanganyika, Uganda, and Egypt. The body was charged with harmonizing the support from African nations and managing the special fund.

The principal organs of the OAU Liberation Committee are the Standing Committee on Information, Administration, and General Policy; the Standing Committee on Finance; the Standing Committee on Defense; and the Executive Secretariat. Representatives of the nationalist groups are accredited to it. Because recognition implied direct access to the Council of Ministers and of course eligibility for aid, the proliferation of political organizations tended to render the work of the committee unnecessarily difficult.

The South West African People's Organization (SWAPO), the Partido Africano de Independencia de Guinea e Cabo Verde (PAIGC), and the Frente de Libertação de Moçambique (FRELIMO) easily emerged as the dominant and authentic nationalist movements in the corresponding territory. For this reason the OAU had no difficulty in granting offical approval.

The problem posed by the Territory of the Afars and Issas (French Somalia, otherwise known as Djibouti) seemed peculiar. Less than thirteen thousand square kilometers and largely arid, its value lies in its command of the southern entrance to the Red Sea and Suez Canal, and in its position on the sea route to French-occupied Réunion in the southern Indian Ocean. The OAU had to contend with the additional task of staving off partition of the country by its neighbors after the departure of the colonial power. To preserve the frontiers of an independent Djibouti, the OAU persuaded Ethiopia and Somalia to sign an undertaking to respect the sovereignty of the territory. Thereafter, the five nationalist groups in the territory held a joint meeting in Accra from 28 to 31 March 1977 under the auspices of the OAU. Following agreement to coordinate their anticolonial exertions, the country secured its freedom in June 1977.

Unlike Djibouti, the existence in Angola and Southern Rhodesia of several hostile and almost equally popular liberation movements proved a serious obstacle to the emergence of a common front against the foreign ruler. Not surprisingly, the OAU often changed its mind on the matter. Thus in 1963 it accepted Roberto Holden's Frente Nacional de Libertação de Angola (FNLA) rather than the Movimento Popular de Libertação de Angola (MPLA), whose initial revolt in Luanda had just misfired. Barely a year later, the committee switched its support to the rival MPLA as the FNLA's fortunes declined and its narrow ethnic base became more and more apparent. Then in 1972 the OAU extended recognition to the FNLA as well. And just before the withdrawal of Portugal from the country, the OAU gave its blessing to yet a third party, Jonas Savimbi's Uniao Nacional Para a Independencia Total de Angola (UNITA). In the end the MPLA won the struggle for power, thanks to Cuban and Soviet military backing.

As in Angola, so too, in Southern Rhodesia (Zimbabwe) the Liberation Committee's efforts to reconcile the competing nationalist associations proved unavailing. With the collapse of the fragile merger of Robert Mugabe's Zimbabwe African National Union (ZANU) and Joshua Nkomo's Zimbabwe African People's Union (ZAPU) under the umbrella of the Patriotic Front (PF), the OAU turned to the Zimbabwe People's Revolutionary Army (ZIPRA) operating from Mozambique.

OAU's fear that the white minority administration in Southern Rhodesia might seize power was vindicated in November 1965 when Ian Smith unilaterally declared the dominion independent of British control. An emergency meeting of the OAU Council of Ministers held in Addis Ababa from 3 to 5 December 1965 threatened that if Britain did not crush the rebellion and pave the way for majority African rule in Southern Rhodesia by the middle of that month, the member states of the OAU would sever diplomatic relations with Britain forthwith. However, only nine of the thirty-six members of the OAU actually did so, among them Ghana and Tanzania. The economies of many of the independent African states were too closely linked to that of Britain for them to obey the call.

Since the British government refused to use sanctions against South Africa and force on Southern Rhodesia, clashes with the African members of the Commonwealth became unavoidable. The African leaders resented Britain's double standard in the application of the principle of self-determination in different parts of the continent. The machinery of both the United Nations and the Commonwealth afforded them an unusual opportunity for bringing pressure to bear on Britain and Portugal. For instance, the Commonwealth Prime Ministers' Meeting invariably attracted much attention in the British press "and customarily enabled the Africans not only to present their own case but also to marshal opinion among their sympathizers in Britain."[13]

Reflecting on the proceedings of the 1964 Commonwealth Prime Ministers' Meeting, the Kenyan nationalist Tom Mboya declared:

> It is evident that the African States tried to secure agreement on issues which concerned them most and on which they were due to report to the OAU at the Cairo Conference. These included the question of Southern Rhodesia, South Africa and even the Portuguese territories. . . .
>
> At the second meeting of the Council of Ministers of the OAU, the African members of the Commonwealth were specifically asked to raise certain matters at the Commonwealth Conference and to use their influence with Britain on the Southern Rhodesian question.[14]

Similar use was made of the machinery of the United Nations General Assembly. Having accepted the legitimacy of the nationalist struggle launched by African liberation movements, the United Nations General Assembly in its resolution 2555 called upon all specialized agencies of the United Nations family to give material assistance to the liberation movement. At meetings of such specialized agencies as the United Nations Educational, Scientific, and Cultural Organization (UNESCO) and the International Labor Organization (ILO), where Portugal, South Africa, and Southern Rhodesia continually came under fire, "the communist and Latin American states and most of those in Asia and the Middle East normally voted with the Africans on African issues."[15] It was the same concerted action by the OAU member states that led the United Nations Security Council to hold a special session on African territory from 28 January to 4 February 1972.

The white settler regimes and their friends in the West pointed to the "abysmal failure" that is postcolonial Africa. They were silenced by Nkrumah's reply that Africans preferred freedom with danger to servitude in tranquility.

However the Lusaka Manifesto, which sought to clarify the stand of thirteen states in East and central Africa on colonialism and racism in southern Africa, was more accommodating than Nkrumah's retort. The manifesto was promulgated at the end of the OAU's fifth summit conference in Lusaka from 14 to 16 April 1969. The signatories—Burundi, Central African Republic, Chad, Congo, Ethiopia, Kenya, Rwanda, Somalia, Sudan, Tanzania, Zaire, and

Zambia—conceded that none of them would claim "that within our states we have achieved that social, economic and political organization which would ensure a reasonable standard of living for all our people and establish individual security against avoidable hardship or miscarriage of justice."[16] They were not hostile to the white-controlled administrations because they were manned by European elements. They were hostile to them

> because they are systems of minority control which exist as a result of, and in pursuance of doctrines of human inequality. What we are working for is the right of self-determination for all the people of these territories. We are working for a rule in those countries which is based on the will of all the people, and an acceptance of the equality of every citizen.[17]

The signatories "would prefer to negotiate rather than destroy, to talk rather than kill." And if there was to be any dialogue, it must be between the white-dominated regimes and the people being oppressed and exploited.

The Lusaka Manifesto was endorsed by the OAU summit in Addis Ababa in 1969. President Ahmadou Ahidjo, who served as chairman, was directed to present it to the UN General Assembly. That body not only adopted it in November 1969 with its resolution 2505 but also recommended it to the attention of all states and peoples. Southern Rhodesia, South Africa, and Portugal ignored it. The three governments must have drawn a considerable measure of security from the fact that earlier in the year (3 February 1969) FRELIMO's Leader Eduardo Mondlane had met his death while opening a parcel bomb presumably sent by colonialist agents. The party found an able successor in General Samora Machel. On 20 January 1973 Portuguese-sponsored infiltrators succeeded also in assassinating Amilcar Cabral of Guinea-Bissau. Like Che Guevara, he was a distinguished theorist and practitioner of revolution.[18] The PAIGC, whose founder and general secretary he had been, continued the struggle, winning freedom for Guinea-Bissau barely eight months later.

No doubt the emancipation of Guinea-Bissau gave a new impetus to the exertions of the liberation movements elsewhere, as well as the diplomatic onslaught of the OAU. Actually, in 1974 the independent African states nearly succeeded in pushing South Africa out of the UN, "a move thwarted by British, French and American vetoes in the Security Council."[19] The same year witnessed the overthrow of the Caetano-led fascist regime in Lisbon in April 1974. The coup brought to power a left-wing administration bent on de-colonization. The new regime fulfilled its promise to dismantle what remained of the Portuguese colonial empire. Angola and Mozambique became self-governing in 1975 after a massive exodus of white settlers from both countries.

The administrations that took over when colonial rule ended in Angola and Mozambique were socialist-oriented and therefore hostile to South Africa. Matters were not helped by the installation of African majority rule in Southern Rhodesia (now Zimbabwe) in 1980. Zimbabwe's independence amounted to the removal of the cordon sanitaire shielding South Africa from the rest of the continent. By 1986, after seventy-five years of anarchy and human suffering, perceptive and pragmatic white South Africans began to sense that the days of apartheid were numbered and to toy with the idea of a negotiated settlement. Excepting die-hard Afrikaners, Bantustans have met with universal disapproval. The banning of the ANC had neither deprived it of sanctuary abroad nor affected the capacity of its military wing, the Umkhonto We Siswe, to escalate violence at home.

It was against this background that the OAU and its Committee on South Africa consisting of sixteen heads of state, including President Ibrahim Babangida of Nigeria, met in Harare (Zimbabwe) on 21 August 1989. Also present was Hosni Mubarak, the Egyptian leader and then chairman of the OAU. The committee laid down four conditions that South Africa must fulfill to make good its claim of preparedness to abandon apartheid. They are the release of all political detainees, the lifting of the state of emergency, the termination of all political trials, and the abrogation of the ban on the ANC.

The Harare conference came a week ahead of a proposed meeting between Kenneth Kaunda, president of Zambia, and F. W. de Klerk, who had just taken over as South Africa's interim president following P. W. Botha's sudden illness. The four conditions based on an ANC policy paper formed the subject of discussion. On 2 February 1990 de Klerk promised the South African Parliament wide-ranging reforms, raising expectations of imminent peace in southern Africa to a new peak. Among the core measures announced were the unbanning after thirty years of the ANC, the Pan-Africanist Congress (PAC), and the Communist party of South Africa; the removal of restrictions on thirty-three other organizations, notably the United Democratic Front, the Congress of South African Trade Unions, and the South African National Students' Congress; the revocation of restrictions on 374 freed prisoners; the limitation of detention without trial to six months, with the provision of legal representation and medical treatment; and a moratorium on hanging. The state of emergency imposed by Botha in 1985 was not lifted.

Reactions outside and within the continent were prompt and favorable. British prime minister Margaret Thatcher, who had persistently opposed sanctions for more than a decade hailed the reforms as a

> "historic landmark on the road to a new South Africa" and called on the ANC to respond positively. President Bush [of America] was more cautious but hinted that US policy on South Africa would be subject to review in the light of the projected changes. President Kaunda of Zambia offered de Klerk "hearty congratulations on a job well-done" while the UN Secretary-General, Mr. Javier Pérez de Cuéllar, said the news had "the sound of celestial music" and seemed "like the beginning of the end of apartheid."[20]

President Mikhail Gorbachev of the Soviet Union welcomed the measures as a step in the right direction. Only die-hard Afrikaners such as Andreis Treurnicht, leader of the Conservative party, and Eugene Terreblanche, president of the neo-Nazi Afrikaner Weerstand Beweging (Afrikaner Resistance Movement) thought the reforms a major disaster.

Then on 10 February 1990 Nelson Mandela, a seventy-two-year-old lawyer and deputy leader of the ANC, was released after spending twenty-eight years in prison. The world's most prestigious prisoner of conscience, he had been jailed originally for life for advocating the use of force to overthrow apartheid, which the United Nations had already denounced as a "crime against humanity." His release provided an unusual opportunity for anti-apartheid pressure groups the world over to renew with vigor their campaigns for a nonracial South Africa.

At midnight on March 21, barely six weeks later, South West Africa achieved the distinction of being the last African colony to regain political freedom. Any fears of insecurity and reprisals still lingering in the minds of white settlers there were finally dispelled by SWAPO's leader, Sam Nujoma, during the independence festivities. He saw the presence of Nelson Mandela and de Klerk at the ceremonies as evidence that "a solution can be found to the problem of apartheid." Echoing the sentiments of his host and erstwhile opponent, de Klerk declared, "I stand here tonight as an advocate of peace. The time of violence has passed for Namibia and for the whole of southern Africa."[21]

Against the background of these astonishing developments, the OAU ad hoc Committee on South Africa met in Lusaka toward the end of March 1990. After noting that de Klerk's tone had been positive, the one-day summit organized a monitoring group whose duty it is to follow up the peace moves initiated by Pretoria and enter into dialogue with that government on behalf of the OAU. The willingness of the African leaders to enter into dialogue with the apartheid regime is a departure from their original policy. The change of mind is a measure of the progress being made toward a peaceful settlement.

At the opening of South Africa's 1991 parliamentary session in Cape Town on February 1, President de Klerk announced the intention of his government to remove the remaining pillars of apartheid: the Land Acts, the Group Areas Act, and the Population Registration Act. The Land Acts of 1913 and 1936 reserved 87 percent of the country's land for whites. The paltry balance left to the black majority was for the most part infertile and obviously inadequate. Under the Group Areas Act the different racial groups were segregated, the idea being to make space coincide with race. The Population Registration Act classified persons according to race. In addition de Klerk issued a "Manifesto for a new South Africa" aimed at formulating common values which, according to him, could serve as a point of departure in the search for a solution.

Speaking at a recent summit of the OAU ad hoc committee, President Yoweri Museveni of Uganda, who is both the OAU and committee chairman, commended de Klerk's gesture but urged his government to work toward a popular and freely elected constituent assembly to draft the country's new nonracial constitution.

Museveni also urged Pretoria to draft a land reform program to redress the imbalance in land tenure. African countries that followed the international community in easing sanctions against Pretoria were rebuked because the hasty action had made South Africa unwilling "to meaningfully and seriously negotiate in order to end apartheid."[22] He appealed to the international community to maintain the pressure. Although de Klerk had merely put forward his "intention," and millions of people in the country were still without the vote, the South African question had now moved beyond the academic debate over whether apartheid could ever be scrapped, to how soon it should be abolished completely.

The significance of the role of the OAU in decolonization is sometimes underrated. No doubt in terms of money and materials the contributions of the OAU are manifestly unimpressive. The OAU Cairo summit of 1964 set the year's budget for the Liberation Committee at £809,000.[23] This sum hardly met more than 10 percent of the financial requirements of the freedom fighters.[24] At the 1972 Rabat summit the Liberation Committee's annual budget was raised by 50 percent. But when OAU's sustained diplomatic support and propoganda are thrown into the scale, the picture changes drastically. The OAU's diplomatic support provided much of the legitimacy needed by the armed resistance movements. The organization may justifiably take a large measure of credit for the destruction of apartheid, when it occurs, and the decolonization of the continent.

A considerable measure of success has marked OAU's efforts in the fields of culture and technical cooperation. The organization staged the first all-African cultural festival in Algiers in August 1969, at the end of which a Pan-African cultural manifesto was adopted. The next year, the first workshop on African folklore, dance, and music, also organized by the OAU, took place in Mogadishu. It was attended by many scholars and artists of international repute from OAU member states.

Guided by the Pan-African cultural manifesto as well as "a common determination to strengthen understanding among our peoples and co-operation among our states" and recalling that "cultural domination led to the depersonalization of part of the African peoples, falsified their history, systematically disparaged and combated African values," the OAU summit of 1976 adopted a Cultural Charter for Africa. Among the aims of the charter are to liberate

African peoples from sociocultural conditions that impede their development in order to recreate and maintain the sense and will for progress and development; to rehabilitate, restore, preserve, and promote African cultural heritage; to assert the dignity of the African and the popular foundation of his culture; and to combat and eliminate all forms of alienation and cultural suppression and oppression everywhere in Africa, especially in countries still under colonial and racist domination, including apartheid.[25]

Priority was accorded to the transcription, teaching, and development of national languages with a view to using them for the dissemination and development of science and technology; the recording, conservation, use, and dissemination of information on oral traditions; the adaptation of educational curricula to development needs and to national and African cultural and social realities; the promotion of cultural activities, the protection and encouragement of artists; and research in the field of local African medicine and pharmacopoeia.

To achieve these objectives, the Cultural Charter for Africa recommended the introduction of African culture into all national educational systems, the establishment of appropriate institutions for the development, preservation, and dissemination of culture, the training of competent staff at all levels, and the organization of competitions offering prizes. The African states undertook to create conditions that would enable their peoples to participate fully in the development and implementation of cultural policies.

Far less impressive was the OAU's performance at managing conflicts within and between member states of the organization. As already noted, the European imperialists merged many precolonial communities together, reducing the one thousand odd polities they found to less than fifty colonies. Unfortunately, they paid little or no heed to culture and language. Whether the mistake was by accident or design is hard to say. But the result, as Julius Nyerere rightly observed, is that "there is no one country which does not include areas which would come under another political unit if any principles of political geography were considered, and numerous tribes live in at least two countries or have their origins in some other area of Africa."[26] Between 1963 and 1981, there were roughly thirty cases of border disputes, attempted secession, and alleged subversion by neighboring states.

At the beginning OAU's efforts in the reconciliation of intra-African disputes were commendable. It succeeded in arranging a cease-fire in the Algerian-Moroccan boundary conflict in 1963 and replacing British with African soldiers in Tanzania following a mutiny there in 1964. The next year the OAU diffused the tension between Ghana and its French-speaking neighbors, including Upper Volta (now Bourkina Faso), Ivory Coast, and Togo. A remarkable feature of the Kinshasa summit of 1967 was the successful settlement of quarrels between Chad and Sudan, Kenya and Somalia, and Somalia and Ethiopia. The conference endorsed President Tubman of Liberia's mediation efforts with regard to the squabble between Guinea and Ivory Coast. To crown it all, an OAU committee reported on the successful reconciliation of the Algerian-Moroccan wrangle. Thereafter, under the cover of its principle of noninterference in the domestic affairs of member states, the OAU tended to turn a blind eye to tensions and injustices that threatened the very fabric of those states.

Where the OAU did not completely turn a blind eye to disruptive issues, its attempts at mediation were either belated or halfhearted or both. Thus, at first the OAU watched helplessly while the Nigerian civil war raged on ferociously and secessionist Biafra complained of genocide. Colonel Ojukwu's regime in Biafra based its case on the apparent unwillingness of the federal government of Nigeria to protect the lives and property of the Igbo. But General Yakubu Gowon held the trump card of the established government. Convinced that man-made arrangements do not stand higher than fundamental human rights, Tanzania, Zambia, Gabon, and Ivory Coast recognized Biafra. All the other African states and the OAU as a body continued to insist on the sanctity of the territorial integrity of Nigeria. The OAU set up a consultative mission at its Kinshasa summit of September 1967, and thereafter retained the main responsibility for attempts at mediation. The organization's indecisive and hesitant action made it possible for outsiders to fish in troubled waters. France, Portugal, and Haiti sided with Biafra, while Britain and the Soviet Union supplied arms to Nigeria. In the end Biafra came to the rescue of the OAU by capitulating in Janaury 1970.

Meanwhile two other major wars of secession that began before the inception of the OAU itself are still raging, and the organization does not appear to have any answer to the problem. Unlike Nigeria, Sudan, Zaire, and Ethiopia, where the insurrections were caused by separatist movements seeking to set up independent states of their own, the civil wars in Chad (since 1965), Uganda (since 1966), and Angola (since 1975) sprang from ethnic rivalry for control of the central government. In each case the OAU was slow to act. With regard to Chad, the main initiative in finding a solution was taken by Nigeria, which was instrumental in summoning OAU-sponsored conferences in Kano and Lagos, and subsequently in despatching an OAU peacekeeping force there.

No crisis dramatized the impotence if not irrelevance of the OAU in conflict management more than the Somali irredentism. At the OAU inaugural conference in May 1963, President Aden Abdullah Osman of Somalia described his country's predicament thus:

> Unlike any other border problem in Africa, the entire length of the existing boundaries, as imposed by the colonialists, cuts across the traditional pastures of our nomadic population. The problem becomes unique when it is realised that no other nation in Africa finds itself totally divided along the whole length of its borders from its own people.[27]

This fragmentation of an ethnic community gave rise to Pan-Somali sentiments bent on uniting kith and kin scattered in adjacent territories in a "Greater Somalia" that would encompass the Ogaden province of Ethiopia, the northeast frontier region of Kenya, and Djibouti.

In 1976 the Western Somalia Liberation Front, a guerrilla organization claiming to represent Somali speakers in Ogaden and enjoying official support from the government of Somalia in Mogadishu, launched full-scale military operations against Ethiopia. What started as a local uprising escalated into an explosive international crisis in July 1977, when troops from Somalia crossed the border into Ogaden and joined forces with the WSLF. Again the vacillation of the OAU left the door open for the Soviet Union and the United States—and Cuba—to intervene. In the end Ethiopia managed to repulse the attack thanks to considerable military help from the Soviet Union and Cuba. Needless to add, the conflict nearly tore the OAU apart. As in the Nigeria-Biafra episode, the OAU found the preservation of the territorial integrity of Ethiopia more important than self-determination for Ogaden-Somalia.

One of the notable exceptions to OAU's tendency of rating artificial national boundaries above fundamental human rights is the Western Saharan war between Morocco and the People's Front for the Liberation of Saquiet el-Hamra and Rio de Oro (POLISARIO). Before withdrawing from Spanish Sahara, Spain made an agreement with Morocco and Mauritania to hand over the phosphate-rich colony to them. The larger portion in the north went to Morocco. Neither the inhabitants of the colony nor the independence movement POLISARIO, which had been launched in 1973 and which Spain had refused to recognize, was consulted. When Spain left the scene in February 1976 and Moroccan and Mauritanian soldiers occupied the coastal towns of Western Sahara, POLISARIO with Algeria's support declared the independence of the Sahrawi Arab Democratic Republic (SADR) and intensified the struggle it had already begun to wage against Spain.

"By 1978 Mauritanian forces had been defeated; the country was bankrupt—a situation made worse by a drop in world demand for iron ore; Mauritania was being defended from POLISARIO by Moroccan troops and French air force."[28] These reverses made it easy for a military coup to topple President Ould Daddah's new regime; Mauritania's claim was renounced, leaving the entire territory to Morocco.

The OAU paid little attention to this potentially dangerous development in the mid-1970s, when a settlement might have been much easier. A special summit proposed in 1977 to discuss the crisis never met. A committee appointed the next year recommended a referendum which King Hassan II of Morocco at first rejected. The decision to admit the SADR, now recognized by as many as twenty-six states representing more than half of OAU's total membership, was postponed at the Freetown summit of 1980. The matter was referred to an ad hoc committee following Morocco's threat to leave the OAU. In September the same year, the ad hoc committee announced a cease-fire, including a referendum to be organized by the OAU with the assistance of the United Nations.

In February 1982 two OAU committees assembled in Nairobi to review the Western Saharan and Chad crises. The committee handling the former problem hardly made any progress. Despite agreeing to a plebiscite the previous year, Morocco refused to withdraw its forces during the poll, or to recognize and hold direct talks with POLISARIO. It insisted on negotiating only with Algeria and Libya. The admission of SADR representatives at a foreign ministers' meeting led to a walkout of nineteen members.

The second committee discussed the plight of the peacekeeping force in Chad. Of six states only Nigeria, Senegal, and Zaire had contributed troops. Their ineffectiveness, in part due to their lack of mobility, was compounded by escalating costs, estimated at $160 million annually.[29]

Two attempts to hold a summit in Tripoli later in the year after the above preparatory committee meetings had to be abandoned because of lack of quorum caused by disagreement over the SADR question and U.S. pressure encouraging a boycott. An alternative venue was found in Addis Ababa. SADR delegates agreed to keep away to avoid further deadlock. The conference renewed its call for a referendum and direct negotiations between POLISARIO and Morocco. In 1984 Nigeria became the thirtieth African nation to recognize the SADR, thereby paving the way for the admission of a POLISARIO delegation at the OAU summit held the same year in Addis Ababa. Protesting, Morocco announced its withdrawal from the OAU supported only by Zaire, which withdrew from the summit. Morocco eventually returned to the fold of the organization.

Although the OAU charter provides for a Commission for Mediation, Conciliation, and Arbitration, the organization has tended to ignore its own commission, preferring direct negotiations between the states involved, good offices offered by third parties, ad hoc committees made up of heads of state, and diplomatic negotiations conducted during summits. Thus, Haile Selassie and Modibo Keita handled the Algerian-Moroccan border clash of October 1963. At the end of the Nigerian civil war, Haile Selassie reconciled Nigeria with the four member states of the organization that had recognized secessionist Biafra. And when in September 1972 Nyerere connived at the invasion of Idi Amin's Uganda from Tanzania by armed supporters of ex-President Obote, the Somali leader Muhammad Siyad Barre diffused the tension, averting a major war between the two East African states.

The Commission for Mediation, Conciliation, and Arbitration

was established in 1964, and its twenty-one members, headed by Nigeria's Justice M. A. Odesanya, were appointed by the Accra summit of October 1965. By the time the commission held its first meeting in Addis Ababa two years later, the OAU had devised other means of containing dissension. It is interesting to note that the organization has avoided arbitration and never referred disagreements between member states to the International Court of Justice as it did in the case of South Africa's attempted annexation of Namibia. Commenting on the organization's dislike of judicial settlement, Justice Odesanya said:

> My OAU experience is that States will always show great reluctance in limiting their own political and diplomatic freedom beyond what they regard as absolutely necessary to secure their immediate objectives.[30]

A new dimension in conflict management is the use of regional groupings. With the encouragement and blessing of the OAU, the Economic Community of West African States (ECOWAS) assembled and despatched troops to Liberia in 1990 when President Samuel Doe's government appeared no longer able to maintain law and order in the republic. Although the interventionist force, better known as ECOMOG (ECOWAS Monitoring Group), could not prevent the assassination of Doe by his opponents, its overall effectiveness enabled an ECOWAS summit in Banjul (Gambia) to arrange a ceasefire in November 1990. The same month an ECOWAS-sponsored interim government under the presidency of Amos Sawyer took the oath of office. The transitional administration is made up of the representatives of opposition parties, interest groups, and concerned Liberians. Before the installation of Sawyer, power in Liberia was wielded by Charles Taylor's National Patriotic Front of Liberia, Prince Y. Johnson's Independent National Patriotic Front of Liberia, which captured and killed Samuel Doe, and ECOMOG, depending on which area each controlled.

ECOWAS is among the oldest regional groupings existing side by side with the OAU. Earlier regional associations such as the Mali federation, composed of Senegal and Mali, and the Ghana-Guinea-Mali union, were political groupings. They maintained a precarious existence for only a few years. By 1965 they had all collapsed. The regional economic organizations that succeeded them have fared much better. They filled the vacuum created by OAU's lukewarm attitude to its commitment "to co-ordinate and intensify their co-operation and efforts to achieve a better life for the people of Africa."[31]

Economic organizations have proliferated. In West Africa alone there existed in June 1990 "three economic integration groupings and a whole array of other IGOs [inter-governmental organisations] of lesser pretention, altogether numbering some 40-odd IGOs."[32] Among the major movements for regional cooperation may be mentioned the Economic Customs Union of Central and Equatorial Africa (Union Douanière et Economique de l'Afrique Centrale— UDEAC) linking Cameroon, Central African Republic, Gabon, and the People's Republic of the Congo, the East African Community (EAC) created by the Treaty for East African Cooperation and signed by the heads of state of Kenya, Uganda, and Tanzania in Kampala in June 1967, becoming effective in December; ECOWAS; the Southern African Development Coordinating Conference (SADCC); the Communauté Economique de l'Afrique de l'Ouest (CEAO); and the Conseil de l'Entente.

The EAC grew out of the East African Common Services Organization (EACSO) initiated in 1961 by the British colonial authorities. So even before independence, the East African territories attained a level of economic integration unknown elsewhere in Africa. The essential elements of this integration lay in the existence of a common market, a common currency, an almost identical tax structure, and an impressive array of common services, most notably railways and harbors, ports and telecommunications, airways, and higher education and research facilities. Of these elements the centerpiece was the common market, which ensured a free movement of capital, labor, and goods throughout the region. Among other things the Treaty for East African Cooperation provided for an East African Development Bank and an East African common market, incorporating with substantial modifications the arrangements of the EACSO. The three signatories constituted the East African Authority, assisted by five councils as well as East African ministers appointed by each member country. The East African Legislative Assembly was reorganized and enlarged. The headquarters of the common services were decentralized and shared out among the three states. Under the new arrangements, the East African airways and railways remained in Kenya; the Harbors Corporation and the community headquarters were located in Tanzania; while the newly created East African Development Bank as well as the posts and telegraphs were assigned to Uganda. The objectives were "to strengthen and regulate the industrial, commercial and other relations of the Partner States to the end that there shall be accelerated and balanced development and sustained expansion of economic activities [and] the Benefits shall be equitably shared."[33]

The EAC operated smoothly up till 1971, when President Obote of Uganda was overthrown by his army commander, General Idi Amin. Thereafter, Nyerere's refusal to recognize the Amin regime coupled with ideological differences between capitalist Kenya and socialist Tanzania, as well as conflicts between regional and national interests, began to obstruct the community's work. And since the structure depended on the authority of the three heads of state and government meeting together, the EAC's decline went rapidly downhill after they refused to meet. Henceforth, disagreements and administrative problems remained unsolved. The railway system was the first to break up, Tanzania having taken the rolling stock from the community for its own Tan-Zam railway. The rail link to Uganda was bedeviled by border insecurity, while Kenya expanded its road-haulage industry to the detriment of the railways. The rot soon spread to other common services such as the airways and the harbors, culminating in restrictions on the free movement of people and goods across the frontiers. Disputes over community appointments and the expulsion of Kenyans from Tanzania completed the process of disintegration.

At the time the EAC was falling apart, a similar economic grouping for West Africa, ECOWAS, was being set up. The project was initiated by the United Nations Economic Commission for Africa, headed by the eminent Nigerian economist Adebayo Adedeji. The formation of ECOWAS was made possible by the encouragement and patronage of General Yakubu Gowon and General Gnassingbe Eyadema of Togo, with the support of President Houphouët-Boigny of Ivory Coast. It was launched in Lagos by a treaty signed by the heads of state of fifteen West African nations or their representatives on 28 May 1975. They were Dahomey (now Benin Republic), Gambia, Ghana, Guinea, Guinea-Bissau, Ivory Coast, Liberia, Mali, Mauritania, Niger, Nigeria, Senegal, Sierra Leone, Togo, and Upper Volta (now Burkina Faso). The new organization put an end to the artificial division of the region into English-speaking, French-speaking, and Portuguese-speaking territories, with a combined population estimated at 150 million.

The treaty establishing ECOWAS has sixty-five articles arranged in fourteen chapters. The signatories declared their awareness of an "over-riding need to accelerate, foster and encourage the economic and social development of their states in order to improve the living standards of their peoples." They were convinced that the promotion of harmonious economic development of their states called for effective economic cooperation. They also recognized that progress toward subregional economic integration required an assessment of the economic potential and interests of each state. They accepted "the need for a fair and equitable distribution of the benefits accruing from cooperation. Their ultimate objective was "the creation of a homogeneous society, leading to the unity of the countries of West Africa, by the elimination of all types of obstacles to the free movement of goods, capital and persons."[34] Underlying this aspiration is political unity, even though it is not stated in so many words.

According to article 2 of the treaty, ECOWAS would promote economic cooperation and development, especially in the fields of industry, transport, telecommunciations, energy, agriculture, natural resources, commerce, monetary and financial questions, and in social and cultural matters. These goals would be attained in stages through the elimination between member states of customs duties, the removal of qualitative and administrative restrictions, harmonization of policies, and the implementation of regional projects. The period set out by the treaty for the total liberalization of trade among member countries and the progressive establishment of a customs union was fifteen years.

The institutions of the organization were named in article 4 as follows: the Assemby of Heads of State and Government, the supreme authority, which would meet annually; the Council of Ministers, composed of two representatives from each member country with a chairman from each state in turn; the Executive Secretariat, headed by an executive secretary appointed by the assembly for a four-year term renewable only once; and the Tribunal, charged with the task of interpreting the treaty should disagreements arise. A Fund for Cooperation, Compensation, and Development was established to finance Community projects in member states, help less developed member states, and compensate members who suffered either as a result of trade liberalization or the location of Community projects. "Funding from this would come from member-states' contributions, income from community enterprises, receipts from outside the community, subsidies and contributions from all sources."[35]

The headquarters of ECOWAS and of the Fund were located in Nigeria and Lomé respectively. Aboubakar Quattara was elected the Community's first executive secretary, assuming office in January 1977.[36]

"In 1980, ECOWAS could boast one project which was successfully on course for completion, Panafiel branch telecommunications, for which $50m had been obtained from the EC."[37] By 1990 remarkable progress had been made on the construction of the Trans-West African Highway with interconnecting roads providing landlocked states access to the sea. Road regulation, including the adoption of a common-road vehicle, third-party liability insurance, had been harmonized.

However, the organization's performance in other areas has been far from impressive. As Adebayo Adedeji rightly pointed out in 1990, many of the ECOWAS industries were either primary ones (oil in Nigeria, uranium in Niger, iron ore and bauxite in Guinea, phosphate in Togo), or large- and medium-scale manufacturing establishments, "largely foreign-owned, with generous fiscal privileges and rapid depreciation allowances, tax holidays, carry over losses and permission to repatriate profits."[38] What passed for industry comprised food, beverages, tobacco and textiles, which between them accounted for two-thirds of output in most of the states. For every practical purpose, manufacturing took the form of assembling consumer and capital goods with imported parts and without linkages with key sectors of the economy.

On the whole, ECOWAS has disappointed the initial hopes that it would erase the artificial divisions in the region and terminate underdevelopment occasioned by a century of European colonial rule and exploitation. Sustained competition from a multiplicity of intergovernmental associations and persistent shortage of funds have sapped the collective will of the body to implement the provisions of the Lagos treaty. Because the French-speaking partners belonged also to the Conseil de l'Entente and CEAO, both of which were restricted to only former French colonies, their attitude to ECOWAS tended to be lukewarm. This lack of enthusiasm posed serious problems, since they commanded 63 percent of the total membership of the organization. Of the sixteen constituent nations of the body in 1990, ten were French-speaking.

The CEAO prevented the implementation of trade liberalization in 1989 when it was due for progressive application in all the component territories. Ten years later the executive secretary of ECOWAS, Abass Bundu of Sierra Leone complained in his report that

> contrary to the provisions of Articles 13 and 17 of the ECOWAS Treaty prohibiting discriminatory practices within the community, members of the CEAO on October 24, 1989, adopted a new CEAO protocol (Protocol R) that envisages the levying of a Community Solidarity Tax of 1 per cent on the CIF or Mercurial value of all imports from third countries; non-CEAO ECOWAS Member States are not included in the exemption list.[39]

Another obstacle to the development and expansion of intra-community trade was the absence of a single monetary program. Speaking to a conference of business leaders in Lagos in 1990, Bundu noted that there were nine different national currencies, most of them nonconvertible. Nor were matters helped "by our local banks' entrenched practice of passing their international transactions through external multinational banking institutions."[40]

At the Abuja summit of July 1986, President Babangida of Nigeria warned that delays by member countries in paying their dues had "virtually crippled" the operations of the secretariat.[41] Only Nigeria, Togo, and Ivory Coast had made regular contributions without any record of accumulated arrears. At the Banjul summit held on May 1990 to mark the fifteenth anniversary of the signing of the ECOWAS treaty, the current chairman and host, President Dawda Jawara of Gambia, warned that "it will be difficult, if not impossible for individual members to deal with a united and strong Europe."[42]

So far the Southern African Development and Coordinating Conference (SADCC) appears to be the most promising of the substantial economic groupings in the continent. Composed of nine states—Angola, Botswana, Lesotho, Malawi, Mozambique, Swaziland, Tanzania, Zambia, and Zimbabwe—its principal aims are to reduce economic dependence on South Africa; to create an equitable regional integration; to mobilize resources to implement regional policies; and to secure international support for its economic projects.

Six areas of cooperation were identified: trade and communication, agriculture, energy, manpower, industrial development, and finance. Policy and problems were to be thrashed out at subpresidential and subministerial levels to avoid the kind of high-level confrontation that wrecked the EAC. The supreme organ of SADCC was the summit meeting held at least once a year. A Council of Ministers was empowered to appoint ad hoc committees of ministers for particular program areas. Commissions for sectoral areas and the executive secretary, though appointed at the summit meeting, were directly responsible to the council, whose decisions were nevertheless subject to the approval of the supreme organ. The chairmanship of the summit meeting was held by Botswana from 1979 to 1982; thereafter it became rotational.

Constituent nations of SADCC were at liberty to maintain other ties of cooperation outside the framework of the organization. Thus, Botswana, Lesotho, and Swaziland were also members of the South African Customs Union, of which the Republic of South Africa was a member as well. Members were also not obliged to participate in areas of cooperation within SADCC from which they derived no benefits. This flexibility has saved the organization from intraregional and interstate friction.

Unfavorable world prices for its products, inadequate foreign exchange, high debt-servicing rates, and South Africa's destabilization policy notwithstanding, SADCC partner states had achieved a progressive overall 4.5 percent per capita growth rate by 1989. Assessing the performance of the SADCC on the occasion of its tenth anniversary in 1990, Simba Makoni, who became executive secretary in 1984 after the death of Arthur Bolumeris, expressed satisfaction with developments. The foundation for integrated programs in all sectors had been laid. Technocrats, notably accountants, farmers, bankers, lawyers, and archaeologists, had been trained to implement the programs. "The transport system carries more goods for and from member states than from or through South Africa. The Tazara (Zambia/Tanzania), Beira (Zimbabwe/Mozambique), Benguela (Angola/Zambia) rail and road corridors [have] increased capacity while the Limpopo is soon to be opened."[43] Air, telecommunication, and satellite links now offered direct communication within SADCC instead of routing through Europe or South Africa. Makoni believed that Namibian independence, peace moves in Angola, Mozambique and South Africa, as well as improving relations between the United States and the Soviet Union, and signs of improved world markets offered opportunities for SADCC to focus on implementing many projects for which research had already been completed.

From the foregoing analysis we see that the aspirations of the regional economic groupings in Africa are quite compatible with the economic objectives of the OAU. This is also true of the aims of the African Development Bank (ADB) and the Economic Commission for Africa (ECA), which were not initiated by the independent African states. The ADB is an international institution consisting of fifty self-governing African nations known as the regional members and twenty-five non-African countries designated as nonregional members. As with the OAU, only independent African territories qualify for membership. The ADB began operations in 1966 with headquarters in Abidjan and branch offices in Addis Ababa, Harare, London, Nairobi, Rabat, and Yaoundé. The purpose of the bank is to further the economic development and social progress of its regional members individually and collectively. In discharging its functions, the ADB promotes the investment of public and private capital for development purposes.

The ADB also seeks to cooperate with national, subregional, and regional development institutions in Africa and with other international organizations like the African Development Fund (ADF). According to article 2 of its charter, the purpose of the ADF is to assist the bank to contribute more effectively to the social and economic development of bank members and to foster intra-African economic cooperation and commerce. Since member states of the ADB qualify automatically for admission to the ADF, the two bodies may be described as two international organizations in one, even though they were established by two separate treaties.

After ECA's initial resentment of OAU's efforts at economic cooperation, especially during the Robert Gardiner era, cooperation between the bodies began to grow by leaps and bounds. The amicable relations between the ECA, ADB, and OAU were well illustrated in May 1973 when the three international organizations jointly held the African ministerial conference at Abidjan on trade, development, and economic independence. In 1989 the OAU adopted the African Alternative Framework to Structural Adjustment Programs of Socioeconomic Recovery and Transformation prepared by the ECA.

1. A full text of Emperor Haile Selassie's Welcome Address is printed in *Addis Ababa Summit, 1963* (publication of the Ministry of Information, Addis Ababa, Ethiopia), and in *Journal of Modern African Studies* 1 (September 1963): 281–91.

2. Ibid.

3. *Addis Ababa Summit, 1963*, 47.

4. Domenico Mazzeo, ed., *African Regional Organizations* (Cambridge: Cambridge University Press, 1984), 55.

5. For provisions of the OAU Charter, see Appendix A.

6. *The Illustrated London News*, 15 June 1963, 919.

7. J. D. B. Miller, *Survey of Commonwealth Affairs. Problems of Expansion and Attrition, 1953–1969* (London: Oxford University Press, 1974), 116.

8. The resolutions of the Conference of Independent African States at Addis Ababa at which the OAU was formed are reprinted in V. Bakpetu Thompson, *Africa and Unity. The Evolution of Pan-Africanism* (London: Longman, 1969), 364–69.

9. Ibid., 365.

10. Ibid.

11. Michael Crowder, ed., *The Cambridge History of Africa*, vol. 8, *From c. 1940–1975* (Cambridge: Cambridge University Press), 129.

12. Thompson, *Africa and Unity*, 365.

13. Miller, *Survey of Commonwealth Affairs*, 261.

14. Cited in ibid., 121–22.

15. Ibid., 119.

16. For a text of the Lusaka Manifesto see J. Ayodele Langley, *Ideologies of Liberation in Black Africa, 1856–1970. Documents on Modern African Political Thought From Colonial Times to the Present* (London: Rex Collings, 1979), 782–88.

17. Ibid.

18. For details see Amilcar Cabral, *Unity and Struggle: Speeches and Writings* (London: Heinemann, 1980).

19. Crowder, *The Cambridge History of Africa*, 128.

20. *West Africa*, 12 February 1990, 212.

21. *Newswatch* 2, no. 14 (2 April 1990): 28; *West Africa*, 2 April 1990, 528.

22. *The Guardian* (Lagos), 11 February 1991, 5; *Newswatch* 13, no. 9 (25 February 1991): 19–21.

23. *West Africa*, 6 June 1988.

24. William Tordoff, *Government and Politics in Africa* (London: Macmillan, 1984).

25. See OAU Pan-African cultural manifesto, its Cultural Charter for Africa.

26. Julius Nyerere, "A United States of Africa," *Journal of Modern African Studies* 1 (1963): 89.

27. Cited in Tordoff, *Government and Politics in Africa*, 250.

28. Ali A. Mazrui and Michael Tidy, *Nationalism and New States in Africa* (Heinemann: London, 1984), 352–53.

29. *West Africa*, 6 June 1988, 1029.

30. Cited in Zdenek Cervenka, *The Unfinished Quest for Unity. Africa and the OAU* (London: Julian Friedmann, 1977), 65.

31. See OAU Charter, Article II Section 16.

32. *West Africa*, 11 June 1990, 980.

33. Mazrui and Tidy, *Nationalism and New States in Africa*, 332.

34. See ECOWAS treaty.

35. *West Africa*, 28 May 1990, 882.

36. Ibid., 883.

37. Ibid.

38. Ibid.

39. Extensive extracts from Abass Bundu's "An Overview of Developments in ECOWAS, 1989–90" are reproduced in ibid., 899–902.

40. *West Africa*, 28 May 1990, 884.

41. *West Africa*, 4 June 1990, 938.

42. Ibid.

43. *West Africa*, 9 April 1990, 580.

7

Trends, Problems, and Prospects

From its inception in the closing decades of the eighteenth century to the middle of the twentieth century, people of African origin in the Western Hemisphere as well as Europe actually led the movement articulating the component elements of Pan-African ideology and initiating Pan-African meetings and conventions. With the attainment of self-rule by African nations in the 1950s and the formation a decade later of the OAU, Africans abroad found themselves virtually excluded from Pan-African activities. The annual OAU summits, excepting that of Cairo (17–22 July 1964) attended by the black American civil rights leader Malcolm X, are restricted to "Africans at home." It looked as if the new rulers believed they had enough matters on the continent to tackle and that there was no need to add the wider problems of the black world. At the Cairo summit Malcolm X, who had been sent by the Organization of Afro-American Unity, pleaded:

> We, in America, are your lost brothers and sisters, and I am here only to remind you that our problems are your problems. As the African Americans "awaken" today, we find ourselves in a strange land that has rejected us, and, like the prodigal son, we are turning to our elder brothers for help. We pray our pleas will not fall upon deaf ears. . . .
>
> Your problems will never be fully solved until and unless ours are solved. You will never be fully respected until and unless we are also respected. You will never be recognized as free human beings until and unless we are also recognized and treated as human beings.[1]

A similar plea was made a decade later (1973) by Calvin Lockhart, the Bahamian film actor of *Cotton Comes to Harlem* fame. For many black exiles, he pointed out, Africa was and would remain an important ancestral base from which, from time to time, they could draw inspiration and strength. Today, he went on,

> one of the major psychological problems of the Black man outside the parent continent of Africa is that while he can always say "I have a *country*," he cannot really say "I have a *home*." This is very often his dilemma. He needs a home—an original point of reference. I think that all Black people in the world should have dual citizenship. . . African and that of whatever other country they now live in.[2]

What the proper relationship should be between the continental Africans and the African diaspora was again raised at the second World Black and African Festival of Arts and Culture held in Lagos (January–February 1977) by Murano Ron Karenga. A professor of Swahili at the University of California, San Diego, and leader of the African American contingent to the festival, Karenga urged Africans to look beyond the frontiers of the continent and see "other descendants of black peoples who by accident of history now find themselves in other parts of the world."[3] He suggested four ways by which Africans could do this: (1) setting up a Pan-African university with staff and students drawn exclusively from the black world; (2) granting black communities outside the continent observer and ex-officio status on every OAU committee; (3) providing an all-African peoples' congress (which should exist side by side with the OAU) to discuss common problems; and (4) revising the syllabi of African institutions of higher learning to include courses on the activities of Africans overseas. Karenga revealed that Swahili was introduced to the black American communities in the 1960s "when we recognized that African and black people [elsewhere] needed a tongue to bring them together in close mutual affinity."[4]

Admittedly, several African heads of state have expressed concern about the predicament of their kith and kin in exile. In 1970 Kwame Nkrumah observed that the black disapora lived in a condition of domestic colonialism and suffered class and color prejudice. "The core of the Black Revolution," he insisted, "is in Africa, and until Africa is united under a socialist government the black man throughout the world lacks a national home."[5] Julius Nyerere told the Dar es Salaam Pan-African gathering of 1974 that "as long as black people anywhere continue to be oppressed on the grounds of their color, black people everywhere will stand together in opposition to that oppression in the future as in the past."[6] Two years later General Olusegun Obasanjo of Nigeria, in an interview with the editor in chief of *Africa* magazine, explained that the nation's determination to give material and moral support to the Angolan and other liberation movements in southern Africa was a legitimate duty in the interest of the black man all over the world.[7] Seizing the opportunity of a state visit to the United States in October 1977, Obasanjo reiterated this commitment. "We in Nigeria," he told the American press, "are committed to the task of transforming our young republic into a nation which every black man and woman in the world will be proud of, into the focus and rallying point for all black aspirations."[8]

All the same, it would be misleading to think that the views of Obasanjo, Nkrumah, and Nyerere and one or two other African leaders represent the policy of the OAU on the matter. Until that body begins to treat the disabilities of the diaspora as its own problems by initiating concrete measures not necessarily on the lines of Karenga's proposals, it is reasonable to assume that our leaders are at present more or less concerned with the problems of the continent.

But as Ralph C. Uwechue, the Nigerian ex-diplomat and publicist, has frequently pointed out, there is an urgent need to develop and sustain a dynamic link between Africans and their descendants abroad for the mutual benefit of both parties. He rightly laments that the "Organisation of African Unity, with its interest riveted on African *states*, instead of African *peoples*, avoids the matter altogether."[9] We are reminded that these exiles number some 100 million, that is, approximately a quarter of Africa's present population. Among them are to be found, especially in the United States, the largest concentration of highly trained black labor in the world: scientists, scholars, soldiers, and professional men and women of all descriptions. Uwechue regrets that in what is politically, economically, and militarily Africa's greatest hour of need, "we allow to go to waste such a priceless potential."

However, it would be a mistake to suppose that all contemporary African American civil rights activists feel betrayed by Africa's nonchalant attitude toward their plight. Stokely Carmichael, who in the late 1960s lived in Guinea studying under Kwame Nkrumah, is convinced that the liberation of the black world from racism and economic exploitation depends on the existence of an independent, united, and powerful Africa. In his words: "What we must understand is that until Africa is free, the Black man all over the world is not free."[10] This is an extension of the "land base" argument, the argument that it is only the economic and political power of an independent African land base bent on emancipating the African people internationally that can pressure the United States to end the disabilities of black Americans. Carmichael appears to approve of the tactics of the OAU.

On the other hand, black American observers such as Tony Thomas[11] and Nathan Hare think that success in the struggle on American soil is a prerequisite for the liberation and unification of Africa itself. According to Hare,

> the struggle in America is paramount—not only because Black people (Africans) around the world look to us for leadership. It is also because America, the world's number one imperialist, is an octopus, with tentacles choking other nations all over the world. Though it may be desirable and useful to chop off a tentacle here and there, including its strongest and most destructive tentacles in our Africa, the most lasting and devastating damage will be done in the heart of the octopus.[12]

All this amounts to a shift from the pre-1950 attitude. Up till then, the Pan-African movement concerned itself with the problems of Africans and their descendants in different parts of the globe. But despite the adjective *Pan-African*, the movement during this period was not truly Pan-African in membership. For every practical purpose, Arab North Africa remained outside the pale of Pan-Africanism.

It was left to Nkrumah—and this brings us to a second new Pan-African trend—to reverse the situation. Not only did he marry an Egyptian, but in April 1958 he summoned in Accra a conference of the then eight sovereign African states, five of which are in North Africa.

Cooperation between black Africa and Arab North Africa has led to cooperation between the OAU and the Arab League. Thus in 1968, the OAU, a more respresentative African forum than the Casablanca powers, condemned Israel's refusal to comply with UN Security Council resolution 242 of 22 November 1967 demanding its withdrawal from Arab territories occupied during the 1967 war. With the renewal of hostilities in October 1973, no fewer than twenty black African nations broke off diplomatic relations with Israel. This solidarity was dramatized at the United Nations in 1974 in two controversial issues. One issue was the decision to invite Yassir Arafat, leader of the Palestine Liberation Organization, to the General Assembly. The other was the vote to suspend South Africa from the assembly for the rest of that year's session.

It is misleading to suggest, as some writers have done, that black Africa's increasing identification with the Arabs stems from the former's desire for cheap oil. Africans had already taken sides with the Arabs on the Palestine question before OPEC dramatically raised the price of crude oil in late 1973. By maintaining diplomatic, military, and commercial links with Portugal and South Africa, Israel consciously or unconsciously made itself an accomplice in the suppression of blacks in southern Africa. The explanation for Afro-Arab unity is probably the fact that the African continent and the Arab world are by no means mutually exclusive constructs. The majority of the Arabs, and the most dynamic ones for that matter, are no less African than the other inhabitants of the continent. The African-Arab states of Algeria, Egypt, Libya, Mauritania, Morocco, Sudan, and Tunisia account for three-quarters of the population of the entire Arab world.

African-Arab cooperation was at first essentially political, acquiring a significant economic dimension after the October 1973 war. Thus, at the Arab summit of November 1973 held in Algeria, the Arabs expressed their gratitude to the rest of Africa for supporting them in the conflict with Israel. They also emphasized the need for further economic cooperation and not surprisingly welcomed the formation of the OAU Committee of Seven for Arab-African Cooperation, set up after the October war. Each member country represented a geographical region of the continent. The member states and the regions they represented (in parentheses) are as follows: Tanzania (East Africa), Zaire and Cameroon (Central Africa), Mali (Sahel), Ghana (West Africa), and Sudan (North Africa). One of the major concerns of the committee was the greatly increased economic hardship facing the African countries as a result of the phenomenal rise in oil prices. Not unexpectedly, the Arab summit of November 1973 proposed an African-Arab conference to explore ways and means of developing Afro-Arab solidarity and aiding the African liberation movements.

Accordingly, in January 1974 a meeting was held in Cairo of the seven-member committee representing the OAU and ten oil-producing countries from the Arab world. The result was the establishment of a $200 million Arab Oil Facility Fund. The Cairo summit also agreed to quicken the launching of the Arab Economic Development Bank for Africa (AEDBA).

In addition to the AEDBA and the fund, African countries were enabled to use the facilities of other Arab financial institutions, including the Islamic Development Bank and the Kuwait Fund for Arab Economic Development (KFAED). In March 1975 the KFAED agreed to lend Tanzania $14.4 million to help in the expansion of textile factories.[13]

In response to an OAU appeal for greater Arab assistance, Saudi Arabia seized the opportunity of an Afro-Arab conference held in Cairo in January 1977 to pledge $1 billion in economic aid to black African countries.[14] Following the example of Saudi Arabia, Kuwait also promised $240 million over the next five years to finance African development projects.[15] In addition, Kuwait pledged to increase its contribution to the Arab Fund for African Economic Development by $20 million.[16]

The gradual change of mind on the part of the former critics of Nkrumah's approach to African unity may be taken as another remarkable trend in contemporary Pan-Africanism. Subsequent events, among them the unilateral declaration of independence by the white minority in Southern Rhodesia, the intrigues of foreign powers, and the intensification of apartheid, all helped to demonstrate Nkrumah's political alertness and foresight. In fact, barely two years after the historic inaugural summit of the OAU, Nyerere, easily the most formidable and articulate critic of Nkrumah, turned around and began to preach that functional cooperation could complicate the task of unification. To wait until local differences, distrust, and hostilities no longer existed, he now argued, would amount to waiting forever.[17] As each state developed, more and more barriers were raised; differences inherited from the colonial era hardened, fostering a national pride that could easily prevent the development of a pride in Africa.[18] Nor was it enough, Nyerere further warned,

> for African states to co-operate in dealing with particular problems. We must deliberately move to unity. To the fullest extent possible we must co-operate in our economic development, our trade, and our economic institutions. We must do this despite our separate sovereignties, although we have to recognize that there is a limit to the possibilities of economic integration without political union. When that point comes, then we shall either have to stand still, and thus damage our real hopes for Africa, or we shall have to take the plunge into a merger of our international sovereignties.[19]

When in November 1970 Sékou Touré screamed for military assistance to enable him to dislodge a Portuguese-backed attack on his native Guinea, it took the OAU two weeks to meet in Lagos to consider the situation. General Yakubu Gowon of Nigeria must have spoken on behalf of millions of Africans when he told the conference that "a situation cannot seriously be regarded as an emergency if it has to wait two weeks for a solution."[20] The growing disenchantment with functional cooperation found further outlet in the warm tributes paid to Nkrumah when he died in exile in Romania on 27 April 1972.

Meanwhile in Angola the MPLA continued to bear the brunt of the fighting against the Portuguese colonial regime. With the approach of self-government after the 1974 revolution in Portugal, the Western powers led by the United States tried to prevent the transfer of political power to the MPLA in the new nation. Money and arms were lavishly distributed to the rival nationalist movements UNITA and FNLA, which had previously been almost inactive. The MPLA was obliged to seek help from those who had supported it during the liberation struggle. Cuba and the Soviet Union responded to these requests. These two foreign countries were similarly invited to Ethiopia to assist in the defense of the country against external machinations.

These events drove Nyerere to declare in June 1978 that "it might be a good thing if the OAU was sufficiently united to establish an African High Command and a Pan-African Security Force."[21]

At last, the OAU as a body had awakened not only to the need for an African military alliance, but also for an African security council. At the summit held in Sierra Leone in July 1980, schemes for an OAU defense force and a political security council were discussed and referred back for further study. Proposed by Sierra Leone, the council, if eventually set up, may well be the thin edge of an African parliament. It may also be noted that plans for a Pan-African news agency with headquarters in Senegal are being realized.[22] Taken together, the developments just noted represent a change of direction from functional cooperation to political integration.

Another notable trend is the OAU's decision at the Monrovia summit of July 1979 to start paying serious attention to the economic and social problems of the continent. Hitherto the organization, as shown in the preceding chapter, appeared unwilling to tackle such problems although its purposes include the achievement of "a better life for the peoples of Africa." Hence the question frequently asked by African commentators: whether the OAU is a court of appeals for *all* Africans or just a trade union of incumbent heads of state and government. A Nigerian put the matter more cynically when he observed that Africans have never really had leaders but "rulers" whose achievement so far consists in

> taking our measurements. They know the height of our needs, the depth of our sorrows as well as the breadth of our vision. . . . They should discover the urgency of the re-entrenchment of man's right to live. Our being certainly calls for a transformation into being, not mere existence.[23]

It is this neglect that the Monrovia conference of 1979 sought to reverse. At this gathering, African leaders agreed to discuss economic problems at every annual meeting of the OAU. The organization's secretary-general was ordered to draw up each year, with the assistance of the ECA, appropriate specific measures at both regional and subregional levels. It was also decided that an emergency summit on economic matters be held.

Accordingly, a special economic summit met in Lagos in April 1980. The first such conference in the history of the OAU, it adopted the *Lagos Plan of Action for the Economic Development of Africa: 1980–2000*.[24] In the introduction to the plan, the African leaders lamented that the effect of unfulfilled promises of global development strategies had been more sharply felt in Africa than elsewhere. Instead of improving the economic condition of the continent, successive strategies had made it stagnate, thereby rendering it more suscep- tible than other regions to the economic and social crises plaguing the industrialized nations. Thus Africa is unable to point to any significant growth or satisfactory index of general well-being since the overthrow of colonialism. Faced with this situation and deter- mined to restructure the economic base of the continent, the con- ferees adopted a radical regional approach based on collective self- reliance. Among other things, the proposed measures cover food and agriculture, industry, human and natural resources, science and technology, trade and finance, environment and energy.

A perennial problem to which the OAU appears to have found a solution at last is the reconciliation of the principle of respect for fundamental human rights with that of noninterference in the domestic issues of constituent states. The tendency to subordi- nate the former to the latter had hitherto led the organization to ignore the persistent denial of civil liberties to millions of Africans outside the white-dominated regimes. How can the OAU continue to have the moral authority to condemn the excesses of apartheid South Africa or coordinate and harmonize in any meaningful manner the affairs of its members when it is forbidden to discuss internal factors? The well-known Tanzanian diplomat, Salim Ahmed Salim, who became OAU's secretary-general in July 1990, was making the same point when he declared it a misinterpreta- tion of the charter to assume that noninterference in the internal matters of member countries means indifference to the problems afflicting Africans. The thrust of the charter, he insisted,

> is to preserve the African dignity, to preserve the life of Africans and to promote Africa's welfare.
>   So when that welfare is affected, the Organisation must be involved in one form or another. . . . We cannot keep quiet when people are dying and fighting.[25]

Anticipating the sudden collapse of authoritarian socialist administrations in Eastern Europe and Germany, Salim argued that if African leaders failed to address such problems, they must not complain "when foreigners make it their business to meddle in the affairs of the continent."[26] In the wake of this unexpected development, which had been sparked off by the liberal reforms of President Gorbachev in his native Soviet Union, the Western powers warned African nations not to expect further assistance from them unless they embarked on a similar democratization of their political process. Zaire, Zambia, and Ivory Caost, where the incumbent governments had been in office for at least twenty-five years, were quick to respond positively to the Western threat. Overnight, multipartyism became the vogue.

It is significant that the twenty-sixth OAU summit held in Ethiopia from 9 to 11 July 1990 reviewed the situation of Africa in light of the rapid changes taking place in the world and the perceived threat of the continent being marginalized in the 1990s unless it responded adequately to pressures for change. As far as the attendees could judge, five factors were particularly significant in the present condition of the world: the socioeconomic and political revolutions in Eastern Europe; the movement from confrontation to cooperation in East-West relations; Western Europe's steady progress toward regional integration; the establishment of trading blocs; and advances in science and technology.

The conference ended with a declaration of "The Political and Socioeconomic Situation in Africa and the Fundamental Changes taking place in the World." The heads of state and government said:

> We are fully aware that in order to facilitate this process of socio-economic transformation and integration, it is necessary to promote popular participation of our peoples in the process of government and development. A political environment which guarantees human rights and the observance of the rule of law, would assure high standards of probity and accountability particularly on the part of those who hold public office. In addition, popular-based political processes would ensure the involvement of all, including in particular, women and youth in the development of efforts. We accordingly recommit ourselves to futher democratisation of our societies and to the consolidation of democratic institutions in our countries.[27]

With the new aid conditionality in mind, the summit reaffirmed "the right of our countries to determine, in all sovereignty, their system of democracy on the basis of their socio-cultural values, taking into account the realities of each of our countries and the necessity to ensure develpment and satisfy the basic needs of our peoples. We therefore assert that democracy and development go together and should be mutually reinforcing".[28] The African leaders agreed on steps to rationalize existing regional economic groupings to increase their effectiveness in promoting the eventual creation of an African economic community.

How to make OAU member states fulfill their financial obligations was another chronic problem tackled seriously by the summit. At the time of the meeting, the arrears of members' contributions were estimated at $50 million, the equivalent of funding OAU's budget for two years.[29] In the period before the conference, the staff of the Supreme Council for Sports in Africa had not been paid for ten months due to lack of funds. The Pan-African News Agency rarely received half of its expected annual contributions from member countries.

The summit accepted a number of recommendations made by a subcommittee appointed in February to examine the problem. It recommended that in addition to the application of article 97 of the OAU's financial regulations to defaulting states, other sanctions should be imposed. Article 97 bars such countries with arrears amounting to two years' contributions from voting in OAU meetings. The additional sanctions denied them the right to contribute to discussions during meetings or vie for posts. No concrete proposals were put forward to solve the debt problem. In 1978 Africa owed $48.3 billion in foreign debt, as against $250 billion in 1989.[30]

The trends noted above seem to suggest that, after twenty-five years of rhetoric and indecision, the OAU is beginning to discard its old role of a conservative association afraid of economic and political unity and bent on protecting the vested interests of even corrupt and despotic heads of state who forfeit their mandate to rule. OAU's new image is that of a revitalized organization determined to face internal problems and respond to challenges from abroad. The recent appointment as secretary-general of Tanzania's dynamic, experienced, and resourceful technocrat Salim Ahmed Salim is symbolic.

Two conferences held in the first half of 1991 seem to confirm the emerging new approach to Pan-African aspirations. The Kampala Forum assembled in Uganda between 19 and 22 May. Summoned jointly by General Olusegun Obasanjo's Africa Leadership Forum and the secretariats of the OAU and the ECA, the meeting was hosted by President Yoweri Museveni of Uganda and then chairman of the OAU. Also in attendance were the heads of state of Botswana, Mozambique, Sudan, and Zambia, as well as Julius Nyerere who chaired the plenary session. The purpose of the forum was to discuss and recommend a process that would provide a framework simultaneously for the security and democracy essential to the stability, economic integration, and transformation of African countries.

The conclusions and recommendations of the gathering are contained in the *Kampala Document for the Proposed Conference on Peace, Security, Stability, Development and Cooperation in Africa* (CPSSDCA) to be presented to the OAU summit that would take place two weeks later in Abuja, Nigeria's new federal capital. The *Kampala Document* set out general principles and policy measures as well as processes for implementation after due negotiations. The general principles are sufficiently important to merit reproduction in full as follows:

(i) Every African state is sovereign. Every state respects the rights inherent in the territorial integrity and political independence of African states.

(ii) The peace, security, stability and development of every African country is inseparably linked with those of other African countries. Consequently, instability in one African country reduces the stability of all other African countries.

(iii) The erosion of peace, security and stability in Africa is one of the major causes of its continuing crises and one of the principal impediments to the creation of a sound economy and effective intra- and inter-African cooperation.

(iv) The interdepencence of African states and the link between peace, security, stability and development demand a common African agenda based on a unity of purpose and a collective political consensus derived from a firm conviction that Africa cannot make any significant progress on any other front without creating collectively a lasting solution to its problems of peace, security and stability.

(v) A Conference on Peace, Security, Stability, Development and Cooperation in Africa (CPSSDCA) should be launched to provide a comprehensive framework for Africa's security and stability and should encompass measures for accelerated continental economic integration and socio-economic transformation. CPSSDCA shall encompass four major areas henceforth called calabashes: peace, security, stability, development and cooperation.

(vi) A new order embodied in the framework of CPSSDCA must be created in Africa through a declaration of binding principles and a commitment to ideological independence which will guide the conduct of governance in individual African states as well as the imperatives of intra-African and inter-African relations. The implementation of the new order should seek an active partnership and positive involvement of the rest of the world.

(vii) The fulfillment in good faith of all the CPSSDCA principles must be adhered to by all participating states within the context of any other obligations each participating member may have under international law.[31]

Many of the sentiments expressed in the *Kampala Document* found an echo in the proceedings of the twenty-seventh OAU summit held in Nigeria at the Abuja International Conference Centre from 3 to 7 June 1991. The attendance of thirty-four African heads of state, forty-eight foreign ministers, and three prime ministers is a record. Other prominent participants included Javier Pérez de Cuéllar and Chief Emeka Anyaoku, the secretaries-general of the United Nations and the Commonwealth respectively. Also present was Nelson Mandela.

While giving his progress report as the outgoing chairman of the OAU, President Museveni presented the *Kampala Document* for consideration for acceptance and implementation. The Ugandan leader regretted that four main problems had kept Africa backward. One was the lack of ideological independence, mainfested in the tendency of African leaders to concern themselves with East-West conflicts instead of tackling such issues as science, technology, and modern management skills, each of which was capable of accelerating material advancement. Another obstacle lay in reliance on production of raw materials whose prices were unstable and meagre. A third constraint stemmed from a crippling foreign debt amounting to over $270 billion. Small markets constituted the fourth hindrance. The way forward for Africa, Museveni declared, lay in economic and political unity. To reverse what he saw as the continent's growing marginalization, African states must look more within their continent. The world was moving toward larger, stronger, and more mutually beneficial economic entities. In some cases, presumably as in Europe, political union for the consolidation of economic integration was within reach in a matter of a few years.

Museveni felt that the organization's secretary-general should be allowed more political initiative, the better to be able to tackle problems confronting the region.

The new chairman of the OAU and head of the Nigerian delegation, General Ibrahim Babangida, spoke next. His address, titled "For a Greater and Self-reliant Africa," dealt with internal structural reforms, power and leadership, international indebtedness, South Africa, and regional security. During the preceding ten months no fewer than five African heads of state had been swept out of office: Muhammad Siyad Barre of Somalia, Hissène Habré of Chad, Samuel Doe of Liberia, Moussa Traoré of Mali, and Mengistu Mariam of Ethiopia. It was against this background that Babangida urged African leaders in the name of humanity and the traditional African ethos of familyhood to avoid civil wars, for they unleash unnecessary carnage, turn millions of citizens to unwilling refugees, and retard national development. He believed that

> the cost of maintaining structures of dictatorship, including the energy dissipated and the blood expended in warding off challenges to the monopoly of power all over our continent, makes it imperative that democracy is not only an attractive option but a rational inevitable one. . . . The free choice of leaders by the governed is the essence of representative government.[32]

Babangida demanded reparations from the international community to compensate for the triple tragedy of slavery, colonialism, and neocolonialism spanning some six hundred years. What Africans were seeking, he explained, was neither new nor extraordinary nor unjust. They were merely asking for the same treatment accorded other peoples in recent times, namely, "that the admission of wrong-doing must be accompanied by restitution." Consciously or unconsciously, the delegates made what may well be the first tentative movement away from the prevailing narrow continental Pan-Africanism toward the wider pre-1963 Pan-Africanism when Babangida added:

> On this issue, Africans have embarked on a journey of re-discovery and of solidarity with Africans in Diaspora; for we are linked as much by our history of exploitation as by a common future of hope. We therefore need to reach out to them because we share a common destiny.[33]

Coming from a leader speaking as the chairman of the OAU, the statement is significant. Whether the Arabs, whose trans-Saharan traffic in black people began before the notorious Atlantic slave trade, must also pay reparations and how this could affect Arab North Africa's loyalty to the OAU was glossed over. However, the reparations being demanded will only make sense if they are designed to help the beneficiaries achieve genuine self-reliance.[34]

Babangida advocated setting up an African defense fund that could be used to pay for peacekeeping operations in the continent. When established, the fund would be financed largely from contributions and donations by member states.

Clarence Makwetu, the leader of the PAC, spoke on behalf of liberation movements in South Africa. He presented a distressing report of the latest events in the republic, which he said had led to more deaths there in the preceding fifteen months than ever, before F. W. de Klerk announced the historic reforms. Makwetu maintained that apartheid cannot be reformed but must be uprooted in its entirety. He appealed to the OAU for continued support in the struggle for a nonracial society, and increased material assistance.

The highlight of the Abuju summit was the signing, by forty-eight of the fifty-one member nations of the OAU, of the long-awaited treaty establishing the African Economic Community (AEC). Proposals on economic cooperation had been tabled at many OAU meetings, among them the Algiers summit held in September 1968, as well as the Addis Ababa summits of August 1970, May 1973, and July 1977. And in May 1980 a special summit on economic matters adopted the Lagos Plan of Action, which aimed at establishing an African common market by the year 2000. The long delay in taking steps to implement such an important decision illustrates the conservative, hesitant, and nonchalant attitude of the outgoing generation of leaders to Pan-African aspirations. At the Abuja conference individual heads of state and government emphasized the need for a concerted approach to African economic problems. Individual nation-states were no longer able to look after their citizens effectively. Welcoming the launching of the AEC, Javier Pérez de Cuéllar disclosed that the United Nations had collaborated with the OAU Secretariat in finalizing the draft of the treaty.

The AEC treaty contains twenty-two chapters comprising 106 articles. Article 3 states the principles thus: equality and interdependence of member states; solidarity and collective self-reliance; interstate cooperation, harmonization of policies, and integration of programs; promotion of harmonious development of economic activities among member countries and the observance of the legal system of the Community. The other principles are the peaceful settlement of disputes; the protection of human rights in accordance wih the provisions of the African Charter on Human and Peoples' Rights; and accountability, economic justice, and popular participation in development.

The objectives of the AEC as set out in article 4 are:

• to promote economic, social, and cultural development and the integration of African economies in order to increase economic self-reliance and promote an endogenous and self-sustained development;

• to establish, on a continental scale, a framework for the development, mobilization, and utilization of the human and material resources of Africa in order to achieve a self-reliant development;

• to promote cooperation in all fields of human endeavor in order to raise the standard of living of African peoples, and maintain and enhance economic stability, foster close and peaceful relations among member states, and contribute to the economic progress, development and the economic integration of the continent; and

• to coordinate and harmonize policies among existing and future economic communities in order to foster the gradual establishment of the Community.

Among other measures, the AEC shall by stages ensure the strengthening of existing regional economic communities and the establishment of other communities where they do not exist; the adoption of a common trade policy vis-à-vis third states; the establishment and maintenance of a common external tariff; the establishment of a common market; the harmonization of environmental protection policies; and any other activity that member states may decide to undertake jointly with a view to attaining the objectives of the Community. By the terms of the treaty, the Community will be established gradually in six stages of variable duration over a transitional period not exceeding thirty-four years.

To carry the agreed aims into effect, the AEC treaty set up seven principal organizations similar to those of the European Economic

Community (1958). They are the Assembly of Heads of State and Government, the Council of Ministers, the Pan-African Parliament, the Economic and Social Commission, the Court of Justice, the General Secretariat, and specialized technical committees. Ultimate power rests with the assembly, which has the authority to determine the general policy and major guidelines of the Community and give directives, and coordinate and harmonize the scientific, technical, cultural, and social policies of member states. Only the assembly may appoint the secretary-general and refer any matter to the Court of Justice for advisory opinion.

The AEC is conceived as an economic association with a political content. Underlying the Community are a supranational principle and a commitment to liberal democracy, in sharp contrast to the functionalist and despotic tendencies of yesteryears. A continentally elected parliament is possible only in the context of a democratic culture within national boundaries.

At the end of the summit the African leaders issued a statement, "The Abuja Declaration on South Africa," reaffirming their support of sanctions until the Pretoria regime took concrete steps to remove all obstacles to negotiations, including the ongoing violence in black South African townships. The reference is to the feud between the ANC and Mangosuthu Buthelezi's Inkatha party, which enjoys the sympathy and support of the South African government.

As if in response to the warning of the Abuja declaration, the South African Parliament repealed, barely two weeks later, the Population Registration Act passed in 1950 and regarded as the remaining pillar of apartheid. By the act, all South Africans were classified from birth as either white, mixed-race, ethnic Asian, or black. Whether one could vote, own land, live or work in certain parts of the country, depended on the category to which one belonged. On this classification, up to four million black South Africans lost their homes to white farmers because the laws declared them illegal squatters in areas inhabited by their forefathers over the millennia. Many were separated from spouses classified as belonging to a different race. With the abrogation of the act, followed by attempts by de Klerk to end the quarrel between Inkatha and the ANC, apartheid now appears as good as dead. This is why General Babangida has summoned the OAU ad hoc Committee on South Africa to review the organization's stand on continued sanctions.

Finally, the OAU is to review its twenty-eight-year-old charter to incorporate the operations and laws of the AEC and adopt its clause of noninterference of member states to give the organization a legal authority to set up an African high command. Once the problem of apartheid is completely resolved, the indications are that the OAU will bend its energy toward the attainment of greater economic and political unification on the continent. The emerging image of the body as in the 1990s is that of an international association that has at last rediscovered its proper bearings and is determined to jettison its hiterto reactionary posture, which has become manifestly anachronistic and unrealistic. In several ways, the Abuja summit represents a turning point in the history of Pan-Africanism.

Despite the important decisions taken at the Abuja summit and the achievements recorded by the member states of the OAU individually and collectively since 1960, the year of independence, a quality London newspaper on 29 July 1991 portrayed Africa as a continent "engulfed by economic collapse, war, famine, AIDS and malaria which may bury hopes of freedom, peace and prosperity." The tendency of the Western media to ignore positive development in Africa, particularly black Africa, and to focus on shortcomings and calamities is not new. Thus, the influential, conservative *London Daily Telegraph* in a 28 January 1986 editorial declared that Uganda, "the one-time pearl of Africa, can fairly be described as having become a symbol of everything that has gone wrong in that continent over the past 20 years or so. Since independence it has experienced violence (with hundreds of thousands killed), poverty, misgovernment on an enormous scale, and terrible suffering. Steadily the pillars of government, of law and even economic life have been destroyed." Nigeria's secretary-general of the commonwealth, Chief Emeka Anyaoku, strongly objected to this tendency in a presentation of 9 April 1992 broadcast on a London television network and subsequently published by *West Africa* magazine.[35]

Chief Anyaoku spoke for every African, for the way Africa is projected in the foreign press does matter, especially in the postcold war era when the continent is competing with the emerging democracies of Eastern Europe for "aid which comes from the same basket and is therefore not inexhaustible." Like Edward Wilmot Blyden, the chief recalled how the ancient Greeks regarded the Romans and everyone else as the lesser breed. The Romans in their turn had a high opinion of themselves and their civilization in relation to the Britons, the Gauls, and other subject peoples. Anyaoku regretted that "where the prejudice of the Ancients stemmed largely from ignorance, that of our modern pundits stems in the main from a mixture of motives, not the least of which a reluctance to acknowledge that, for all its afflictions, independent Africa has some achievements to its credit and is working even in inauspicious circumstance to secure its future." The present problems notwithstanding, there were good grounds for Africa's hopes of freedom, peace, and prosperity.

In their craving for the sensational, lamented Anyaoku, Western journalists frequently overlooked the socioeconomic achievements of independent Africa. Upon a rather poor foundation bequeathed by the colonial authorities, self-governing states succeeded in raising the level of adult literacy from 20 to 48 percent within twenty-five years. The figures for Nigeria, Ghana, Tanzania, and Botswana were even more impressive during the same period. In Tanzania the number of *women* who could read and write rose from 18 to 88 percent. Advances recorded in public health were likewise ignored by Western media.

What was true of education and medicine also applied to economic growth before 1973 when the oil crisis appeared on the scene. By then, Malawi, Kenya, Lesotho, Ivory Coast, the Congo, and Gabon had achieved an annual growth rate of 4 percent. A few nations attained even higher heights; they included Nigeria (5.3 percent), Swaziland (5.8 percent), and Botswana (an astonishing 9.3 percent).

This phase of economic buoyancy proved short-lived for many African states. From the 1980s on, escalating prices of oil and manufactured goods reinforced by a continuous fall in the prices of primary "and, not least, mistaken policies in the past" wreaked havoc on the African economy, unleashing the present distress. The Lagos Plan of Action sought to abandon the "mistaken policies" by opting for collective self-reliance through regional economic groupings. Such groupings eventually emerged, notably ECOWAS, SADCC, and the Preferential Trade Area for Eastern, Central, and Southern African States (PTA), which was launched in 1981. The hope that these groups would serve as "building blocks for a pan-African common market" materialized at the Abuja summit where the African leaders signed a treaty establishing an African common market.

It pained Chief Anyaoku that Africa's endeavors to secure peace and prosperity were "often not adequately reflected in the international media, some of which occasionally imply that the continent might benefit from a new round of management from abroad".[36] Regardless of its apparent practical benefits colonial rule was bound to come to an end, making way for the Africans themselves to undertake the task of developing the continent on African terms. Hence, the overthrow of colonial domination and the present clamor for multiparty democracy in which there would be genuine popular participation and effective checks against abuse of power has occurred.

Since the conclusion of the Abuja summit, the movement toward political pluralism has been growing. In more than fifteen countries, among them Angola, Mozambique, Nigeria, Zambia, Sierra Leone, Togo, and Ivory Coast, multiparty politics have either been restored and elections held or preparations for the return to multiparty politics has been far advanced. The current democratic upsurge amounts to a clear break from the recent past.

Though Africans recognized, Anyaoku went on, the essential need for democratization in the interest of political stability and orderly socioeconomic development, they anticipated obstacles "especially in countries made up of different and long established ethnic groups." Their difficulties would be compounded "if they have to contend at the same time with such hostile external factors as having to service a crippling debt burden, earning less and less from exporting the commodities on which their economies depend; and having steadily worsening terms of external trade."[37] That was why, Chief Anyaoku explained, Africans

> are eager for non-African commentators, especially those in the Eurocentric world, to interpret and project Africa's circumstances with greater objectivity and less condescension and despondency than is generally the case. Africans ask for no favours in the reporting of their affairs . . . all that Africans ask is that their strengths and weaknesses should be viewed and interpreted with the same degree of realism and understanding as is applied to other peoples and regions of the world.[38]

1. George Breitman, ed., *Malcolm X Speaks. Selected Speeches and Statement* (New York, 1966), 73–75.

2. *Africa*, no. 7 (November 1973): 15.

3. *Sunday Times* (Lagos), 20 February 1977, 20.

4. Ibid.

5. Kwame Nkrumah, *Class Struggle in Africa* (London, 1970), 87–88.

6. For a full text of Nyerere's speech, see *Black Scholar* 5 (July–August 1974): 16–21.

7. An international business, economic, and political weekly, June 1976.

8. *Daily Times* (Lagos), 7 November 1977, 7.

9. *Africa*, no. 27 (November 1973): editorial. See also his editorial, *Africa*, no. 59 (July 1976).

10. *Africa*, no. 54 (February 1976): 78. See also Stokely Carmichael, "The Highest Political Expression of Black Power is Pan-Africanism," in *Black Poets and Prophets: The Theory, Practice and Esthetics of the Pan-Africanist Revolution*, ed. Woodie King and Earl Anthony (New York: New American Library, 1972).

11. Tony Thomas and Robert Allen, *Two Views on Pan-Africanism* (New York: Pathfinder Press, 1972), 14–21.

12. Nathan Hare, "Wherever We Are," *Black Scholar* (March 1971): 34–35.

13. Ali K. Bakri, "The Economic Factor in African Arab Relations," *A Current Bibliography on African Affairs* 9 (1976–1977): 218.

14. Zdenek Cervenka, *The Unfinished Quest for Unity. Africa and the OAU* (London: Julian Friedmann, 1977), 173.

15. Ibid.

16. Ibid.

17. Julius Nyerere, *Freedom and Socialism* (OUP), 247. See also Opoku Agyeman, "The Osagyefo, the Nwalimu and Pan-Africanism: A Study in the Growth of a Dynamic Concept," *Journal of Modern African Studies* 13 (1975): 672–75.

18. Julius Nyerere, "The Dilemma of the Pan-Africanist," in *Zambian Papers*, no. 2 (Manchester University Press, 1967), 4.

19. Ibid., 7.

20. *African Development*, May 1973, 29. See also *Daily Mail* (Freet OWA), 30 November 1970, 8.

21. *Daily Times* (Lagos), 19 June 1978, 7.

22. *West Africa*, 14 July 1980, 1271.

23. *Daily Times* (Lagos), 18 July 1979, 3.

24. Addis Ababa, 1985. For excerpts from the Lagos Plan of Action, see *West Africa*, 19 May 1980, 870–72, and 2 June 1980, 960–62.

25. *Guardian* (Lagos), 20 May 1990, 1–2.

26. Ibid., 2.

27. *West Africa*, 17 December 1990, 3041.

28. Ibid.

29. *West Africa*, 23 July 1990, 2146.

30. *Guardian* (Lagos), 21 July 1990, 9.

31. See the *Kampala Document*.

32. President Ibrahim Babangida's speech is printed in full in the *Daily Times* (Lagos), 10 June 1991, 34–35.

33. Ibid., 34.

34. The well-known Nigerian publisher and business tycoon Bashorun M.K.O. Abiola reinforced Babangida's contention by drawing attention to specific historical precedents. For extracts from Abiola's address on "Reparations: Progress Report and Future Prospects" delivered in London on 3 May 1992 see *West Africa*, 1–7 June 1992, 910–11.

35. *West Africa*, 27 April–3 May 1992, 718–19.

36. Ibid., 719

37. Ibid.

38. Ibid.

Appendix A

The Charter of the Organization of African Unity

We, the Heads of African States and Governments assembled in the City of Addis Ababa, Ethiopia;

CONVINCED that it is the inalienable right of all people to control their own destiny;

CONSCIOUS of the fact that freedom, equality, justice and dignity are essential objectives for the achievement of the legitimate aspirations of the African peoples;

CONSCIOUS of our responsibility to harness the natural and human resources of our continent for the total advancement of our peoples in spheres of human endeavour;

INSPIRED by a common determination to promote understanding among our peoples and co-operation among our States in response to the larger aspirations of our peoples for brotherhood and solidarity, in a larger unity transcending ethnic and national differences;

CONVINCED that, in order to translate this determination into a dynamic force in the cause of human progress, conditions for peace and security must be established and maintained;

DETERMINED to safeguard and consolidate the hard-won independence as well as the sovereignty and territorial integrity of our States, and to fight against neo-colonialism in all its forms;

DEDICATED to the general progress of Africa;

PERSUADED that the Charter of the United Nations and the Universal Declaration of Human Rights, to the principles of which we reaffirm our adherence, provide a solid foundation for peaceful and positive co-operation among states;

DESIROUS that all African States should henceforth unite so that the welfare and well-being of their peoples can be assured;

RESOLVED to reinforce the links between our states by establishing and strengthening common institutions;

HAVE agreed to the present Charter.

Establishment

ARTICLE I

1. The High Contracting Parties do by the present Charter establish an Organization to be known as the ORGANIZATION OF AFRICAN UNITY.
2. The Organization shall include the Continental African States, Madagascar and other Islands surrounding Africa.

Purposes

ARTICLE II

1. The Organization shall have the following purposes:
   a. to promote the unity and solidarity of the African States;
   b. to co-ordinate and intensify their co-operation and efforts to achieve a better life for the people of Africa;
   c. to defend their sovereignty, their territorial integrity and independence;
   d. to eradicate all forms of colonialism from Africa; and
   e. to promote international co-operation, having due regard to the Charter of the United Nations and the Universal Declaration of Human Rights.
2. To these ends, the Member States shall co-ordinate and harmonize their general policies, especially in the following fields:
   a. political and diplomatic co-operation;
   b. economic co-operation including transport and communications;
   c. educational and cultural co-operation;
   d. health, sanitation, and nutritional co-operation;
   e. scientific and technical co-operation; and
   f. co-operation for defence and security.

Principles

ARTICLE III

The Member States, in pursuit of the purposes stated in Article II, solemnly affirm and declare their adherence to the following principles:

1. the sovereign equality of all Member States;
2. non-interference in the internal affairs of States;
3. respect for the sovereignty and territorial integrity of each State and for its inalienable right to independent existence;
4. peaceful settlement of disputes by negotiation, mediation, conciliation or arbitration;
5. unreserved condemnation, in all its forms, of political assassination as well as of subversive activities on the part of neighbouring States or any other State;

6. absolute dedication to the total emancipation of the African territories which are still dependent;
7. affirmation of a policy of non-alignment with regard to all blocks.

Membership

ARTICLE IV

Each independent sovereign African State shall be entitled to become a Member of the Organization.

Rights and Duties of Member States

ARTICLE V

All Member States shall enjoy rights and have equal duties.

ARTICLE VI

The Member States pledge themselves to observe scrupulously the principles enumerated in Article III of the present Charter.

Institutions

ARTICLE VII

The Organization shall accomplish its purposes through the following principal institutions:
1. the Assembly of Heads of State and Government;
2. the Council of Ministers;
3. the General Secretariat;
4. the Commission of Mediation, Conciliation and Arbitration.

The Assembly of Heads of State and Government

ARTICLE VIII

The Assembly of Heads of State and Government shall be the supreme organ of the Organization. It shall, subject to the provisions of this Charter, discuss matters of common concern to Africa with a view to co-ordinating and harmonizing the general policy of the Organization. It may in addition review the structure, functions and acts of all the organs and any specialized agencies which may be created in accordance with the present Charter.

ARTICLE IX

The Assembly shall be composed of the Heads of State and Government or their duly accredited representatives and it shall meet at least once a year. At the request of any Member State and on approval by a two-thirds majority of the Member States, the Assembly shall meet in extraordinary session.

ARTICLE X
1. Each Member State shall have one vote.
2. All resolutions shall be determined by a two-thirds majority of the
    Members of the Organization.
3. Questions of procedure shall require a simple majority. Whether or not
    a question is one of the procedure shall be determined by a simple
    majority of all Member States of the Organization.
4. Two-thirds of the total membership of the Organization shall form a
    quorum at any meeting of the Assembly.

ARTICLE XI
The Assembly shall have the power to determine its own rules of procedure.

The Council of Ministers

ARTICLE XII
1. The Council of Ministers shall consist of Foreign Ministers or such other
    Ministers as are designated by the Governments of Member States.
2. The Council of Ministers shall meet at least twice a year. When re-
    quested by any Member State and approved by two-thirds of all Mem-
    ber States, it shall meet in extraordinary session.

ARTICLE XIII
1. The Council of Ministers shall be responsible to the Assembly of Heads
    of State and Government. It shall be entrusted with the responsibility
    of preparing conferences of the Assembly.
2. It shall take cognizance of any matter referred to it by the Assembly. It
    shall be entrusted with the implementation of the decisions of the
    Assembly of Heads of State and Government. It shall co-ordinate inter-
    African co-operation in accordance with the instructions of the Assem-
    bly and in conformity with Article II (2) of the present Charter.

ARTICLE XIV
1. Each Member State shall have one vote.
2. All resolutions shall be determined by a simple majority of the members
    of the Council of Ministers.
3. Two-thirds of the total membership of the Council of Ministers shall
    form a quorum for any meeting of the Council.

ARTICLE XV
The Council shall have the power to determine its own rules of procedure.

General Secretariat

ARTICLE XVI

There shall be an Administrative Secretary-General of the Organization, who shall be appointed by the Assembly of Heads of State and Government. The Administrative Secretary-General shall direct the affairs of the Secretariat.

ARTICLE XVII

There shall be one or more Assistant Secretaries-General of the Organization, who shall be appointed by the Assembly of Heads of State and Government.

ARTICLE XVIII

The functions and conditions of services of the Secretary-General, of the Assistant Secretaries-General and other employees of the Secretariat shall be governed by the provisions of this Charter and the regulations approved by the Assembly of Heads of State and Government.

1. In the performance of their duties the Administrative Secretary-General and the staff shall not seek or receive instructions from any government or from any other authority external to the Organization. They shall refrain from any action which might reflect on their position as international officials responsible to the Organization.
2. Each member of the Organization undertakes to respect the exclusive character of the responsibilities of the Administrative Secretary-General and the Staff and not to seek to influence them in the discharge of their responsibilities.

Commission of Mediation, Conciliation and Arbitration

ARTICLE XIX

Member States pledge to settle all disputes among themselves by peaceful means and, to this end, to decide to establish a Commission of Mediation, Conciliation and Arbitration, the composition of which and conditions of service shall be defined by a separate Protocol to be approved by the Assembly of Heads of State and Government. Said Protocol shall be regarded as forming an integral part of the present Charter.

Specialized Commissions

ARTICLE XX

The Assembly shall establish such Specialized Commissions as it may deem necessary, including the following:

1. Economic and Social Commission;

2. Educational and Cultural Commission;
3. Health, Sanitation and Nutrition Commission;
4. Defence Commission;
5. Scientific, Technical and Research Commission.

ARTICLE XXI

Each Specialized Commission referred to in Article XX shall be composed of the Ministers concerned or other Ministers or Plenipotentiaries designated by the Government of the Member States.

ARTICLE XXII

The functions of the Specialized Commissions shall be carried out in accordance with the provisions of the present Charter and of the regulations approved by the Council of Ministers.

The Budget

ARTICLE XXIII

The budget of the Organization prepared by the Administrative Secretary-General shall be approved by the Council of Ministers. The budget shall be provided by contributions from Member States in accordance with the scale of assessment of the United Nations; provided, however, that no Member State shall be assessed an amount exceeding twenty percent of the yearly regular budget of the Organization. The Member States agree to pay their respective contribution regularly.

Signature and Ratification of Charter

ARTICLE XXIV

1. This Charter shall be open for signature to all independent sovereign African States and shall be ratified by the signatory States in accordance with their respective constitutional processes.
2. The original instrument, done if possible in African languages, in English and French, all texts being equally authentic, shall be deposited with the Government of Ethiopia which shall transit certified copies thereof to all independent sovereign African States.
3. Instruments of ratification shall be deposited with the Government of Ethiopia, which shall notify all signatories of each such deposit.

Entry into Force

ARTICLE XXV

This Charter shall enter into force immediately upon receipt by the Government of Ethiopia of the instruments of ratification from two-thirds of the signatory States.

Registration of the Charter

ARTICLE XXVI

This Charter shall, after due ratification, be registered with the Secretariat of the United Nations through the Government of Ethiopia in conformity with Article 102 of the Charter of the United Nations.

Interpretation of the Charter

ARTICLE XXVII

Any question which may arise concerning the interpretation of this Charter shall be decided by a vote of two-thirds of the Assembly of Heads of State and Government of the Organization.

Adhesion and Accession

1. Any independent sovereign African State may at any time notify the Administrative Secretary-General of its intention to adhere or accede to this Charter.
2. The Administrative Secretary-General shall, on receipt of such notification, communicate a copy of it to all the Member States. Admission shall be decided by a simple majority of the Member States. The decision of each Member State shall be transmitted to the Administrative Secretary-General, who shall, upon receipt of the required number of votes, communicate the decision to the State concerned.

Miscellaneous

ARTICLE XXIX

The working languages of the Organization and all its institutions shall be, if possible, African languages, (or, if not, then) English and French.

ARTICLE XXX

The Administrative Secretary-General may accept on behalf of the Organization gifts, bequests and other donations made to the Organization, provided that this is approved by the Council of Ministers.

ARTICLE XXXI

The Council of Ministers shall decide on the privileges and immunities to be accorded to the personnel of the Secretariat in the respective territories of the Member States.

Cessation of Membership

ARTICLE XXXII

Any State which desires to renounce its membership shall forward a written notification to the Administrative Secretary-General. At the end of one year from the date of such notification, if not withdrawn, the Charter shall cease to apply with respect to the renouncing State, which shall thereby cease to belong to the Organization.

Amendment of the Charter

ARTICLE XXXIII

This Charter may be amended or revised if any Member State makes a written request to the Administrative Secretary-General to this effect; provided, however, that the proposed amendment is not submitted to the Assembly for consideration until all the Member States have been duly notified of it and a period of one year has elapsed.

Such an amendment shall not be effective unless approved by at least two-thirds of all the Member States.

IN FAITH WHEREOF, We, the Heads of African States and Governments have signed this Charter.

Done in the City of Addis Ababa, Ethiopia, this 25th day of May, 1963.

Algeria	*President Ben Bella*
Burundi	*King Mwambutsa*
Cameroon	*President Ahmadou Ahidjo*
Central African Republic	*President David Dacko*
Chad	*President François Tombalbaye*
Congo (Brazzaville)	*President Fulbert Youlou*
Congo (Kinshasa)	*President Joseph Kasavubu*
Dahomey	*President Hubert Maga*
Ethiopia	*Emperor Haile Selassie*
Gabon	*President Léon M'ba*
Ghana	*President Kwame Nkrumah*
Guinea	*President Sékou Touré*
Ivory Coast	*President Félix Houphouët-Boigny*
Liberia	*President William V. S. Tubman*
Libya	*King Idris I*
Malagasy Republic	*President Philibert Tsiranana*
Mali	*President Modibo Keita*
Mauritania	*President Makhtar Ould Daddah*
Niger	*President Hamani Diori*
Nigeria	*Prime Minister Alhaji Sir Abubakar Tafawa Balewa*
Rwanda	*Foreign Minister Callixte Habamenshi*
Senegal	*President Léopold Senghor*
Sierra Leone	*Prime Minister Sir Milton Margai*
Somalia	*President Abdullah Osman*
Sudan	*President Ibrahim Abboud*

Tanganyika	*President Julius Nyerere*
Tunisia	*President Habib Bourguiba*
Uganda	*Prime Minister Milton Obote*
United Arab Republic	*President Gamal Abdel Nasser*
Upper Volta	*President Maurice Yaméogo*

Appendix B

Organization of African Unity

*Declaration of the Assembly of Heads of State and Government
of the Organization of African Unity
on the Political and Socio-economic Situation in Africa
and the Fundamental Changes Taking Place in the World*

11 July 1990   Addis Ababa

1.   We, the Heads of State and Government of the Organization of African Unity, meeting at the Twenty-sixth Ordinary Session of our Assembly in Addis Ababa, Ethiopa from 9–11 July 1990, have undertaken a critical review of the political, social and economic situation of our Continent in the light of the rapid changes taking place in the world and their impact on Africa as presented in the *Report of the Secretary General on the fundamental changes taking place in the world and their implications for Africa: Proposals for an African Response.*

2.   In particular, we have noted the changing East-West relations from confrontation to cooperation, the socio-economic and political changes in Eastern Europe, the steady move towards political and monetary union of Western Europe, the increasing global tendency towards regional integration and the establishment of trading and economic blocs as well as the advances in science and technology. These we found constitute major factors which should guide Africa's collective thinking about the challenges and options before her in the 1990s and beyond in view of the real threat of marginalisation of our Continent.

3.   We noted with satisfaction, the achievements of Africa in the struggle for the decolonization of the Continent and in the fight against racism and apartheid, as well as the positive role played by the OAU in this respect. The independence of Namibia has pushed further Africa's frontiers of freedom.

4.   We took note of the measures taken by Mr. de Klerk which provide

ground for optimism. We caution, however, that these changes fall far short of our common objective of totally dismantling apartheid. Unless and until the racist minority Government is irreversibly committed to the eradication of this anachronistic system, the International Community must continue to exert all forms of pressure including, in particular, economic sanctions against South Africa. This, our collective view, is also the demand of the National Liberation Movements of that country. We wish at the same time to reaffirm our solidarity with the oppressed people of South Africa and to assure them of our undivided support at this crucial phase in their struggle. At the same time, we urge them to close their ranks and unite their forces.

5.   The socio-economic situation in our Continent remains precarious today despite the many efforts made by our countries, individually and collectively. At our Second Extra-Ordinary Assembly in Lagos, Nigeria, in April 1980, we adopted the *Lagos Plan of Action* for the Economic Development of Africa up to the Year 2000 and the *Final Act of Lagos*. At the Twenty-first Ordinary Session of our Assembly held here in Addis Ababa in July 1985, we also adopted the *Africa's Priority Programme for Economic Recovery 1986–1990*. Equally, in the face of the excruciating external debt burden, we convened the Third Extra-Ordinary Session of our Assembly and adopted the *African Common Position on Africa's External Debt Crisis*. In all these endeavours, we were guided by the principle of collective self-reliance and self-sustaining development.

6.   These represented our collective attempt to institute measures to arrest and reverse the steady decline in Africa's economic performance. Despite these attempts and strong political commitment to them, it has not so far been possible to achieve our objective of laying a firm foundation for self-sustained development of our countries. On the contrary, throughout the decade of the 1980s most of our productive and infrastructural facilities continued to deteriorate. The per-capita incomes of our peoples fell drastically and so did the volumes of our exports as well as imports. There has been sharp decline in the quality of life in our countries as spending on public health, housing and education and other social services had to be severely curtailed. Food production has also fallen in proportion to the expanding population. All this contrasted sharply with the alarming rise in Africa's external debt stock which shot up from about 50 billion US Dollars in 1980 to about 257 billion US Dollars by the end of 1989. As a result of this combination of acute economic problems and external indebtedness, the number of African Member States classified as least developed rose from 21 to 28 during the same period.

7.   Our countries have made serious efforts to cope with the most adverse consequences of this difficult economic situation. Most of our countries

have entered into structured adjustment programmes with the international financial and monetary institutions—mostly at heavy political and social costs. But we realize that these are short term measures and are by themselves insufficient to completely restore our economies to sound footing and lay firm foundation for future growth. We are very much concerned that, in addition to these problems, there is an increasing tendency to impose conditionalities of political nature for assistance to Africa.

8. We reaffirm that Africa's development is the responsibility of our governments and peoples. We are now more than before determined to lay solid foundation for self-reliant, human-centered and sustainable development on the basis of social justice and collective self-reliance so as to achieve accelerated structural transformation of our economies. Within this context we are determined to work assiduously towards economic integration through regional cooperation. We are also determined to take urgent measures to rationalize the existing economic groupings in our Continent in order to increase their effectiveness in promoting economic integration and establishing an African Economic Community.

9. These are objectives we set for ourselves in Lagos in 1980. We reaffirm their continued validity as well as the fundamental principles of the Lagos Plan of Action and Africa's Priority Programme for Economic Recovery, including the sectoral priorities contained in them, in particular, the urgent need to attain self-sufficiency in food production, to promote science and technology for development and to establish a viable industrial base on the Continent. In this context, we commit oursleves to the pursuit of sound population and environmental policies conducive to economic growth and development of our Continent.

10. We are fully aware that in order to facilitate this process of socio-economic transformation and integration, it is necessary to promote popular participation of our peoples in the processes of government and development. A political environment which guarantees human rights and the observance of the rule of law would assure high standards of probity and accountability particularly on the part of those who hold public office. In addition, popular-based political processes would ensure the involvement of all, including in particular women and youth in the development efforts. We accordingly recommit oursleves to the further democratisation of our societies and to the consolidation of democratic institutions in our countries. We reaffirm the right of our countries to determine, in all sovereignty, their system of democracy on the basis of their socio-cultural values, taking into account the realities of each of our countries and the necessity to ensure development and satisfy the basic needs of our peoples.

We therefore assert that democracy and development should go together and should be mutually reinforcing.

11.   We realize at the same time that the possibilities of achieving the objectives we have set will be constrained as long as an atmosphere of lasting peace and stability does not prevail in Africa. We therefore renew our determination to work together towards the peaceful and speedy resolution of all the conflicts on our Continent. The resolution of conflicts will be conducive to the creation of peace and stability in the Continent and will also have the effect of reducing expenditures on defence and security thus releasing additional resources for socio-economic development. We are equally determined to make renewed efforts to eradicate the root causes of the refugee problem. It is only through the creation of stable conditions that Africa can fully harness its human and material resources and direct them to development.

12.   At this crucial juncture when our Continent is emerging with difficulty from a phase in its history that focussed mainly on political liberation and nation building, and is about to embark on a new era laying greater emphasis on economic development, we need to strengthen the Organization of African Unity so that it may also become a viable instrument in the service of Africa's economic development and integration. Consistent with this goal, we rededicate ourselves to the principles and objectives enshrined in its Charter, to our faith in ourselves and to our Continent, with greater determination to be masters of our destiny. In this spirit, we reaffirm our commitment to revive the ideals of Pan-Africanism and commit ourselves, individually and collectively, on behalf of our governments and peoples to maintain and strengthen our unity and solidarity and to pool our resources and wisdom in order to face the challenges of the decade of the 1990s and beyond, change the bleak socio-economic prospects of our continent and guarantee a better life for all peoples and future generations yet unborn. These objectives are well within our capabilities. We, therefore, pledge to apply ourselves fully to the achievement of these objectives.

13.   The achievement of these objectives will also require international cooperation and solidarity as well as fundamental changes in the international economic system. The continuing plummeting of the prices of Africa's commodities, skyrocketing of prices of manufactured goods and the growing burden of external debt and the attendant reverse flow of resources constitute external factors which severely constrain our efforts for economic recovery. The developed countries bear a major responsibility for the transformation of the present inequitable international system. On our part, we will continue to strive for the establishment of a just and equitable inter-

national economic system. In this connection, a revitalised Non-Aligned Movement can play a decisive role.

14.   We recommit ourselves to strengthen the South-South Cooperation and to play a lead role in this regard. We also wish to express our readiness to work in concert with other countries and regions of the developing world to reactivate North-South dialogue and cooperation. We do believe that an increasingly interdependent world calls for greater international solidarity and that peace and prosperity should be shared for the common good of humanity.

15.   We request the Secretary General to monitor the implementation of this declaration and to take all necessary actions in this respect in collaboration with the United Nations Economic Commission for Africa, African Development Bank and other African and International Institutions. We also request him to ensure the widest possible dissemination of this declaration and to sensitize African public opinion and the International Community on its content.

Bibliography

Primary Material

Manuscript

1. *Bridgeman Collection* (in owner's possession). The papers contain some correspondence, but thin, from the West African Students' Union and Marcus Garvey; newspaper cuttings on the Italo-Ethiopian crisis; some publications of the West African Students' Union and Marcus Garvey's Universal Negro Improvement Association and African Communities League. The papers also contain some early numbers of *The Negro Worker* edited by George Padmore and a substantial amount of material on the League Against Imperialism.

2. *C.O. 554/49* (Public Record Office, London). Contains material relating to the National Congress of British West Africa.

3. *C.O. 554/50* (Public Record Office, London). Contains material relating to the National Congress of British West Africa.

4. *C.O. 554/51* (Public Record Office, London). Contains material relating to the National Congress of British West Africa.

5. *Gold Coast ARPS Papers* (Cape Coast Archives, Ghana). They are probably the richest single source on the 1945 Manchester Pan-African Conference and the activities of the West African National Secretariat. They also contain some correspondence from the West African Students' Union, the Negro Welfare Association, the International African Service Bureau and the Pan-African Federation. The Sekyi Papers form an integral part of the Gold Coast ARPS Papers.

6. *F.O. 403/363* (Public Record Office, London). Memorandum by Dr. Blyden on the Liberian situation communicated to the British Foreign Office on 24 May 1905.

7. *Morel Papers* (London School of Economics). Miscellaneous correspondence F.9/B. They include a few letters from Edward W. Blyden.

8. *Moorland Collection* (Howard University Library, Washington D.C.) contains some publications of the UNIA; letters of Booker T. Washington relating to Pan-Africanism; material on DuBois's Pan-African interests; and a copy of R. N. Duchein's *The Pan-African Manifesto*.

9. *Booker T. Washington Papers* (Library of Congress, Washington D.C.) contains several letters from Henry Sylvester Williams in connection with the activities of the African Association (London) and the Pan-African Conference of 1900. It also contains a few letters from Marcus Garvey concerning the UNIA.

10. *Wallace Johnson Collection* (Institute of African Studies, Legon, Ghana). The collection is in the form of a thirty-page typescript. It comprises, in the main, some details about the personal life of Wallace Johnson; Wallace Johnson's comments—surprisingly sketchy—on the NCBWA, the Negro Welfare Association (London), the PAF, as well as a substantial amount of material on the West African Youth League and the attitude of the league to the Italo-Ethiopian crisis.

11. *Schomburg Collection* (New York City Library). Contains quite a number of letters from Mojola Agbebi as well as his *Inaugural Sermon* of 21 December 1902; John Edward Bruce Papers; Alexander Crummell Papers; an almost complete file of the IASB's *International African Opinion*; Mbonu Ojike's *My Africa*; some publications and tracts of Benito Sylvain; *The Crisis*, organ of the NAACP; *Without Bitterness: Western Nations in Post-War Africa* by A. A. Nwafor Orizu; Alexander Walter's autobiography, *My Life and Work*, as well as many tracts by Edward W. Blyden including *Liberia's Offering: Being Addresses, Sermons, etc.*

Printed Material

12. *The African Repository* (American Colonization Society). Vols. 1–68 (March 1825–January 1892). Washington, D.C. (Fourth Bay College, University of Sierra Leone). Contains most of the tracts of Edward W. Byden.

13. *Publications of the Abyssinia Association* (Bridgeman Collection)
    (a) *Nemesis*. London, 1939.
    (b) *Memorandum on the Policy of His Majesty's Government Toward Ethiopia*. London, 1941.

14. *British Official Publications* (London University Library, Senate House)

(a) *West Indian Royal Commission 1938–1939: Recommendations*. Cmd. 617. 1940.

(b) *Statement of Policy on Colonial Development and Welfare*. Cmd. 6175. 1940.

(c) *West Indian Royal Commission Report*. Cmd. 6607. 1945.

(d) *Report of the Commission on Higher Education in the Colonies*. Cmd. 6647. 1945.

(e) *The Colonial Empire (1939–1947)*. Cmd. 7167. 1947.

(f) *Parliamentary Debates*, 1929–1948.

15. *Publications of the International African Service Bureau*

(a) *International African Opinion* (George Padmore Research Library, Accra). Vo. 1, no. 1 (July 1938)–vol. 1, no. 5 (November 1938).

(b) Pamphlets (George Padmore Research Library, Accra; British Museum).

    (i) Lewis, W. Arthur. *The West Indies Today*. London, 1938.

    (ii) Padmore, George. *Hands Off the Protectorates*. London, 1938.

    (iii) Cunard, N., and G. Padmore. *The White Man's Duty*. London, 1943.

    (iv) Kenyatta, Jomo. *Kenya, Land of Conflict*. London, 1945.

    (v) Williams, Eric. *The Negro in the Caribbean*. London, 1945.

    (vi) Michelet, R. *African Empires and Civilizations*. London, 1945.

    (vii) Padmore, George, ed. *The Voice of Coloured Labour*. London, 1945.

    (viii) Cunard, N., and G. Padmore. *The White Man's Duty* enlarged ed. London, 1945.

(c) *Colonial Parliamentary Bulletin* (British Museum). Vol. 1, no. 3 (March–April 1946)–vol. 3, no. 6 (September 1948).

16. *Publications of the League Against Imperialism* (Bridgeman Collection)

(a) *The Anti-Imperialist Review*. Vol. 1, no. 1 (September–October 1931).

(b) *Abyssinia*. London, 1935.

17. *Publications of the League of Coloured Peoples*. Mostly in the British Museum. Copies of many of them as well as useful newspaper cuttings are also in the possession of Dr. Christine Moody.

(a) *The Keys* (July 1933–September 1939). Continued as *News Notes*, no. 1 (October 1939). Continued as *L.C.P. Letter*, no. 2 (November 1939)–no. 6 (March 1940). Continued as *News Letter*, no. 7 (April 1940)–no. 104 (December 1948).

(b) Buxton, Charles R. *Impressions of Liberia, Nov. 1934: A Report to the League of Coloured Peoples*. London: League of Coloured Peoples Publication, n.d.

    (c)   Annual Reports
        (i) *Seventh Annual Report*, March 1938; previous annual reports were printed in *The Keys*.
       (ii) *Eighth Annual Report*, March 1939.
      (iii) *Ninth Annual Report*, March 1940.
      (iv) *Tenth Annual Report*, April 1941.
       (v) *Eleventh Annual Report*, March 1942.
      (vi) *Twelfth Annual Report*, March 1943.
     (vii) *Thirteenth Annual Report*, March 1944.
    (viii) *Fourteenth Annual Report*, March 1945.
      (ix) *Fifteenth Annual Report*, March 1946
    (d)   Papers and Correspondence Relating to Appointments in the Colonial Service. Published in *The Keys*.

18.   *Publications of the League of Nations* (British Museum)
    (a)   *International Commission of Enquiry in Liberia* (official no. C. 658 M. 272. 1930 VI). Geneva, 1930.
    (b)   *Dispute Between Ethiopa and Italy, Request by the Ethiopian Government* (official no. C. 230 [1] M. 114 [1]. 1935 VII). Geneva, 1935.
    (c)   *Dispute Between Ethiopia and Italy. Memorandum by the Italian Government on the Situation in Ethiopia* (official no. C. 340. 171 1935 VII). Geneva, 1935.

19.   *Publication of the National Association for the Advancement of Coloured People* (George Padmore Research Library, Accra) *The Crisis*, 1918–1934 (microfilm).

20.   *Publication of the Pan-African Association*. London (British Museum) *The Pan-African*. Vol. 1, no. 1 (October 1901).

21.   *Publications of the Pan-African Federation*. The publications are widely dispersed in Cape Coast Archives, Ghana; George Padmore Research Library, Accra; Rhodes House Library, Oxford; the National Library of Scotland, Edinburgh; and the British Museum. The largest concentrations are in the George Padmore Research Library, Accra, and the British Museum.
    (a)   *Pan-African Congress: Declaration and Resolutions Adopted at the Fifth Pan-African Congress at Manchester, England*, October 13–21, 1949.
    (b)   Open Letter to Clement Attlee (British Prime Minister), September 1945. Printed as a leaflet.
    (c)   *Pan-Africa*. Vol. 1, no. 1 (January 1947); vol. 11, no. 4 (April 1948).
    (d)   Padmore, George, ed. *Colonial and . . . Coloured Unity: A Programme of Action*. Manchester: Pan-African Service, 1947.

22.   *Publications of the Universal Negro Improvement Association and African Communities League*

(a) *Petition of the Universal Negro Improvement Association and African Communities League to the League of Nations.* New York, 1922.

(b) *Renewal of Petition of the Negro Universal Improvement Association and African Communities League to the League of Nations.* London, 1928.

(c) "The Case of the Negro for International Racial Adjustment, Before the English People." Speech delivered by Marcus Garvey, Royal Albert Hall, London, England, on Wednesday, 6 June 1928. London: Poets' and Painters' Press, 1968.

23. *Publication of the West African National Secretariat.* Cape Coast Archives, Ghana.
   The New African. Vol. 1, no. 1 (March 1946); vol. 1, no. 3 (May 1946).

24. *Publications of the West African Students' Union* (British Museum)
   (a) *Wasu* (WASU Magazine). No. 1 (March 1926); vol. 12, no. 3 (1947).
   (b) *United West Africa (or Africa) at the Bar of the Family of Nations.* London, 1927. (Also available at National Library of Scotland, Edinburgh).
   (c) *The Truth About Aggrey House: An Exposure of the Government Plan for the Control of African Students in Great Britain.* London, 1934.
   (d) Annual Reports (published in *Wasu*):
      (i) *The Annual Report up to the Year Ended 31st December 1938.*
      (ii) *The Annual Report up to the Year Ended 31st December 1939.*
      (iii) *The Annual Report and Audited Accounts for the Year Ended 31st December 1940.*
      (iv) *W.A.S.U. Annual Report and Audited Accounts for the Year Ended 31st December 1941.*
      (v) *W.A.S.U. Annual Report and Audited Accounts for the Year Ended 31st December 1942.*
      (vi) *W.A.S.U. Annual Report and Audited Accounts for the Year Ended 31st December 1943.*

25. *Publications of the Government of Ethiopia*
   (a) *Second Conference of Independent African States*, Addis Ababa, 14–26 June 1960. Addis Ababa, 1960.
   (b) *The Fourth PAFMECA Conference Held in Addis Ababa February 2nd to 10th 1962* (speeches and statements). Addis Ababa, n.d.
   (c) *Addis Ababa Summit*, 1963.
   (d) *OAU Perspective. Third Regular Assembly.* Addis Ababa, 1966.

26. *Publications of the Press and Information Division of the General Secretariat, Organization of African Unity*
   (a) *OAU Charter and Rules of Procedure.* Addis Ababa, 1982.
   (b) *OAU Convention Governing the Specific Aspects of Refugee Problems in Africa.* Addis Ababa, 1983.

(c) *OAU: Short History*. Addis Ababa, 1983.
(d) *African Charter on Human Rights and Peoples' Rights* (adopted by the Eighteenth OAU Summit, Nairobi, June 1981).
(e) *Cultural Charter for Africa* (Port Louis, 1986). Addis Ababa, n.d.
(f) *The Lagos Plan of Action*. Addis Ababa, 1985.
(g) *Twenty-fifth Anniversary OAU*. Addis Ababa, 1988.
(h) *Declaration of the Assembly of Heads of State and Government of the Organization of African Unity on the Political and Socio-Economic Situation in Africa and the Fundamental Changes Taking Place in the World*. Addis Ababa, July 1990.
(i) Statement by His Excellency Yoweri Kaguta Museveni, President of the Republic of Uganda and Current Chairman of the Organization of African Unity at Its Twenty-seventh Summit, Abuja, Nigeria.
(j) *Treaty Establishing the African Economic Community*. June 1991.
(k) *The Kampala Document for Proposed Conference on Peace, Security, Stability, Development and Cooperation in Africa* (Jointly produced by the OAU Secretariat, United Nations Economic Commission for Africa, and Africa Leadership Forum). Kampala, 1991.
(l) *Report of the Secretary-General on the Activities of the Regional and Sub-Regional Offices Covering the Period July 1990 to Febraury 1991*. CM/1633 (LIII), part III. Addis Ababa, February 1991.
(m) *Report of the Secretary-General on the Activities of the OAU Regional Offices Covering the Period February to May 1991*. CM/1660 (LIV), part III. Abuja, Nigeria, June 1991.

27. Articles

Azikiwe, Nnamdi. "Realities of African Unity." *African Forum* 1 (Summer 1965).
Du Bois, W. E. B. "Pan-Africanism." *Voices of Africa*, June 1961.
Greg, W. R. "Dr. Arnold." *Westminster Review* 39 (January 1843).
Kenyatta, Jomo. "African Socialism and African Unity." *African Forum* 1 (Summer 1965).
Logan, Rayford. "The Historical Aspects of Pan-Africanism: A Personal Chronicle." *African Forum* 1 (Summer 1965).
Nyerere, Julius. "The Nature and Requirements of African Unity." *African Forum* 1 (Summer 1965).
———. "A United States of Africa." *The Journal of Modern African Studies* 1 (1963).
Olympio, Sylvanus. "African Problems and the Cold War." *Foreign Affairs*, October 1961.
Padmore, George. A collection (4 vols.) of most of George Padmore's

articles is available at the George Padmore Research Library, Accra.

———— . "Forced Labour in Africa." *The Labour Monthly*, April 1931.

———— . "Hands Off the Colonies." *The New Leader*, 25 January 1933.

———— . "The Struggle for Bread." *The Negro Worker*, June–July 1933.

———— . "Colonial Fascism in the West Indies." *The People* (Trinidad), 21 May 1938.

———— . "The Colonial Question." *Empire*, May 1939.

———— . "A Negro Surveys the Colonial Problem." *The African Morning Post* (Accra), 30–31 January, 1 February 1939.

———— . "The Revolt in Haiti," *The Labour Monthly*, June 1939.

———— . "Colonials Demand Britain's War Aims." *The New Leader*, 15 February 1941.

———— . "Whither the West Indies." *The New Leader*, 29 March 1941.

———— . "No Atlantic Charter for Colonies." *The New Leader*, 24 January 1942.

———— . "Uncle Sam's Black Ward." *Tribune*, 23 October 1942.

———— . "Britain Follows Mussolini." *The New Leader*, 17 July 1943.

———— . "Russia and the Colonial Question." *The Socialist Leader*, 25 January 1947.

28. *Contemporary Books and Tracts*

Abrahams, Peter. *Tell Freedom*. London, 1954.

Adams, H. G. *God's Image in Ebony: Being a Series of Biographical Sketches, Facts, Anecdotes, etc. Demonstrative of the Mental Powers and Intellectual Capacities of the Negro Race*. London, 1854.

Adera, Teshome. *Nationalist Leaders and African Unity*. Addis Ababa: Berhanena Selam Printing Press, 1963.

Agbebi, Mojola. *Inaugural Sermon, Delivered at the Celebration of the First Anniversary of the "African Church," Lagos, West Africa, December 21, 1902* (in Schomburg Collection).

Ali, Duse Mohamed. *In the Land of the Pharaohs: A Short History of Egypt From the Fall of Ismail to the Assassination of Boutros Pasha*. London, 1911; reprint London: Frank Cass, 1968.

Angell, Norman. *The Great Illusion*. London, 1910.

———— . *The Fruits of Victory*. London, 1921.

———— . *This Have and Have Not Business*. London, 1936.

Aptheker, Herbert, ed. *W. E. B. Du Bois, The Correspondence of W. E. B. Du Bois: Selections, 1877–1934*. Vol. I. Amherst, Mass.: University of Massachusetts Press, 1973.

Armistead, Wilson. *A Tribute for the Negro: Being a Vindication of the Moral, Intellectual and Religious Capabilities of the Coloured Portion of*

Mankind: With Particular Reference to the African Race. Manchester, 1848.

Azikiwe, Nnamdi. *Renascent Africa.* Lagos, 1937.

Blyden, Edward W. For other tracts of E. W. Blyden see the *African Repository,* 1862–1892.

———. *The West African University.* Freetown, 1872.

———. *Christianity, Islam and the Negro Race,* 2nd ed. London, 1888.

———. *Liberia's Offering: Being Addresses, Sermons, etc.* New York, 1892.

———. *African Life and Customs.* London, 1908.

Bowen, J. W. E., ed. *Africa and the American Negro: Addresses and Proceedings of the Congress on Africa.* Atlanta, 1896.

Cabral, Amilcar. *Unity and Struggle: Speeches and Writings.* London: Heinemann, 1980.

Casley-Hayford, J. E. *Ethiopia Unbound, Studies in Race Emancipation.* London, 1911.

Congress on Africa. *Chicago Congress on Africa, 1894* by Frederick Perry Noble (in Schomburg Collection).

Crummell, Alexander. *The Future of Africa.* New York. 1862.

Cudjoe, S. D. *Aids to African Autonomy.* London: College Press, 1949.

Cunard, Nancy, ed. *Negro Anthology.* London, 1934.

Delaney, Martin R. *The Condition, Elevation, Emigration and Destiny of the Coloured People of the United States Politically Considerd.* Philadelphia, 1852.

———. *Official Report of the Niger Valley Exploring Party.* New York and London, 1861.

Du Bois, W. E. B. *Dusk of Dawn: An Essay Towards an Autobiography of a Race Concept.* New York, 1940.

———. *The Negro.* Home University Library, 1915.

———. *The World and Africa.* New York: International Publishers, 1965 (contains a full list of the works of Du Bois).

Equiano's Travels. Abridged and edited by Paul Edwards. London, 1967.

Ferris, William H. *The African Abroad, or His Evolution in Western Civilization Tracing His Development Under Caucasian Milieu.* New Haven, 1913.

———. *Alexander Crummel: An Apostle of Negro Culture.* Occasional Papers no. 20. Washington D.C.: American Negro Academy, 1920.

Garvey, Amy Jacques, ed. *Philosophy and Opinions of Marcus Garvey.* 2 vols. New York, 1923–26.

———. *Garvey and Garveyism.* London: Collier-Macmillan, 1970.

Garvey, Marcus. *The Tragedy of White Injustice.* New York, 1927.

Germany Speaks. By 21 leading members of Party and State. With a Preface by Joachim von Ribbentrop, Reich Minister of Foreign Affairs, London, 1938.

Gregoire, H. *An Enquiry Concerning the Intellectual and Moral Faculties and Literature of Negroes.* Translated by O. B. Warden. Brooklyn, 1810.

Hailey, Lord. *An African Survey.* Oxford, 1938.

———. *World Thought on the Colonial Question.* Johannesburg, 1946.

Hill, H. C., and Martin Kilson, eds. *American Leaders on Africa From the 1880s to the 1950s.* London, 1969.

Holly, James Theodore. *A Vindication of the Capacity of the Negro Race for Self-Government and Civilized Progress, As Demonstrated by Historical Events of the Haitian Revolution and the Subsequent Acts of That People Since Their National Independence.* New Haven, Conn., 1857.

Horton, J. A. B. *West African Countries and Peoples . . . A Vindication of the African Race.* Introduction by George Shepperson. Edinburgh: Edinburgh University Press, 1969.

James, C. L. R. *The Black Jacobins: Toussaint L'Overture and the San Domingo Revolution.* New York: Dial, 1938; rev. ed. New York: Random House, 1963; London: Allison and Busby, 1980.

———. *A History of Negro Revolt.* London, 1938.

Johnson, J. C. de Graft. *Towards Nationhood in West Africa.* London, 1928.

Kenyatta, Jomo. *Facing Mount Kenya.* London: Mercury Books, 1962.

Lewis, W. Arthur. *Labour in the West Indies.* Fabian Society Research Series. London, 1939.

———. *The West Indies.* London, 1946.

Locke, Alain, ed. *The New Negro.* New York: Atheneum, 1969.

McKay, Claude. *Harlem: Negro Metropolis.* New York: E. P. Dutton, 1940.

Mellon, M. T. *Early American Views on Negro Slavery.* New York: New American Library, 1969.

Moody, Harold A. *Youth and Race.* London, 1936.

———. *Christianity and Race Relations.* London, 1943.

———. *Freedom for All Men.* London, 1943.

———. *The Colour Bar.* London, 1945.

Mudgal, H. G. *Marcus Garvey: Is He the True Redeemer of the Negro?* New York: African Publication Society, 1932.

Nembhard, L. S. *Trials and Triumphs of Marcus Garvey.* Jamaica, 1940.

Nkrumah, Kwame. *Africa's Challenge: A Time of Danger and Hope.* Accra: Government of Ghana, 1960.

———. *Ghana: The Autobiography of Kwame Nkrumah.* Edinburgh: Thomas Nelson, 1961.

———. *Towards Colonial Freedom.* London: Heinemann, 1962.

———. *Africa Must Unite.* London: Heinemann, 1963.

———. *Neo-colonialism.* London: Heinemann, 1965.

————— . *Class Struggle in Africa*. London: Heinemann, 1970.

————— . *Revolutionary Path*. London: Panaf, 1973.

Ojike, Mbonu. *My Africa*. New York: John Day, 1946.

Orizu, A. A. Nwafor. *Without Bitterness: Western Nations in Post-War Africa*. New York: Creative Age Press, 1944.

Padmore, George. *The Life and Struggles of Negro Toilers*. London, 1931.

————— . *How Britain Rules Africa*. London, 1936.

————— . *Africa and World Peace*. London, 1937.

————— . *How Russia Transformed Her Colonial Empire*. London: Dennis Dobson, 1946.

————— . *Pan-Africanism or Communism? The Coming Struggle for Africa*. London: Dennis Dobson, 1956.

————— . *History of the Pan-African Congress*, 2d ed. London: Susan Tulley, 1963.

Spiller, G., ed. *Papers on Inter-Racial Problems Communicated to the First Universal Races Congress Held at the University of London, July 26–29, 1911*. London: King and Son, 1911.

Vaughan, D. *Negro Victory: The Life Story of Dr. Harold Moody*. London, 1950.

Walters, Alexander. *My Life and Work*. 2 vols. New York: Fleming H. Revel, 1917.

White, Walter. *A Man Called White: The Autobiography of Walter White*. New York: Viking Press, 1948.

Willkie, Wendell, *One World*. London: Cassell, 1943.

Woolf, Leonard. *Imperialism and Civilization*. London, 1928.

————— . *Mandates and Empire*. London, 1928.

————— . *The League and Abyssinia*. London, 1936.

Work, F. E. *Ethiopia: A Pawn in European Diplomacy*. New York, 1935.

29. *Newspapers (British Museum)*
      African Morning Post (Accra)
      Daily Herald
      Daily News (London)
      Daily Times (Lagos)
      Gold Coast Chronicle (Accra)
      The Guardian (Lagos)
      Lagos Standard
      Manchester Guardian
      New Leader (London)
      New Statement and Nation
      Socialist Leader (London)
      Sunday Times (Lagos)
      The Times (London)

West African Pilot (Lagos)
Western Mail (Cardiff)
Yorkshire and Leeds Mercury

30. *Periodicals (British Museum)*
Abyssinia
Africa (An International Business, Economic and Political Monthly
[Fourah Bay College Library])
African Times and Orient Review
African World
Colonial Parliamentary Bulletin (ed. by George Padmore)
Labour Monthly
Lagos Weekly Record
Listener
Negro Worker (George Padmore Research Library, Accra: Bridgeman
Papers)
New Times and Ethiopia News
Peace
Sierra Leone Weekly News
Voice of Africa (Africana, University of Ghana, Library)
West Africa

Secondary Sources

31. *Articles*
Agyeman, Opoku. "The Osagyefo, the Mwalimu and Pan-Africanism:
A Study in the Growth of a Dynamic Concept." *Journal of Modern
African Studies* 13 (1975).
Akindele, R. A. "The Organization of African Unity, 1963–1988." *Jour-
nal of the Nigerian Institute of International Affairs* 14 (1988): 1–358.
Bakri, Ali K. "The Economic Factor in African Arab Relations." *A
Current Bibliography on African Affairs* 9 (1976–1977).
Bennett, George. "Pan-Africanism." *International Journal* 28 (Winter
1962–63): 91–96.
Drake, St. Clair. "Rise of the Pan-African Movement." *Africa* (Special
Report) 3 (April 1958): 5–9.
Garigue, P. "The West African Students' Union: A Study in Culture
Contact." *Africa* 23 (1953): 55–69.
Geiss, Imanuel. "Notes on the Development of Pan-Africanism." *Jour-
nal of the Historical Society of Nigeria* 3 (June 1967): 719–40.
———. "Pan-Africanism." *Journal of Contemporary History* 4 (January
1969): 187–200.

Hare, Nathan. "Wherever We Are." *Black Scholar* (March 1971).

Irele, Abiola. "Negritude or Black Cultural Nationalism." *Journal of Modern African Studies* 3 (October 1965): 321–48.

Isaacs, H. R. "The American Negro and Africa: Some Notes." *Phylon* 33 (1959): 219–33.

Pankhurst, Richard. "Ethiopia and Africa: The Historical Aspect." *Ethiopia Observer* 3 (1964): 155.

Shepperson, George. "Notes on Negro American Influence on the Emergence of African Nationalism." *Journal of African History* 1 (1960): 299–312.

32. *Books*

Adams, P., and L. Solomon. *In the Name of Progress: The Underside of Foreign Aid*. London: Earthscan Publications Ltd., 1991.

Agbi, S. O. *The OAU and African Diplomacy: 1963–1979*. Ibadan: Impact Publishers, 1986.

Armah, Kwesi. *Africa's Golden Road*. London: Heinemann, 1965.

Asante, S. K. B. *Pan-African Protest: West Africa and the Italo-Ethiopian Crisis 1934–1941*. London: Longman, 1977.

Austin, Dennis. *Politics in Ghana, 1946–1960*. London: Oxford University Press, 1964.

Ayandele, E. A. *Holy Johnson: Pioneer of African Nationalism, 1836–1917*. London: Frank Cass, 1970.

Azikiwe, Nnamdi. *The Future of Pan-Africanism*. London: Nigeria High Commission, 1961.

Baeta, C. G., ed. *Christianity in Tropical Africa*. London: Oxford University Press, 1968.

Boahen, A. Adu, ed. *General History of Africa, UNESCO*. Vol. 7, *Africa Under Colonial Rule, 1880–1935*. London: Heinemann, 1985.

Boxer, C. R. *Race Relations in the Portuguese Colonial Empire*. London: Oxford University Press, 1963.

Barraclough, G. *An Introduction to Contemporary History*. London: C. A. Watts, 1964.

Bracey, John G., Jr., August Meier, and Elliott Rudwick, eds. *Black Nationalism in America*. Indianapolis: Bobbs-Merrill, 1970.

Broderick, F. L. *W. E. B. Du Bois: Negro Leader in Time of Crisis*. Stanford: Stanford University Press, 1957.

Buell, Raymond L. *The Native Problem in Africa*. 2 vols. New York: Macmillan, 1928.

Calvocoressi, P. *Independent Africa and the World*. London: 1985.

Carr, E. H. *International Relations Between the Two World Wars, 1919–1939*. London, 1947.

Cartey, Wilfred, and Martin Kilson, eds. *The Africa Reader*. Vol. 2, *Independent Africa*. New York: Random House, 1970.

Cervenka, Zdenek. *The Unfinished Quest for Unity: Africa and the O.A.U.* London: Julian Friedmann, 1977.

Chinweizu. *The West and the Rest of Us*. London: Nok, 1978.

Cohan, D. W., and J. P. Green. *Neither Slave nor Free*. Baltimore: Johns Hopkins University Press, 1972.

Coleman, James. *Nigeria: Background to Nationalism*. Berkeley and Los Angeles: University of California Press, 1958.

Cronon, Edmund D. *Black Moses: The Story of Marcus Garvey and the Universal Negro Improvement Association*. Madison: University of Wisconsin Press, 1972.

Crowder, Michael, ed. *The Cambridge History of Africa*. Vol. 8, *From c. 1940–1975*. Cambridge: Cambridge University Press, 1984.

Curtin, Philip D. *The Image of Africa*. London: Macmillan, 1965.

Davidson, Basil. *Africa: History of a Continent*. London: Weidenfeld and Nicolson, 1966.

Davis, John A., ed. *Africa Seen by American Negroes*. Paris: Présence Africaine, 1962.

Decraene, P. *Le Panafricanisme*. Paris, 1959.

Delf, George. *Jomo Kenyatta*. London: Victor Gollancz, 1961.

Diop, Cheik Anta. *The Cultural Unity of Negro Africa*. Paris: Présence Africaine, 1962.

Fishel, Leslie H., and Benjamin Quarles, eds. *The Black American: A Documentary History*. Glenview, Ill.: Scott-Foresman, 1977.

Franklin, John Hope. *From Slavery to Freedom*. New York: Alfred A. Knopf, 1948.

Frenkel, M. Y. *Edward Blyden and American Nationalism*. Moscow: Africa Institute, Academy of Sciences, 1972.

Freyre, Gilberto. *The Masters and the Slaves: A Study in Brazilian Civilization*. Translated by Samuel Putnam. New York: Alfred A. Knopf, 1955.

———. *The Racial Factor in Contemporary Politics*. Occasional Papers of the Research Unit for the Study of Multi-Racial Societies. Sussex: University of Sussex, Herts, 1966.

Fyfe, Christopher. *Africanus Horton: West African Scientist and Patriot, 1835–1883*. London: Oxford University Press, 1972.

Hansen, E., ed. *Africa: Perspectives on Peace and Development*. London: Zed, 1987.

Hodgkin, Thomas. *Nationalism in Colonial Africa*. London: Frederick Muller, 1956.

Hooker, James. *Black Revolutionary: George Padmore's Path from Communism to Pan-Africanism*. London: Pall Mall Press, 1967.

————. *Henry Sylvester Williams: Imperial Pan-Africanist*. London: Rex Collings, 1975.

King, Woodie, and Earl Anthony, eds. *Black Poets and Prophets: The Theory, Practice and Esthetics of the Pan-Africanist Revolution*. New York: New American Library, 1972.

Kohn, Hans. *The Idea of Nationalism*. New York: Collier Books, 1967.

Kohn, Hans, and Wallace Sokolsky, eds. *African Nationalism in the Twentieth Century*. New York: Van Nostrand, 1965.

Langley, J. Ayodele. *Pan-Africanism and Nationalism in West Africa, 1900–1945: A Study in Ideology and Social Classes*. London: Oxford University Press, 1973.

————. *Ideologies of Liberation in Black Africa, 1856–1970*. London: Rex Collings, 1979.

Legum, Colin. *Pan-Africanism: A Short Political Guide*. New York: Frederick A. Praeger, 1962.

Little, Kenneth. *Negroes in Britain: A Study of Racial Relations in English Society*. London, 1948.

Lowenthal, D. *West Indian Societies*. London: Oxford University Press, 1972.

Lusignan, Guy de. *French Speaking Africa Since Independence*. London: Pall Mall Press, 1969.

Lynch, Hollis R. *Edward Wilmot Blyden: Pan-Negro Patriot, 1832–1912*. London: Oxford University Press, 1967.

Mathurin, Owen Charles. *Henry Sylvester Williams and the Origins of the Pan-African Movement, 1869-1911*. Westport, Conn.: Greenwood Press, 1975.

Mazrui, Ali A. *Towards a Pax Africana*. London: Weidenfeld and Nicolson, 1967.

————. *Africa's International Relations*. London: Heinemann, 1977.

————. *The African Condition*. London: Heinemann, 1982.

Mazrui, Ali A., and M. Tidy. *Nationalism and New States in Africa*. London: Heinemann, 1984.

Mazzeo, D. *African Regional Organizations*. Cambridge: Cambridge University Press, 1984.

Meier, August, and Elliott Rudwick. *From Plantation to Ghetto*. New York: Hill and Wang, 1976.

Moon, P. T. *Imperialism and World Politics*. New York: Macmillan, 1961.

Otite, O., ed. *Themes in African Social and Political Thought*. Enugu: Forth Dimension Publishers, 1978.

Pan-Africanism. A publication of the British Information Services. London, 1962.

Pan-Africanism Reconsidered. Edited by the American Society of African

Culture. Berkeley and Los Angeles: University of California Press, 1962.

Redkey, Edwin S. *Black Exodus: Black Nationalist and Back-to-Africa Movements 1890–1910*. New Haven, Conn.: Yale University Press, 1969.

Rodrigues, Jose Honorio. *Brazil and Africa*. Berkeley and Los Angeles: University of California Press, 1965.

Rout, Leslie B., Jr. *The African Experience in Spanish America*. London: Oxford University Press, 1976.

Stuckey, Sterling. *The Ideological Origins of Black Nationalism*. Boston: Beacon Press, 1972.

Sylvester, A. *Arabs and Africans: Cooperation for Development*. London: Bodley Head, 1981.

Tannenbaum, F. *Slave and Citizen*. New York: Vintage Press, 1947.

Thomas, Tony, and R. Allen. *Two Views on Africanism*. New York: Pathfinder Press, 1972.

Thompson, V. Bakpetu. *Africa and Unity: The Evolution of Pan-Africanism*. London: Longman, 1969.

Thorpe, Earl E. *The Mind of the Negro: An Intellectual History of Afro-Americans*. Westport, Conn.: Greenwood Press, 1970.

Tordoff, W. *Government and Politics in Africa*. London: Macmillan, 1984.

Vincent, Theodore, *Black Power and the Garvey Movement*. Berkeley: Ramparts Press, 1971.

Wallerstein, I. *Africa—The Politics of Unity: An Analysis of a Contemporary Social Movement*. London: Pall Mall Press, 1968.

Wauthier, Claude. *The Literature and Thought of Modern Africa*. London: Pall Mall Press, 1966.

Weisbord, Robert G. *Ebony Kinship: Africa, Africans and the Afro-Americans*. London: Greenwood Press, 1973.

33.   *Unpublished Dissertations*

Contee, Clarence Garner, "W. E. B. Du Bois and African Nationalism, 1914–1945." Ph.D. dissertation, The American University, Washington, D.C., 1969.

Desta, Mengiste. "The Evolution of the Pan-African Movement." M. A. thesis, Howard University, 1960.

Index